SKIN DEEP

Ajay Monga is the writer of critically acclaimed films, such as *Fashion* and *Corporate*, which earned him nominations for several prestigious awards in the film industry.

SKIN DEEP

AJAY MONGA

RUPA

Published by
Rupa Publications India Pvt. Ltd 2019
7/16, Ansari Road, Daryaganj
New Delhi 110002

Sales centres:
Allahabad Bengaluru Chennai
Hyderabad Jaipur Kathmandu
Kolkata Mumbai

Copyright © Ajay Monga 2019

This is a work of fiction. Names, characters, places and incidents are either the product of the author's imagination or are used fictitiously and any resemblance to any actual person, living or dead, events or locales is entirely coincidental.

All rights reserved.
No part of this publication may be reproduced, transmitted, or stored in a retrieval system, in any form or by any means, electronic, mechanical, photocopying, recording or otherwise, without the prior permission of the publisher.

ISBN: 978-93-5333-505-2

First impression 2019

10 9 8 7 6 5 4 3 2 1

This book is sold subject to the condition that it shall not, by way of trade or otherwise, be lent, resold, hired out, or otherwise circulated, without the publisher's prior consent, in any form of binding or cover other than that in which it is published.

To Shivang, Simran and Varun

Beauty is abstract, yet it is physical. It is temporary, yet its permanence is delusive. When combined with youth, beauty is a heady concoction. It possesses everyone and everyone wants to possess it. But can beauty be possessed?

Before

1

'Can you see the black dot glinting in the centre? The one which is less faint than the other stones? That's a spy camera.' Anirudh handed Simran an embellished brooch, shaped like a lily.

The video went static momentarily, and then flickered.

'The footage will be stored in this receiver,' Anirudh pointed at her brooch and then at a little white device he was holding. 'The receiver will transfer data to your laptop via Bluetooth,' he explained as Simran fiddled with the brooch pinned to her dress.

If there ever was an award for Ballsy Beauty with Brains, Simran Thapar would have won it hands down. She was never one to overplay her appearance, but even her large spectacles couldn't subdue the brilliance of her caramel eyes. Her chic bob drew attention to her affable smile. She had the remarkable quality of always speaking her mind. Though she hosted a trite celebrity show, she hoped to make a mark in the field of investigative journalism someday.

'Rudy, I have to leave for the pageant tomorrow morning and your annoying boss hasn't even confirmed if I am to carry out the sting-op or not,' Simran grumbled.

'Sims, we need to prepare ourselves. We will not have enough time to understand the technicalities later on,' Anirudh reasoned with her, sensing her irritability. 'See, this camera is going to be close to your heart. Actually, closer to your boobs,' smirked Anirudh and put his hand inside her top to fix the camera.

Simran raised an eyebrow and narrowed her eyes. 'You seem to be having an awful lot of fun fixing this camera.'

Just then a knock on the door startled them, making them swear.

'Hey! Oh, I'm so sorry,' Divya, the post-production supervisor, was mortified to walk in on the two of them in such a compromising position. Uncomfortable, she stalled at the doorway, waiting for the earth to swallow her up...or, them.

'It's okay! Divya, you can come in. Rudy was just having his quota of fun before he faced the imminent doom,' Simran quipped.

Anirudh had not wanted anyone else in the office to know about the sting-op, but it seemed like Simran didn't share the same concerns. He fidgeted with the brooch briefly before excusing himself to make a call.

'Hi, sir, I wanted to know if we can go ahead with the op,' Anirudh's voice instantly turned servile.

'I will give the green signal only after the party in the evening. Karmarkar will be there as well. In fact, I am supposed to have a separate meeting with both Karmarkar and Nimesh Mehta.' Gul Mohammad's voice conveyed a sense of self-importance and pomposity.

'Sir, Simran is getting worked up because we have kept her in the dark. She doesn't even know if she's leaving for the pageant tomorrow or not.' Anirudh tossed the ball in Gul's court, but the plan backfired.

'Anirudh, you have to decide whether you are doing this for her or for me. I don't think your relationship with her should come in between professional work. Get it through your girlfriend's dense skull that such things can get sticky at times. She has no choice but to be patient,' Gul reacted acidly. 'And one more thing, Anirudh. Keep her on a tight leash. If things go awry under any circumstance and she names the channel, I will raise my hands and feign complete ignorance.'

'I have already briefed her, Gul sir. She has understood the implications and has agreed to bear the consequences,' assured Anirudh, caught in the crossfire between his girlfriend and his boss.

Meanwhile, in the editing room, Divya and Simran were watching the footage from an old episode of the chat show in which Nimesh Mehta was the guest. Anirudh joined them.

'Haven't you reduced beauty to a commodity?' Simran demanded.

'If I wasn't doing it, someone else would. There is an inconceivable craze for beauty pageants. Girls as young as five want to wear a crown. So why shouldn't I cash in on that? If I am labelled a trader or a dealer, so be it,' answered Mehta, nonchalantly.

'But isn't that encouraging a system which projects women as objects of desire? That, too, in a sex-starved society. Won't this lead to more rapes and atrocities against women?'

'What you are talking about is a law and order problem. That is not my responsibility.'

Unable to endure the appalling statements that this unscrupulous man was making all over again, Simran fast-forwarded the video.

'We will take a short break here. Don't go anywhere. We are in conversation with Mr Nimesh Mehta, the proud owner of the India Beauty Queen pageant.'

Unbeknownst to Mehta, the cameras were still rolling. 'This business is very tricky. Jo dikhta hai vo bikta nahi, aur jo nahin dikhta vo bikta hai. What you see doesn't sell, and what you don't see sells.'

'What do you mean by that?'

'A beauty pageant is a game of fillers.'

'How so?'

'You will get it at some point. You're quite sharp. In fact, you're the perfect combination of beauty and brains. Why don't you compete in my pageant? You will win hands down.'

'How can you be so sure?'

'I will give you a position in the final five straightaway. From there on, it will all just be a cakewalk.'

'Are you making me a proposition, Mr Mehta?'

'How much more clearly can I spell it out for you?'

Simran paused the video and turned on the lights. She looked at Anirudh, who was trying to read her mind.

'That's all the information I needed, Divya. Thanks for your help.'

'Ok, Simran, let me know if you need anything else.' Divya paused briefly before adding, 'Wish you all the best for the beauty pageant.'

Simran smiled politely and thanked her. *I need good luck for the fucking sting-op, not the pageant,* she reflected.

Anirudh handed the iPad and groceries to Simran as he rummaged in his pocket for their house keys. A great swell of mess greeted them in the living room—cameras, monitors and a web of wires that took up most of the space. Simran simply grimaced and made her way to the bedroom, stepping gingerly through the tech landfill. The bedroom was no better. She cursed her maid, Shantabai, who clearly hadn't paid a visit during the day, and started cleaning up herself.

On one of the monitors in the living room, Anirudh watched a pixelated image of Simran packing her dresses for the pageant. He ducked under the monitor to refit the visual data cable, and shouted, 'Why don't you change before you pack your bags?'

Simran had just walked into the living room in search of her phone. She came to a sudden halt as her eyes registered what was being displayed on the monitor.

Anirudh emerged from behind the table and the smirk on his face disappeared. 'I can explain,' he said.

'You sleazy bastard! You voyeuristic pervert!' She paced ahead with every word, and eyed him like Shantabai did when she was ready to squash a cockroach. 'You want to have a peep show?'

Just as Anirudh was about to make a dash for it, Simran pounced on him and pinned him down. She flashed her claws at him before the attack. Anirudh sputtered and choked on hysteric laughs as she tickled him relentlessly. Satisfied with the punishment, Simran rolled over, sniggering. 'You are such a *kamina*. I'm a little nervous, Rudy. Scared actually. Will I be able to pull this off?'

'There is no compulsion, Simran. You can still back out.' He tried to allay her fears. 'You wanted to do something worthwhile in investigative journalism. What could possibly be better than this sting-op?'

'Of course, I agree, but my nervousness stems from your fickle boss. Where is your goddamn boss, Gul? He has still not given the final go-ahead.'

'Be a little sympathetic. He has to talk to the channel owners.'

'What rubbish! Isn't he himself the owner of the channel?'

'Don't be naïve, Sims. He barely owns 4 per cent of the channel and that too only through stock options. The Chandarias own the channel.'

'But I don't think the Chandarias even care what happens to this channel. Gul doesn't need a pat on the back to do a piddly little sting-op.' Simran was walking back to the bedroom when she realized something. 'But isn't Gul at Karmarkar's party?'

'Ya! So? He is waiting for a call from the Chandarias.' Anirudh was running out of patience and Simran could sense it. Offering him a peace sign, she backed away into the room.

Simran finished her packing in no time, dumping the contents of her entire wardrobe in two huge suitcases. 'I am changing,' she announced teasingly.

Anirudh, who was typing a message to Gul, grinned. He could see Simran on the monitor. She was prancing around in her undergarments and making faces at him through the camera. 'Sorry to bother you, Gul, but she is getting very jittery,' he read out the message aloud before hitting 'send'. 'Without a final go-ahead, she is not even willing to understand how the cameras function.'

'Fine by me,' she shouted. 'That should put some pressure on the fucker.'

Anirudh was more or less through with fixing the cameras. He had checked the reception on Simran's laptop and had even edited it successfully. He cross-checked and then triple-checked everything. It was in order. He walked into the room to update Simran, but she had nodded off by then. He lay down beside her, taking care not to jostle her. He gently kissed a freckle on her shoulder, buried his nose in the crook of her neck and hugged her tightly.

2

Ensconced in the driver's seat of his Honda Accord, Mithun had a look of euphoria on his face. In a basement parking, he was being given a treat that most guys loved. A tangle of long, wavy hair curtained off what was happening underneath. He let out short, heavy breaths as he ran his fingers through the silky tresses. His expression instantly changed as the alarm on Shikha's phone went off. She had set it on, as she had to head home and start packing for the pageant. She lifted her head to turn it off.

'You can't do this, Shikha!' Mithun whined.

'But I have to go, sweety,' she insisted, her voice laced with a thick Punjabi accent.

Shikha's voluptuous body, coupled with the crude edges of her personality, made for an outrageously funny combination.

'But you promised me.'

'It has been fifteen minutes, Mithun. Next time! I can't stay here forever *na*, baby.'

Mithun would be damned if he let her go after all that he had bought for her. 'What next time, Shikhu? You'll be away for almost a month. And you clearly told me not to come to Mumbai during your pageant. This is not fair. You have to…' He made a sad face, pretentious though.

Shikha interrupted him. 'But, Mithun, I have to concentrate on the pageant. Why don't you understand? Let's go.'

'Just give me two more minutes.'

Mithun jerked himself off really hard. His grunts and groans in Marathi made Shikha laugh. She instinctively pulled out a bunch of tissues from the dispenser on the dashboard.

Shikha was a Punjabi-Marathi fusion by blood. She belonged to a middle-class family which had moved to Pune from Chandigarh just a couple of years back. She had lost her father to cancer after a prolonged fight which hugely drained the family of its finances. They had been living in Chandigarh at the time he was diagnosed with evidence of malignancy in his pancreas. Now all that remained was her father's ancestral home in Pune.

Shikha, her two younger sisters—fourteen-year-old Prajakta and nine-year-old Shilpi—and their mother lived in a boxy but neat house. Their mother worked as an admin assistant at an export firm. Being the sole breadwinner in a family of four, she spent most of her days breaking her back, trying to provide for her daughters and securing a better future for them. But during the last couple of years, weighed down by the burden of responsibilities, she had drifted away from her daughters. She had lost sight of the kind of people they were turning into.

Shikha used to work as a receptionist at a four-star hotel in Pune. Although her job was a temporary one, the drastic change it brought about in her seemed permanent. Whenever problems came knocking at her door, she developed the habit of taking the easy way out. During her short stint at the hotel, she had several flings before she was flung out for her unprofessionalism.

A big believer in not-putting-all-her-eggs-in-one-basket, Shikha employed her 'multitasking abilities' in three different cities. Currently, she had four boyfriends—two in Pune and one each in Mumbai and Delhi. She was an expert at making each one of them believe that he was *the one* for her. In turn, they would shower her with gifts.

Shikha walked home carrying an assortment of shopping bags, her hands struggling to hold all of them. Prajakta ogled the bags and quickly started sifting through the dresses with excited squeals. She was trying on one of the miniskirts when Shikha cornered her. 'Keep your hands off my clothes. I have to pack right away.'

'I will help you na, Didi.'

'There's absolutely no need for that. You just stay put and remove that skirt.'

'Let me see myself in the mirror na, Didi.'

'No! Take it off right away.'

Little Shilpi was distracted by what was happening in the hall. She ambled across to the passage between the living room and the bedroom. Shikha was so busy trying on one of the dresses, she didn't notice it when Prajakta wore the skirt under her dress and disappeared into the bedroom.

'Prajakta, remove that skirt immediately!' Shikha snapped.

At that very moment, their mom entered the house. '*Haai main mar javaan*. Where have you got all these clothes from? Whom have you borrowed from this time?' Her mother was absolutely livid.

'I have not borrowed or stolen anyone's money, Mummyji. These are gifts from Mithun. I don't have to pay him back.'

'How much has he spent? We will return his money as soon as possible.'

'About 50k.'

'What? FIFTY THOUSAND?' Her mother thundered. 'Why the hell would someone buy you such expensive things?'

'He is my boyfriend, Mummyji.'

'*Kanjari*, just last week that Munish was your boyfriend. He bought all those things for you. Now it's some new monkey performing the same tricks? I don't understand what is happening in your life.' Her mom held her head in her hands. She saw Shilpi and Prajakta peeking and ordered them to go inside. Sensing their mother's anger, they hurriedly scuttled in.

'Look, Shikha, I am giving you one last warning...'

'Mummyji, you have given me so many "last warnings",' Shikha interrupted. 'What are you going to achieve by these threats?' Just then Shikha's phone rang and disrupted their conversation. 'Hi, Sania. What's up! Yes, I'll be ready on time. What time are you going to reach? Cool. I'll be ready by four. Bye! Wait...wait...wait, Sania. Don't forget those tops you said you'd be getting for me. Thanks! See you in a bit.'

Shikha looked at her mom, who still had an agitated vein pulsating on her forehead. 'Mummyji, try and understand. We aren't well off...'

'So what?'

'So nothing.'

'No, you will have to answer me today. Are we so poor that you have to take favours from strangers? Will you like it if your younger sisters start following in your footsteps? If you were in my position, how would you stop your daughter from getting out of hand?'

'I wouldn't. I would let her have all the fun in the world. Life is too bloody short. Take Papaji's case, for instance. What was the use of being so careful about his habits and preferences? He had to dies so he died. Did he have a little bit of fun in his life? He kept slogging to make us happy. And then, he left us with a huge debt for which *you* will have to keep working all your life. I don't want to lose out on my life. So spare me your Moral Science class.'

Whack! Shikha's face throbbed where her mother slapped her. She juddered with anger and her ears turned puce—just as her cheek would in a while.

'This house that you are living in is because of your father's hard work. If he slogged, he did it for us. At least he tried to give us a good life. If he had died a gambler or an alcoholic, would you have any respect for him? He earned respect and love in the eyes of his children.' Her mother's voice choked with emotion.

Shikha wondered dismissively why some parents slapped their children and then cried. This kind of emotional spiel had stopped working on her a year ago. Now, she could not and *would* not see beyond herself.

3

Sania took out the tops she had kept aside for Shikha and bundled them in a separate handbag. Rechecking if she had packed everything she needed, Sania called out to Zubeida, a chirpy adolescent girl, who was their house help.

'Zuby, take all these bags to the main door, please. Abdul chacha will help you load the bags in Abbu's car.' Sania's mellifluous voice complemented her serene countenance.

Thick, straight lustrous hair that fell to her narrow waist framed her porcelain face. Her rosy lips were always curved upwards in a gentle smile and her dark eyes brimmed with kindness. She was the epitome of pristine beauty. Everyone who knew her held her in high regard, not just for her beauty but also for her benevolence.

'Ok, Aapa,' said Zubeida.

'I will go meet Ammi and then leave immediately.'

'Sania aapa!' Her younger brother, Ayub, called out to her. He hit the Pause button of a show he was watching online, removed his headphones and spoke to her in a grim manner. 'There is a lot of tension at Mamu's. They are not happy that you are going for this pageant.'

Of all the contestants in the pageant, Sania probably faced the steepest challenge—that of fighting radically orthodox views.

'So should I live by their diktats? Just because you and Sajid bhaijaan are employed by Mamujaan doesn't mean he can control my life as well.' Sania did not mince her words.

'We are not employed by him. We are partners in the business,' Ayub corrected Sania.

'That is what *he* makes you think. If you were partners, you would know how much money he makes. Mamujaan cheated Abbu.'

'Why do you have to dig up the past every time, Aapa?'

'Because we have given Mamujaan too much of a say in our lives.

Just because Sajid bhaijaan does not get along with Abbu, Mamujaan has created a rift in our family. Open your eyes! Fortunately, Abbu has moved on and is doing quite well. I don't care about anyone else's opinion other than Abbu's. He has given me his blessings and that is the only thing that matters to me.'

'I just wanted to give you a heads-up. Sajid bhaijaan is coming to talk to you. Even Rashid miyaan is coming along.'

Sania looked at Ayub bleakly and groaned. She sought her mother who was watching a cookery show. Her father was also sitting there, explaining to her mom the importance of going for walks.

'Abbu has a point, Ammi. Considering your weight and acute diabetes, you will have to take care of your health,' Sania lectured Shamim.

'Not you too! I am tired of listening to sermons.'

Sania tried to hug her mother but found that even her long, slender arms were unable to wrap around her ammi's circumference. 'Ammi, you better get huggable by the time I return from the pageant.'

'*Inshallah*, God willing! I will try. But once you're there, I want you to remain focused on whatever you are required to do. *Jazakallah Khair*. May God reward you with goodness.'

Sania thanked her mother and took her leave.

Shiraz sensed trepidation on his wife's face. 'Don't worry, Shamim. We're doing the right thing by giving her the freedom to decide what she wants to do with her life. I shudder when I think about what happened to Sakina. She is the worst off.' Sakina was their eldest child, who had been languishing at home since the day she got a divorce.

'I agree. We did not allow her to enrol for the catering course that she so desperately wanted to do. We should have known better than to bend our will to Sajid's pressure.'

'Not Sajid but your splendid brother Yousuf. I vehemently opposed his interference but to no avail. That incident sowed the seed of our differences. I regret making him a part of my business. I regret that we didn't educate Sakina well.'

'That poor girl is equated to a maidservant by her very own brothers just because we did not let her pursue her dreams.' Shamim's eyes were moist. She realized how important it was to fight chauvinism, and was glad that Sania stood up against it.

As Sania was walking towards their car, an Endeavour screeched to a halt next to her. Sajid, her elder brother, got out of the car and stood right in front of her. He carried his well-built body with a menacing look.

Rashid alighted from the driver's seat and stood at a distance, watching the proceedings. Rashid, a lanky fellow with a poxy face, was Sania's cousin who wanted to get married to her. Despite his slight physique, his demeanour was an authoritative one.

Sania looked at Sajid with an air of defiance which made his blood boil. He held her arm tightly and jerked her. Sania tried to resist him, but he overpowered her. 'What the hell do you think you are doing? You are disgracing our community!' Sajid ground his teeth as he spoke.

'Why is it disgraceful?' Sania dared him.

'Because girls are paraded nude over there. I'll be damned if I let my sister strut around half-naked! It is an insult to a woman's decency, and as your brother, I will *not* let you shame yourself like this.'

'So, it's okay for guys to get into bodybuilding, wearing nothing but Speedos?'

'Don't argue for the sake of arguing. Women will never be at par with men. That is the reality.'

'Who gave birth to you? A woman. Who nursed you as a child? A woman. Stop using force and interfering with our lives. We can do better than you.'

Unable to counter his sister's reasoning and spurred by Rashid's presence, Sajid used his might to quell Sania's defiance and pushed her into a corner. 'You are finally showing your true colours to me, you whore. I will not tolerate it! Not in my house,' he bellowed.

'Since when is this your house?' Sania roared back at him.

Hearing the commotion, Shiraz rushed out and saw Sajid manhandling Sania. 'You worthless blockhead!' he thundered. 'How dare you interfere in her life when you can't even support your sorry ass! Go and offer your yeoman services to your beloved mamujaan. Tell him that I don't want you or his useless son to come to my house and do moral policing. You don't have any right whatsoever to determine what Sania does or what anybody else does. Each person is free to make the decisions that he or she wants.'

'Look who's talking; the king of extravagance. How is your second wife by the way? I heard she ran away. Serves you right! You didn't even ask for my mother's permission when you got married a second time.'

'Who are you to pass judgements? I am on excellent terms with your mother and you don't need to poke your filthy nose in anyone's life. Sania will do what she wants. All this because your boss's son, this incompetent Rashid, wants to marry her?'

'Don't you dare utter derogatory remarks about Rashid or Mamujaan!' Sajid walked up to his dad and glowered at him with animosity. His hostile posture was enough to indicate how bellicose he was.

'What will you do? Will you hit me? Come on, you little shit, HIT ME!' Shiraz's voice boomed.

Shamim and Sakina rushed out, as did some of the neighbours, which made Sajid retrace his steps.

'If you even dare to open your mouth against your sisters or your mother, I will take you to task. Drill it in your brain that till the time I am running this house, my word is the law. Even when I am not here, I get regular updates.' Shiraz turned to leave.

Abdul chacha, their driver, got the cue. He loaded the bags in the trunk, while Shiraz and Sania seated themselves in the car. They were off within no time. Sajid was left high and dry. A fuming Rashid tried to reassure him.

'We're under your building, Shikha,' Sania whispered on the phone. She tried to keep her voice down, so as not to disturb her dad, who was snoozing away. But he woke up all the same.

'Come up na. Get your daddy also. You can freshen up here.' Shikha's Punjabi-*tadka* accent was as strong as ever. She and her mom were standing in the balcony of their three-storey flat, while her sisters were peering down from the adjoining window.

Sania gestured to Shiraz if he wanted to go up and he nodded in response. 'We can stretch out a little and have a cup of tea if they offer,' he grinned.

Encouraged by her genial smile, Prajakta and Shilpi were immediately swarming around Sania.

'What's your name?' Sania asked the youngest one.

'My name is Shilpi Azgaonkar. I am studying in St. Mary's High School in Class 2B.' Shilpi regurgitated, thanks to rote learning.

'Did she ask you which school and which class you are studying in? *I am in Class 2B.*' Prajakta mimicked Shilpi's slow lilting style of speaking.

Sania was amused by the playful rivalry between the two sisters.

'And what is *your* name?' Sania asked the other sister.

'Prajakta Azgaonkar,' she replied confidently.

'Which school do you go to?' Sania's question evoked a chuckle from Shilpi who seemed to have scored over Prajakta.

'See that? It's better if you say which school you go to and which class you are in—all at once.'

'I study in St. Mary's too but in the ninth grade,' Prajakta revealed, a little embarrassed.

'What do you want to do when you grow up?'

'I want to be a beauty queen, a Miss India,' responded Prajakta, almost instinctively.

'Wow! What about you, Shilpi?'

'Even I want to be Miss India!' Shilpi beamed with excitement.

'They fit me really well.' Shikha walked in, adjusting the strap of a turquoise-blue halter top. 'Where did you get these tops from, Sania?'

'My dad keeps travelling to the Middle East for business. He gets most of my clothes from there.'

'Hey! Stop bothering her.' Shikha pulled up her sisters.

'Oh! They are not. Your sisters are very cute,' Sania said light-heartedly. 'I think India will miss them if they don't become Miss Indias.'

They all giggled.

In sharp contrast, the mood in the living room was grim. A garlanded picture of Shikha's dad adorned one of the walls. Her mother was telling Shiraz about how she had lost her husband and how it had been a struggle ever since to bring up her three daughters.

'I am at my wit's end as far as this Shikha is concerned. She has been borrowing from her friends and making them shop for her. I don't know how she is going to repay them. The most worrisome part is that the younger ones are getting influenced by her.'

'These girls belong to the new generation and are determined to achieve whatever they set out for. God willing, everything will fall in place.' Shiraz got up to leave as he heard the rumbling of footsteps from the inside room. 'I think they are ready to leave. But let me tell you, Mrs Azgaonkar...'

'Gurpreet. Please call me Gurpreet.'

'Gurpreet, I think you're a brave woman. Don't be too hard on yourself.' Shiraz tried to mollify Shikha's apprehensive mom.

As they were about to leave, Gurpreet called Shikha into the other room. 'Shikha, you are the apple of my eyes. It is the pressure of work and home, and of raising your two little sisters that gets to me. I tend to lose my cool with you. But please don't get me wrong. I really love you and wish you the very best, sweetheart.' The tears in her mother's eyes broke Shikha as well.

Shikha hugged her mother like her life depended on it. 'You don't worry, Mummyji. I will win the title. Our lives will change after that. I promise you.'

The car entered a posh apartment in the upscale Juhu area of Mumbai. Shikha, who was accompanying Sania and her dad, was quite surprised when she got off the car and walked through an ostentatious lobby to a sleek modern elevator. Sania's dad's apartment was on the fifteenth floor of the building, which was done up immaculately. She was soaking in the décor of the apartment when her filmi ringtone prompted her to answer the call.

'I have just reached, baby. Where are you? Yeah, we are also at Juhu. Just hold on a second.' Shikha covered the mouthpiece with her hand and asked Sania what the name of the building was. Sania was already set to retire for the day. 'I am just calling this guy over to pick me up.'

'Where are you going so late?' Sania inquired in a low voice. 'I don't want Abbu to get the wrong impression about you.'

'We are going to Enigma at Marriott. He is my Mumbai-wala boyfriend,' Shikha replied with a wink.

'Mumbai-wala boyfriend?' Sania asked in amazement.

'Ya, I already have two boyfriends in Pune, yaar. But in Mumbai, I totally depend on this guy Deepak. I don't like to mix Pune and Mumbai.'

'Yup, it seems better to keep them apart,' Sania replied hesitantly, unsure of how to react.

'Vaise Deepak is also very warm and caring. You know he is getting a birthday present for me. It is supposed to be a surprise!' The excitement in Shikha's voice was palpable.

'But if you know about it, how is it a surprise?' Sania wondered out loud.

'I get surprised very easily...like if you give me a gift just now, I'll be surprised.' Her answer convinced Sania that she wasn't the brightest bulb.

'Sania, your mom has been trying to call you. Here, talk to her,' said Shiraz, handing the phone to Sania. He acknowledged Shikha with a slight nod and left.

'Yes, Ammi. Sorry, Ammi. I was just talking to Shikha. Yeah, she has come along. I am absolutely fine, Ammi.' Sania stepped out of the room to talk to her mom as Shikha changed.

By the time Sania returned to the room, Shikha was decked up in a short off-shoulder dress.

'So, when was your birthday?' Sania asked her, picking the safest topic.

'Oh! It was a few months back,' Shikha replied casually as she brushed her long, wavy hair. 'Poor Deepak could not meet me. He wanted to come to Pune but like I mentioned, I don't think it's wise to mix Mumbai and Pune *friends*. So, I told him I am really busy and that when we meet, he should get me a solid birthday gift. Poor guy went and bought some shoes and dresses for me.'

'How do you know this poor guy?'

'FB. Where else? And he is actually not a poor guy. He drives an Audi R8.'

'Wow! Have you known him for long?'

'This is my first birthday with him. He added me on FB...'

'He added you randomly?'

'No, no. He was a client at the Marriott. I was at the front desk for about three months. So, I hi-ed and hello-ed him when he came to stay at the hotel. He added me and I accepted his friend request.'

'Have you met him often before?'

'I haven't met him outside many times, but I've spent time with him at the hotel...in his room.'

'Oh! Was it allowed in your job to go to the clients' rooms and meet them there?'

'Actually, I got to know later that the hotel people did not like it, because they asked me to leave one day.'

Just then, the doorbell rang. 'I'll get it. It must be your friend Deepak, right?' Sania was beginning to understand Shikha's frivolity.

Deepak had a huge gift-wrapped box in his hands. Shikha ran to the door and grabbed it, barely acknowledging Deepak. She ripped open the gift, squealed at the sight of a Mango dress and Aldo shoes, and only then did she hug Deepak. 'You have made my day. Thank you so much, Deeps.'

Shikha was showing her gratitude to Deepak by snogging

him when Shiraz walked in on them. She straightened up, feeling uncomfortable, and Shiraz went straight back to his room, maintaining a poker face.

'Deepak, this is Sania, my best friend. Sania, this is Deepak, my boyfriend.'

After they exchanged greetings, Shikha took Sania into the room to talk to her. 'Sania, we are leaving now. How do I enter the house later? I'll probably be back late in the night,' Shikha whispered.

'Never mind, you just call me on my cell. I will come and open the door. I do this often for my younger brother.'

'You are sure you don't want to get joint with us? It will be fun.' Deepak asked in a tone that told Simran he didn't actually want her to 'joint' them.

'No, no, thanks. Sleep trumps everything else. We are supposed to be reporting in the morning for the pageant. And you keep that in mind too, Shikha.'

4

A deep and heavy beat thumped inside Enigma. Technicolour lights revealed a variegated crowd gyrating on the dance floor. At the centre of this group was Karmarkar's only child, Sunidhi. She had not only inherited the media magnate's vast fortune but also his striking good looks. Clad in a slinky burgundy dress, her long legs were strapped in skyscraper heels and her perfectly highlighted hair brushed against her back as she swayed.

That night, Sunidhi's friends had organized a send-off party for her. And what a party it was! They had popped mollies like M&M's. She felt the manic energy surging through the marrows of her bones and she thrust her fists in the air as she surrendered herself to the euphoria.

She felt someone jerking her arm. Her pupils were so dilated that only a thin ring of her stormy grey eyes was visible. 'Your dad is calling. He wants you to go to the party at your house,' Jai shouted in Sunidhi's ears.

'What the fuck will we do over there? On whose phone has he called now?'

'Mine. Talk to him.'

'You tell him I am busy right now!' Sunidhi yelled back at him and tried to shrug her arm off. But Jai pulled her aside to a relatively quiet part of the club, made her sit down, unmuted his phone and handed it to her.

Sunidhi scowled and reluctantly accepted the call. 'Yes, I know. No, you listen to me first. But for me this party is equally important, Pops. My friends have travelled quite a distance to see me off. I won't be meeting them for over three weeks. What will I do there? Meet Nimesh Mehta for what? Pops, I'm telling you again I don't want any favours. I will win this on my own, you just wait and...'

Sunidhi collapsed on the couch, her hand dangling limply from the edge. Jai wasn't surprised by Sunidhi's behaviour. He quickly rescued his phone that was about to slip from her fingers and answered it. 'Sir, we are leaving right away. She's a little tipsy but don't worry, I'll bring her back safe. No, of course, none of us will drive. The driver is here. Yes, sir.'

Sunidhi slumped over Jai's shoulder and he had to drag her out like a rag doll. They finally stepped out of the hotel at a painfully slow pace and Jai summoned the driver.

No sooner had Jai opened the rear door than Sunidhi crash-dived on the plush seat of the BMW, leaving no room for him. Left with no choice, he shut the door, a little harder than he had intended to and made his way to the passenger seat in front.

Jai emptied an entire gallon of water on Sunidhi's head. She came to her senses with a start, and screamed her lungs out.

'You have to freshen up, babe.' Jai dealt with her noncompliance like a mother dealt with her irritatingly irrational infant—with infinite patience.

'Fuck the hell off,' she screamed.

By now, he knew well how to deal with her. Belatedly, Sunidhi realized that she was in her bed.

'The biggest names in the media industry are here, only because your dad invited them.' He continued in the same patient tone.

'Pops has nothing better to do. I don't give a rat's ass about them,' yelled Sunidhi.

'Just meet them, babe. They are the ones calling the shots.' Jai tried but failed to convince her.

'Don't be so fucking dumb. *They are the ones calling the shots.*' She mocked him. 'They are just waiting for the opportunity to kiss Dad's ass. They'll do anything to get business and favours from him. Don't be so deluded.'

'Your dad told me that tonight's party is only a formality to pacify Nimesh Mehta so that he takes special care of you. He wants you to meet him before the pageant and tonight is the only chance you have. It will be conspicuous if Nimesh Mehta is seen talking to you once the pageant commences. People will jump to the worst-possible conclusion and think that your dad has made a deal with him.'

'I have told my father very clearly that I don't want any favouritism. If I have to win the pageant, it will be on my merit alone.'

'But at the same time, you can't take the risk of offending Nimesh Mehta. I hope you understand that. Your dad has invited Mehta for a specific reason—to introduce you. So you better be on your best...'

'That's enough of your lecture.' Sunidhi cut him off and slowly stripped out of her wet dress. She preferred to go commando most of the time. She looked at him defiantly, challenging him with her stare, which made Jai go weak in the knees. He should've known better than to fall for her tricks every time, but he couldn't help himself; she was like a bad habit. He took a wary step towards her. She didn't stop him, and that was all the encouragement he needed. Jai took off his shirt in one swift motion and was about to unzip his jeans when Sunidhi put her hand on his and stopped him. She quietly led him to the bed and nudged his head between her thighs. He welcomed the taste that he had become so familiar with. She squirmed and moaned with pleasure. The drugs in her system heightened the sensations Jai stirred within her, and she held his head firmly between her quivering thighs. Her release came so hard that she went completely limp and drifted into a slumber. She turned her back towards Jai. He didn't have the nerve to wake Sunidhi up and ask her to take care of him. Once she was satisfied, she detested being disturbed.

Jai pulled down his jeans, along with his boxers, and lay next to her. Even from the back, she was a sight to behold. He marvelled at the smooth expanse of her skin, the way her back tapered down only to expand and accommodate her derrière. He lightly traced the dimples on her lower back. Unable to hold back any longer, he stroked himself.

5

The network which lies behind a media blitzkrieg is a complicated one. The broadcasting channel, the radio partner, the on-ground and on-air sponsors, the various co-sponsors, the venue partners—a plethora of parties usually come to the negotiating table with excess baggage. Wheeling and dealing in the back rooms of such events is a norm.

Luckily, the India Beauty Queen (IBQ) pageant had a rather smooth journey the last few years, mainly because they had an on-going sponsor, year after year, in the form of Yogesh Karmarkar's company, Desire—an umbrella company for various multinational brands.

The suave and charming Karmarkar carried himself with flair. His salt-and-pepper hair and chiselled features made him look like an Indian version of George Clooney. Even though Karmarkar was well aware that he aged like a fine Single Malt Scotch, he never took advantage of the fact. He was loyal to a fault when it came to his wife, and doted on his daughter, Sunidhi.

By virtue of being one of the biggest ad-spenders in the country, he had catapulted into the circle of the most powerful personalities in India.

Almost all the media companies, including leading newspapers and TV channels, wouldn't bat an eyelid before licking Karmarkar's boots. Event management companies, like Nimesh Mehta's, had experienced a complete change of fortune ever since Karmarkar had come on-board. It was thus a given that Nimesh Mehta would go to any length to keep Karmarkar happy.

But this year, things were different. Karmarkar's daughter was participating in the pageant. As a result, Karmarkar's company could not sponsor the event since it would be a conflict of interest. So Karmarkar had brought his protégé, Khambatta, in the fray. Of course, the idea was to have a handle; not that Mehta would have gone against Karmarkar's wishes. But still, Karmarkar did not want an external brand to hijack this property.

Khambatta had worked as Karmarkar's CEO for a good eight years. He had then branched out on his own, launching some mid- and low-market segment products. Karmarkar had been so supportive of this enterprise that he had helped Khambatta set up the venture. Although sponsoring Nimesh Mehta's pageant was a small favour Karmarkar was asking for, it took significant persuasion to convince Khambatta. Karmarkar had assumed that Khambatta would readily do what was asked of him, but he was sorely mistaken. As the negotiations commenced, Khambatta revealed he had his own set of priorities and preferences. Nimesh Mehta, who was used to working with Karmarkar, now found it difficult to deal with Khambatta's style of working and his idiosyncrasies.

Not distracted by the magnificent view of the Arabian Sea juxtaposed with the Mumbai skyline, the group was having a debate on the lawn terrace of Karmarkar's sprawling mansion. The topic of discussion was Dastak—Gul's television channel where Simran worked.

'Without beating around the bush, Gul is offering me 1,500 seconds of free commercial time over and above what Raman's channel, Galaxy TV, is,' said Khambatta, emptying his glass of liquid courage.

'Wait! Are you trying to reopen the negotiations for the sponsorship now? At this juncture, when the pageant starts tomorrow?' an inebriated Mehta asked incredulously, trying his best to tamp down the urge to throttle Khambatta.

'Why not? If there is such a vast difference between the two channels, why shouldn't I reconsider it?' Khambatta persisted.

Mehta took another sizable gulp of his drink and asked him what the difference was.

Khambatta briefly looked at Gul Mohammad, who gave him the slightest nod possible. 'Does ₹15 crore sound like a small amount to you?'

Mehta broke into a delirious laughter. 'You think 1,500 seconds of Dastak are worth ₹15 crore? That means he is selling at ₹1 lakh a second. ₹1 lakh a second?' Mehta laughed like a maniac.

Gul jumped in the debate to side with Khambatta. 'Khambatta is right, that is our rack rate.'

'How many seconds do you sell at your rack rate? Even with the most sporadic ads that come to your channel, forget the regular ones. 8,000? At the most 10,000 to the one-off advertisers. The regular ones you have sold at a bulk rate of ₹3,000–5,000 a second. Am I right?' Mehta looked intently at Gul and Khambatta. 'Am I right or not, Gul?'

Gul maintained silence.

'It still makes a difference,' Khambatta continued, inviting trouble.

'For fifty odd lakhs, you want to switch channels? That too on the eve of the pageant? It is starting tomorrow, Brother. Galaxy TV has been my broadcast partner for the last seven years, Khambatta.'

'For the last seven years, Karmarkar had been sponsoring the event. But this year, you have a new sponsor, so why not a new broadcast partner?'

'Where will all my co-sponsors go?'

'Get them to Gul's Dastak.'

'Neither I nor my co-sponsors are interested in the down-market Dastak. It is way below our standard and my class.'

'Watch your language, Nimesh. Just because I have a stronger viewership in the low-income segment does not mean that I am downmarket.'

'I don't even want to talk to you, Gul. You're a fucking scumbag. IBQ is my property. Only I can decide which channel will air my show,' Nimesh snapped.

Gul's face contorted, but he countered the accusation in an unusually calm manner. 'I seriously object to your offensive snubs, Nimesh. Even at the press conference held a few days ago, you insulted my channel. You better watch your tongue or you'll have to start watching your back.'

'Does it look like I care? You and your channel are a septic tank. Ask anyone! Don't you agree, Mr Karmarkar?' Nimesh attacked. Without even waiting for a reply, he resumed his belligerent tirade. 'Isn't this guy and his channel worse than horseshit?'

'I would beg to differ, Nimesh. There are brands which cater to the lower-income segment, so this channel can be of use to them,' contradicted Karmarkar, polite as ever.

'Exactly! You all know my company has ventured into lower-end soaps and detergents. For me, Gul's "downmarket" Dastak channel is good enough.'

'But, Khambatta, having said that, this emotional blackmail at the eleventh hour is not justified.' Karmarkar made his stand crystal clear.

'That's my point. The pageant is starting tomorrow. We have already aired three curtain-raisers. You cannot wake up at the last moment and make comparisons and demands which are totally unwarranted.' Nimesh went a little easy on his diatribe, opting for Karmarkar's diplomatic stance instead.

'I'm sorry, Mr Karmarkar. You are my ex-boss. I respect you. But the fact is, you withdrew from the sponsorship only because your daughter, Sunidhi, is participating, not as some magnanimous gesture for me. I want value for the money I am spending. Period.' Khambatta was adamant.

Everyone looked at Khambatta with disbelief. Karmarkar excused himself and tried to steer Nimesh to the side but to no avail.

'If he wants to back out, let him do so. He is doing this now when he is supposed to be paying the rest of the sponsorship fee. And he is trying to push me for a bargain. But bear in mind that I will not budge from my stand, Khambatta. Your ₹4-crore advance will be forfeited. I will find someone overnight.' Nimesh Mehta's reaction hit Khambatta like a bolt; he was dumbstruck.

'You can't do that,' Khambatta stuttered.

'Please go through your terms and conditions. You can ask your legal department to cross-check.' Nimesh was ready to demolish him.

Sensing trouble, Karmarkar intervened. 'Nimesh, I don't want any bad blood. Give him 500 seconds more on Galaxy.'

Nimesh tried to protest, but Karmarkar gestured him to do as said. Nimesh complied grudgingly.

A sharp knock on the door lurched Jai from his sleep. 'Hey! I think your dad has sent someone for you,' he said as he prodded Sunidhi and hastily made himself decent. She stirred feebly but did not want to break out of her stupor.

'Sunidhi,' Karmarkar's crisp voice carried through the door. 'Sunidhi!' That seemed to do the trick as she jolted awake.

'Yes, Pops! Um... I'm in the loo. I'll be out in five.' Sunidhi stumbled across her room in a jiffy. Her father was her lifeline and she couldn't displease him at any cost. She spritzed herself with her favourite Coco Mademoiselle, pulled on a strappy lace dress and shook her hair out as she finger-combed it. And just like that, in a couple of minutes, she looked like a Goddess.

'Bring it on!' she announced as she walked out of the room with Jai at her heels.

'How long do you take to get ready, princess?' Karmarkar enveloped Sunidhi in his arms and kissed her forehead. 'Hi, Jai. You did well to get her back.' He signalled at one of his senior company executives. 'Come, let's go.' With his daughter tucked in his arm and Jai trailing somewhere behind, he marched towards the lush terrace lawns.

6

The alarm woke Simran up, but Anirudh continued to sleep, unperturbed. She threw the final lot of her things in the bags and locked them up. She found the spy camera Anirudh, the peeping tom, had used last night. He had placed it strategically on a low almirah so the entire room was visible. She went out to see what it had recorded, out of curiosity. She connected it to her laptop and saw Anirudh talking to someone on his phone. She paused it and plugged in a pair of headphones.

'Gul sir, she was persistently chewing on my brains. Yes, yes, she is super enthusiastic about it. No, don't worry. Ya, I know Karmarkar's daughter, Sunidhi. She is participating in the pageant too. Okay, I will brief Simran. Yes, in detail.'

Simran closed the window of the laptop before shutting it down. Then she strode back to her bedroom. She yanked the quilt off the bed only to find a neat column of pillows. Anirudh emerged with a shout from behind her.

'You bastard! You scared me shitless!' she screamed, clutching on to her chest. 'What the hell were you talking to Gul about? I have your entire conversation recorded. I have persistently chewed on your brains, is it?' said she, teasingly.

'I told him the truth. What else would I have told him?' Anirudh defended himself. 'He is my boss, Sims. You have to keep your boss updated.'

Simran rolled her eyes and headed for the bathroom. 'It's time for me to get ready and leave.'

'First, understand properly how the cameras function.' Anirudh stopped her. 'You know you can transfer files from your camera to your iCloud without even connecting it to your Mac, right? Keep sorting your videos date-wise and also incident-wise. Like, if you have any major incident that you feel should be highlighted, mark it separately. So when you have to search for it, you will be able to locate the file easily.'

Simran's big eyes suddenly got bigger and sheened with nervousness. She hugged Anirudh fiercely. 'Tell me you're going to be with me through this.'

'Of course, love, don't ever doubt that.'

'I'm going to get lonely there.' She held him tighter, wishing she could crawl inside his chest. Instead, she settled for breathing his scent in, a smell she had started to associate with home.

'You will be surrounded with more people than you can handle.' He stroked her back soothingly. 'And mark my words, you will have all of them eating out of your hand in no time. Most of these girls are just airheads. You can easily manipulate them to get what you want. But don't ever forget why you are going there. Never get carried away and stay focused on the job.'

'Are you sure I'll be able to pull it off?'

'A hundred and ten per cent.' He lifted her chin and bussed her lips passionately.

While Simran showered, Anirudh methodically packed all her sting-op equipment. She stepped out in a wrap knit-dress which accentuated her form, and minimal make-up.

'You're so beautiful, Simran.' Anirudh trailed his fingers along her cheekbone, admiring her dewy skin.

'I have to leave.' No compliment could soothe Simran's nerves.

'Stay calm. And call me once you get there.'

'Welcome to the 7th IBQ Contest, Sponsored by Belleza' read the banner at the entrance of the hotel lobby as it swayed merrily in the breeze. Contestants were being received with a cold pressed juice of pomegranate, chia seeds and mint, which Simran accepted gratefully.

The hotel's atrium was magnificently sumptuous—a majestic fountain being the highlight. An ornate chandelier hung over the reception, casting bursts of iridescent light around it. The hotel was perched right across the vast Arabian Sea. In the bustle of Mumbai, this was easily the most scenic view one could get—ships and boats slowly faded from the glittering horizon, and waves competed with themselves as they crashed against the coast. The contestants had slowly started to trickle in and gather in the lobby. Some were being dropped by family, but most of them had their boyfriends tagging along. Simran fleetingly wondered as to how many of these relationships would survive the test of time. Where she was coming from, all the glitz and glamour seemed like a big sham. The overwhelming craze that possessed these girls completely discombobulated her. She saw quite a few of them who looked anorexic; their faces marked with a perpetually famished look. *You will be spending the next three weeks of your life in their company*, said a terrified voice inside her head.

Suddenly her heart started to palpitate and her head began to throb. A wave of self-doubt crashed on her, drowning all her confidence. Just then her phone started buzzing. Her spirits lifted a little as she saw the name flashing on the screen.

'It's performance anxiety, sweetheart.' Anirudh spoke as if he was an expert on psychology.

He was right, of course. Anirudh knew her better than she thought he did.

'I am nervous as hell, Rudy. What if I get caught? I will be disqualified. It will be the most humiliating thing ever.' A thousand doubts came charging into her mind.

'Calm down, Simran. Switch on the spy cams, at least the one I fixed onto your sling bag, and get acclimatized to your surroundings. The earlier you come to terms with it, the better.' Anirudh's solutions were always pragmatic, but right now, what Simran needed was to hear motivational fluff.

Anirudh had sewn a camera in Simran's sling bag which could be easily switched on with a snap switch fixed onto the side of her bag. A tiny bump was all that could be seen. She had three back-up cameras as well. One of them was right in the frame of her glasses, one in the pendant that she was wearing and the third one on her belt. She felt like she could give *Miss Congeniality*'s Sandra Bullock a run for whatever she was worth and challenge the gallantry of the James Bonds of the world.

The girls were listening with rapt attention to the announcements being made by Neelam, one of the organizers of the pageant. She was calling out the participants' names and their respective room numbers. Rohit, a rotund balding manager, was standing next to her. His team of two boys and three girls held the placards which read: 'A to I: Room Nos 101–105', 'J to R: Room Nos 106–110', 'S to Z: Room Nos 111–115'. 'Ankita Raichura, Aashna Jhaveri, Archana Joglekar and Bhuvaneshwari Rao: Suite 101–102.' 'Sania Ahmed, Shikha Azgaonkar, Simran Thapar and Sunidhi Karmarkar: Suite 111–112.'

Simran could feel the gaze of her roommates as she entered their suite. She lugged her trolley bag and placed it near the foot of her bed. As she turned to keep her handbag on the side table, she made eye contact with one of her roommates and offered her a polite smile. 'Hi, I'm Simran Thapar.' She extended her hand to her roommate.

'I am Sania Ahmed from Aurangabad,' she replied with a genuine smile that exuded warmth. Sania shook Simran's hand and held it for a second longer than the latter would have expected her to. 'Are you from Mumbai?' she enquired.

'Not really. I'm originally from Delhi. I stayed for a couple of years in New York, but now, I'm trying to make my career in Mumbai.' Simran turned to the other girl in their room, who was listening in on their conversation and greeted her with a smile.

'I am Shikha Azgaonkar. I live in Pune now but at first, I was from Chandigarh.' She walked right up to Sania and Simran to introduce herself. As hard as Simran tried not to form an opinion about Shikha, she couldn't help it; right from her articulation to her body language, everything about her screamed inanity.

The fourth roomie was at the far-end corner of the suite. She had her earphones plugged in and seemed least bothered about introducing herself or meeting the rest of them. But being the bubbly person that she was, Shikha wanted to talk to her.

'Excuse me! Hello?' Shikha's voice was obscured by the music blasting through the earphones, so she went up to her and gave her a typical Punjabi nudge, which was more of a push. Shikha managed to startle her. 'We were trying to just hi-hello each other,' Shikha explained, almost apologetic when she saw how offended the girl was. 'Myself Shikha, Shikha Azgaonkar. I want to talk something to you.'

'What is it?' she replied tersely.

'What is your name?'

'Sunidhi.'

'Hi, Sunidhi. Myself Shikha, Shikha Azgaonkar.'

'I didn't think you would change your name in the last five seconds,' Sunidhi responded tartly.

'I like sea. Can we do *adla-badli*?' Shikha's tone was such that Simran could barely control her laughter.

'What? What is adla-badli?' Sunidhi was blunt to the point of being rude, but Shikha remained unfazed by her tone.

'Adla-badli means exchange, yaar,' she continued. 'You are from Yo-Yo land or what? I will take your bed and you take my bed,' Shikha simplified.

'Fuck off!' Sunidhi flipped her the bird and plugged her earphones in again.

That's when it struck Simran that the fourth girl was Sunidhi Karmarkar, daughter of the biggest media magnate in India.

Sunidhi Karmarkar is the most prized contestant this time around. Be friends with her and target her for some inside stories about her dad and Nimesh Mehta. You might just scrape the real underbelly of this ugly beauty business. Anirudh's words came ringing back to her ears.

'Shikha, why don't you take my bed? I am not so keen on the

sea view.' Simran realized that she wouldn't get a chance like this again and decided to capitalize on the situation.

'Great! Thank you so much, Simran!' gushed an overjoyed Shikha.

Simran could feel discomfiture radiating off Sunidhi's body when she moved next to her. 'I hope you don't have any problem with me shifting next to you.' Simran tried to allay her uneasiness, but Sunidhi chose to ignore her completely and traipsed to the refrigerator to pick up a Diet Coke instead.

'Don't have that Coke!' Shikha screamed from the other end. 'Neelam madam announced that they will charge extra for it, that too at five-star rates. You have to be very careful of such traps in these fancy hotels. I know because I used to work at the Marriott in Pune.'

Sunidhi threw a withering look at Shikha. 'Whatever, loser!' She gulped down the Coke, crushed the can and trashed it. She did not even spare a second look at Shikha, who was visibly offended.

Shikha glanced at Simran and then at Sania, and tried to salvage her reputation. 'Who are you showing so much attitude, madam?'

'To you, dumbfuck. "Can we do adla-badli?"' Sunidhi blatantly mocked Shikha. 'Don't you dare speak to me. You not only talk like a *gavar*, but you even look like a *rastachhaap*.'

'I am rastachhaap. So what is the big deal? I pick up all my designer clothes from the roadside stalls. How does it matter to you?' Shikha retorted, incensed.

'It matters! Dumbfucks like you rubbing shoulders with *me* and sharing the same room with *me*. Yuck.' Sunidhi continued to spew vitriol.

'So good, na? We have become equal now. Can we say cheers to that?'

'Fuck off, bitch,' Sunidhi bellowed.

'Hey, cool down, Miss Karmarkar.' Simran decided it was time to intervene.

'Why should I cool down? And who are you to conduct the

proceedings here? Some talk-show host of that downmarket Dastak TV? Mind your business.'

'Honey, your dad's achievements seem to be taking an ugly shine on you. Do you think just because you're some big shot's daughter, you have a license to shoot off your mouth?'

'Did I talk to you or anyone else in this room? It must be a happy family union for all of you. I don't want to be dragged into any of your lame conversations.'

'So will you talk like that? Using that kind of abusive language?'

'I will talk the way it suits me. Do you understand? Now fuck off.'

'Mr Yogesh Karmarkar's daughter, you must be incredibly secure because of having a father like that. After all, he is calling the shots in this pageant. He has got his pet dog, Khambatta, as a proxy. But remember one thing, if you rub people the wrong way, you will soon be on the wrong side of your luck. Then even your dad's dogs, like Khambatta and Nimesh Mehta, will not be able to do anything for you.' Simran lashed out at Sunidhi. Simran mentally cursed herself when she realized that she had successfully antagonized the one person who was crucial for her sting-op.

'What makes you think that I am riding my dad's luck, you bitch?'

'Let it be na yaar, Simran. Don't get into unnecessary *pangas*.' Shikha tried to douse the fire.

'You must be thinking I am Karmarkar's daughter and so I will win this pageant...' She deliberately paused, waiting for Simran to react to her rhetorical frippery. But Simran knew better than to reply. 'I might be Karmarkar's daughter, but I am *not* going to use his shine to get my glory. I am here on my own. And I will prove myself on my own steam.'

Simran instinctively started clapping slowly. 'Wow, a self-righteous girl stinking of her dad's filthy money talks of proving herself on her own steam. That is just precious. I couldn't give a fuck about whether you win or lose, you prove yourself or don't. But you will not talk to anyone in this tone, especially not to anyone in this room. Do you get that? Or should we ask your daddy to pay for your brain implants? I want you to apologize to Shikha.'

'What if I don't? Are you going to complain about me to the organizers?' Sunidhi scoffed.

'Do you really think I am so unimaginative? Now *that* is an insult. You assume too much and too soon. You think I don't know what has been going on behind the scenes? A brand like Belleza doesn't become the sponsor of IBQ for no rhyme or reason unless it is backed by your dad. After all, the owner of Scrub has been your dad's faithful dog! And I am sure you haven't gone through the elimination rounds like all the others. So if I raise the bogey, it might give you and your dad a taste of a new medicine called Nepoto-mycin,' Simran continued to lambast her.

'So you want to show me down?'

'Not at all! I want to show you your new reality, which is us, your roommates for the next three weeks. And yes, we might not be shitting money, like your father, but that doesn't mean you can treat us like doormats.'

For the first time in her adult life, Sunidhi was flabbergasted. Simran figured nobody had given her a good upbraiding in a while and that was the root cause of her obnoxious nature. Sunidhi stared at Simran for a few more seconds before walking up to Shikha and apologizing to her in a rather gruff and reluctant manner.

7

At the pageant, the girls had a hectic regimen in place for them. They had to wake up at six every morning and start the day with yoga followed by meditation. After a quick breakfast, they had a session of Pilates followed by lunch and then, more workout at the gym. The only difference between a beauty pageant and a boot camp is that the former has prettier-looking people who live on 'grass'.

The girls were allowed to have only soups, green juices, leafy salads and lean proteins. They weren't even allowed to look at carbs and glutens because that could apparently result in weight gain. Each contestant was required to drink at least two litres of water every day, along with a puke-worthy concoction of ginger and some arcane herbs that was supposed to give the skin a radiant glow.

Back in Pune, Prajakta and Shilpi were inexplicably excited to see their big sister on TV. They called out to their mom, who ventured out from the kitchen to watch Shikha.

'She looks really nice na, Mummyji? Next time, I will be in Miss India Beauty Queen.' Prajakta stoked up her passion as she spoke.

Not wishing to be left behind, Shilpi chimed in vehemently, 'I am going to be Miss India Beauty Queen!' and placed her cardboard crown on her head.

'Then who will do your homework and your studies? We will get someone from the neighbourhood to do your homework, okay? Or should I start going to school in your place?' Their mother rambled on, appalled by their aspirations.

In Aurangabad, Shamim, Sakina and Sajid's wife, Zeenat, watched Sania's interview, enraptured. Even Ayub stood at the threshold and watched intently, refusing to sit down.

The most excited member, though, was Zubeida, the house help. 'Look at Didi! She is looking so pretty. *Khuda kare kisi ki nazar na lag jaaye*,' she said, wiping away happy tears with her dupatta.

When Ayub saw Sajid bhaijaan heading towards them, he immediately switched off the television and pretended to read a book. An awkward silence descended on the room as the others too tried to keep a blank face. Sajid sensed something was off, but he was not in the mood for a tussle. Zeenat gestured to Zubeida to fetch Sajid a glass of water, but she gave her an apologetic shrug and started off in the opposite direction. Zeenat was left with no choice but to get it herself.

8

A big, round glass jar rotated slowly on a table. There was a palpable brouhaha in the air. The girls, who had gathered near the poolside, listened to Neelam's announcement with rapt attention. 'What you see here is a voting jar. Each one of you will vote for your top three contestants from amongst yourselves. And *remember*, you cannot vote for yourself.'

The girls knew that this was a mock round and the results of this poll hardly mattered. They were in a playful mood, gossiping with each other. The voting chits were distributed and when it was time to pen down their thoughts, the girls keenly deliberated over their choices before jotting down three names on three separate pieces of paper.

As Neelam and Rohit tallied the votes, some of the girls waited with eager anticipation, while the others were least bothered.

Neelam didn't waste a single second playing the Guessing Game. 'The maximum number of votes has gone to Simran Thapar!' she announced.

A loud cheer erupted as everyone clapped excitedly for Simran. She stepped onto a small stage to collect a certificate which read 'The winner of the IBQ mock poll is Simran Thapar'. Neelam requested her to give a customary speech. In an attempt to mask her surprise and unpreparedness, Simran laughed as she spoke to the girls. 'I just can't believe it! I am deeply honoured. Thank you for your love and support,' she finished with a dazzling smile and the girls cheered for her yet again.

'The second favourite is Dhwani Mehra!' Neelam's announcement brought a tumult of applause and whistles yet again. 'And the third place goes to Sania Ahmed!' Neelam's final announcement evoked a mix of ovation and barely concealed derision. It was a shocker of a win, as Sania was bracketed in the orthodox category. But on closer inspection, one realized that her thoughts were extremely progressive, given her background.

Back in Suite 111, Sania, Simran, Shikha and Sunidhi were in the middle of a conversation. Sunidhi was rarely a part of such debates, but that day's mock poll had caused a stir in her mind. She wanted to understand why she had not been considered among the top three contenders. On some level, she knew the reason, but she needed to hear it from someone else to fully accept it.

'The mock poll results are totally misleading. I got more votes because I have been interacting with everyone. I consider myself completely ordinary and undeserving of this. Just lucky perhaps...'

'You should have given this speech there. There's no need to be so diplomatic. I've heard you fart and snore,' Shikha jested.

'But I have to admit, you have a way with words, Simran. You know how to make people feel at ease and extract information out of them.' Sunidhi's compliment took everyone by surprise, especially Simran. She thanked her and for the first time in all these days, gave Sunidhi a heartfelt smile.

'Hosting a TV show has made Simran smart,' Shikha explained between glugging down her Diet Coke. She paused only to burp loudly, making the others laugh.

'But honestly, I am convinced that everyone voted in an emotional state of mind,' Simran tried to justify her victory.

'Emotion or no emotion, it is a verdict. And why should you feel guilty about winning? You should take pride in the fact that you have been voted *the best*.' Sunidhi's insecurity manifested itself.

'Not the best, the most popular perhaps. And I don't have an iota of guilt. I was just being honest when I said that this verdict was completely misleading. It was the opinion of a small group. I can bet my ass that the final results are not going to be even remotely close to this.'

'I'm willing to bet 50k,' challenged Sunidhi, pouncing on the first opportunity.

'That's cute,' Simran chortled. What makes you think I have that kind of money?'

'Let's bet 5k then?' Sunidhi counter-proposed.

'I am totally against bet...'

'What are the stakes?' Shikha interjected.

'The bet is not for a child like you. And I will offer ten times the amount if I lose the bet. So the maximum you will lose is 5k. But if you win, you will get 50k. Deal, Simran?'

'What is the bet about?' Sania decided to be a participant in the conversation.

'The winner of the pageant will not be from the top three of today's mock poll.' Sunidhi's tone was laced with malice and conceit.

'But that is exactly what I am also saying, that the winner will be someone else, not me,' Simran clarified.

'Then that is no bet at all,' Shikha opined.

'I will win the IBQ title this year,' Sunidhi declared.

Sania and Shikha were stumped by Sunidhi's belligerence. Simran was surprised by her overconfidence, but she knew better than to verbalize it.

'Are you in or out?' Sunidhi demanded.

'Okay, you lose, you pay 50k,' Simran conceded.

'Deal.'

Sunidhi was the first one to turn off the alarm next morning. She sprung off her bed and dashed to the bathroom to get dressed. This zappy new attitude was a drastic departure from the everyday routine she had followed previously of snoozing till she was significantly tardy. The other three woke up groggily, trying to squeeze lethargy out of their eyes. They were astonished to see a new, vibrant and enthusiastic Sunidhi, all geared up.

At the gym, much before the scheduled time, a pair of feet pounded on a treadmill's belt. Sunidhi was running furiously on it. She perspired profusely but remained committed to the task. She had not felt so alive in a while.

The bet Sunidhi had made with Simran was a calculated move. It helped her become more focused and driven. It was an old ploy she had used during school and in college; whenever she knew she had to push herself, Sunidhi would challenge herself in front of her friends and colleagues. It was her way of pushing the bar for herself.

While she was jogging, Sunidhi saw her phone's backlight blink. Placing her feet on the side panels of the treadmill, she paused the machine and answered the call. 'Did you read the message I sent you, Pops?' she mumbled into the phone and walked towards the washroom.

'I did. What help do you need?' Karmarkar asked, cutting straight to the chase.

'Do whatever you can, but you have to do this much for me,' Sunidhi implored desperately. She looked around to check if anyone else was there in the washroom. 'Please, Pops…'

'Okay, princess. Let me see what I can do. Just promise me that you'll be calm and relaxed. Don't take any undue stress.'

Karmarkar sat up in his bed, deeply troubled after his conversation with Sunidhi.

His wife was anxious to know what had happened. 'Why is she panicking so much?'

'That's precisely what is bothering me as well. She has never put so much pressure on me for anything.' Karmarkar was grim.

'She probably wanted to show off to her friends. She used to do this in college as well. She would brag about something and then struggle to prove her tall claims.'

'She should be making all these claims on her own merit. She shouldn't expect her father to swoop in and save her every time,' Karmarkar muttered crossly. 'She had laid it on thick about succeeding on her own, especially without my "interference". And now, as soon as things are a little shaky, she has reversed her own stand.'

'It's a once-in-a-lifetime opportunity for her. If she wants to win the title, please help her,' his wife entreated.

'I will help her only if she is willing to help herself. She can't make a habit of having everything served to her on a silver platter. I would rather she loses respectfully than wins unjustly,' Karmarkar said with a steely finality.

Karmarkar's office was meticulously organized, to the point of being cold. He planted himself in a dark-umber leather chair and checked his phone. It displayed a call he had missed from his wife. He didn't need to call her back to know what she wanted. He dialled a number. 'Hey, do you have a couple of minutes to spare?'

'Of course, Mr Karmarkar. Nimesh Mehta is always at your service.'

'I need to talk to you about something very personal and confidential. I hope that whatever I discuss with you today will remain strictly between us.'

'Rest assured, sir; you needn't even mention it. You are my provider, my mentor, my spirit guide. I can't even dream of offending you.' Mehta was the most toadyish lickspittle Karmarkar had the unfortunate pleasure of knowing. Most of the times, Karmarkar would avoid dealing with him directly and delegate the work to someone else. But this time, as much as he hated the superlatives Mehta used for him, he couldn't. So he just braced himself for Mehta's sycophancy.

'I am in a sticky situation.'

'Please be absolutely frank with me, Mr Karmarkar,' Nimesh prodded him on.

'Sunidhi... What are Sunidhi's chances in the pageant?'

'You mean on merit?'

'Yes, of course, on merit.'

'Can you please give me about half an hour to get back to you?'

'Sure.'

Nimesh immediately called up Rohit. 'I want the complete low-down on Sunidhi Karmarkar. I want it emailed to me. In fact, give me a comparative picture of the top ten contenders. Send me the worksheet you have on that.'

Within a few minutes, Nimesh was going through Rohit's email. He called up Karmarkar and briefed him. 'Sir, for personality, she scored a 6, for natural beauty a 7, for attire a strong 9, but for likeability a low 2. She scored a 5 for talent. Wit and humour have not been assessed as yet and Q&A is also pending.'

'So her chances are bleak.'

'Well, you could say so, unless there is a drastic improvement.' Mehta hesitated before adding, 'From what I have heard, she is very unsocial and arrogant with her colleagues as well as the staff.'

Karmarkar expelled an exhausted sigh. 'My sincere gratitude for your help. I will get back to you.' He hung up on Mehta and gazed out of the empire he had created, concerned.

Back at Suite 111, the girls were back after a hectic day. They were knackered to the bone.

'Who's up for some tea?' Sunidhi's voice evoked an amused shock on Simran's face. She called out to Sania and Shikha.

By the time Sania and Shikha reached Simran's bed, she pretended to have passed out. Sunidhi brought green tea for everyone. Seeing Sunidhi's generosity, Sania's and Shikha's eyebrows shot up as well.

'Can we go to dinner together?' Sunidhi was transparently pretentious, but the others appreciated that she was at least making an effort.

'We go together every day. But you can join us if you like,' offered Sania, politely.

'Yes, I would like to come along if it's okay with you guys,' Sunidhi replied meekly and hugged Sania and Shikha with moist eyes.

Soon, they made their way to the buffet downstairs. Most of the girls were already there and Sunidhi's courteousness and gentility left them all flabbergasted. Some passed audible barbs, but Sunidhi remained unfazed.

'She is really trying to win the bet,' Sania remarked. 'Good for her though. I would be the happiest person if she does win.'

Shikha overheard them. Insidious tendrils of insecurity wrapped themselves around her mind and left her reeling.

9

It was well past midnight when Rohit staggered towards his room, intoxicated. He vaguely registered the sound of muffled footsteps behind him, but he couldn't be bothered. He opened the door to his room with the key card. Just as he was about to shut the door, somebody pushed it. Rohit was startled and let out a yelp. As his eyes focused, he was even more shocked to see it was Shikha standing in front of him.

'Hi, Rohit sir. I wanted to have a word with you,' Shikha said nervously.

Rohit tried his best to sober up. 'What do you want to say at this hour?'

'If you can spare just a couple of minutes, sir. Please.'

'Would you like to come in?'

'Yes, that would be better.' Shikha tipped her head in both directions of the passage to make sure that no one was watching.

'Why don't you sit down?' he urged Shikha and switched the coffee maker on.

'What is it you want to talk about?'

Shikha, who had parked herself on a chair, was a little reluctant to talk. 'I feel a little odd to ask you for a favour.'

'I have shut the door. There is no one who will hear us. So feel free to say whatever you want to.' Rohit handed a cup of coffee to her and took one for himself.

'I belong to a middle-class background. My mother is the only one who supports the family. I lost my father three years ago.'

'I am really sorry to hear that.'

'I have two younger sisters. I hope you understand how important it is for me to achieve something in life.'

'I completely understand that, but what is it that you want from me? At least be frank about it, so you know we can deal with it.'

Shikha took a deep breath and mustered all the courage she could. 'I want to meet Nimesh sir.'

'What for?'

'I want to get my Beauty Queen title confirmed.'

'What? How will you get your title confirmed from Nimesh sir?'

'I will convince him. You leave that to me. Can you please get me in touch with him?' Shikha said despondently.

'Don't be stupid, Shikha. Every participant has come for that. They all go through this low phase of self-doubt. I have seen it year after year. There is no need to worry. And don't forget you're only seventeen. We have forged some of your documents, we can't take a bigger risk.'

'But, sir, everyone tampers with their age. So many twenty-eight-year-olds pose as twenty-four.'

'If someone gets to know that you are underage, you will be disqualified,' said Rohit, gruffly.

'Rohit sir, I need to meet Nimesh sir anyhow. Please, I beg you.'

'Look, Shikha, suppose I put you on to Nimesh sir and he helps you, what will I get in all this?' Rohit lewdly eyed the curve of her breasts and wondered how they would look bare.

'I will pray for you, sir, for your entire family.'

'When you meet Nimesh sir, do you plan to pray for him and his family also in return?'

'Yes, sir. I will pray with all my heart. We go to Vaishno Devi every two years. I will pray to Mata Rani as well.'

Rohit was still looking at the mounds which encased her heart when he set aside his cup and lay down on his bed. 'You think I am some moron who has been faffing all this while? You are not as dumb as you pretend to be,' said Rohit, removing his shoes, socks and belt. The roughness of his tone sent a shiver of apprehension down Shikha's spine. 'Do you want to meet Nimesh sir?'

'Yes, sir. I want to meet him anyhow.'

'Do you know what a toll bridge is?'

She gave him a nod.

'I am a toll bridge. You can't go ahead until you pay the toll. So do you want to pay now or later?'

'Can I pay you later?'

'Then you will cross the bridge later.'

'Okay then. I will pay it now,' she conceded with utmost reluctance.

Shikha avoided Rohit's lips when he tried to kiss her. She put her cheek in front instead. 'My boyfriend will feel bad.'

Rohit grasped her neck with his hairy, fleshy fingers and brought his face just inches near hers. His grip was so tight that Shikha choked and gasped for air.

'I don't care about your boyfriend.'

'But what is the guarantee that you will make me meet Nimesh Mehta after this?'

'That is the risk you will have to take.' His breath reeked of cheap liquor, cigarettes and coffee.

Shikha averted her face and squeezed her eyes shut.

Shikha's phone beeped with a message from an unknown number. 'Marriott Lobby, 5 p.m.' Shikha and Sania were crammed in a car with four other contestants. Five cars with twenty-five contestants and four moderators cruised along the Western Express Highway, on their way to Palladium Mall. The girls were out on a shopping spree courtesy the sponsors and co-sponsors of the pageant. They were handed sizable gift vouchers to spruce up their wardrobe. The girls cackled with excitement as they got off from the cars.

Although Shikha was a hardcore shopaholic, she couldn't appreciate this excursion. She had to be at the Marriott at five in the evening, which meant she barely had an hour to shortlist what she wanted to buy.

'What's wrong? You look worked up,' Sania asked Shikha, who had been scampering from store to store in a frenzied state.

'I have to meet someone in Juhu, which will take more than an hour to reach,' Shikha replied in a state of panic. 'Can you please help me decide what to pick?'

As obliging as ever, Sania agreed, and within half an hour, Shikha had finished her quota of shopping. In fact, she had surplus clothes. She knew she had to do away with a couple of things to remain in the voucher limit unless she wanted to pay for them from her own pocket, which was highly unlikely.

As she stepped out of the trial room in search for Sania, she saw the mad ruckus that the girls had created. Clothes were strewn on the floor like rags, shoes were tossed around haphazardly and accessories jangled angrily as they were being tried on. Shikha was tempted to shop more, but she knew she could not. She told herself that if this meeting went well, she'd be making many such shopping trips. She then sneaked out of the mall and took a cab to Juhu. Shikha kept checking her phone every two minutes, awaiting further instructions. She quickly texted Sania to remind her, yet again, to not forget her shopping bags. That did scarce to distract her from all the thoughts whizzing through her mind.

Meanwhile, in another corner of the store, Anirudh was in tears as he watched Nimesh Mehta scratching his underparts with one hand deep inside the back of his pants, on Simran's iPad. It was a small part of the extensive footage Simran had recorded. 'Now that's a scoop.' Anirudh and Simran had met each other after two gruelling weeks and both had a lot to share.

Anirudh was stunned by the bizarre and shocking things Simran had managed to capture. There were girls dressed in their underwear, candidly chatting with each other. Some of them talked about going to the mountains to attain nirvana by cutting themselves off from the world and smoking A-grade hash. Anirudh's eyes did a double flip when he saw Karmarkar's daughter snorting coke with another contestant. He paused the visuals. 'This is mind-blowing stuff, Simran. I want a copy of these visuals to show Gul.'

'No freaking way. Not until I'm back and I've had the time to edit them.'

10

During the IBQ pageant days, Nimesh Mehta conducted most of his meetings in a lavish suite at the JW Marriott. An entire wall of the suite overlooked the breathtaking Arabian Sea. In the antechamber of his suite, sat an imposing L-sectional couch and a solid, modern mahogany table. On that day, the table top was covered under a blanket of official papers because Mehta had visitors.

'I don't want to disappoint her,' Karmarkar told Nimesh, his voice thick with feeling.

'I totally understand, Mr Karmarkar. I will not let you down. In fact, Sunidhi will be proud of you.'

'I wanted it to be the other way around, but sometimes, emotions get the better of you,' Karmarkar said stiffly.

'I am completely obligated to you, sir. I will do whatever you want me to.' Karmarkar was appalled by Mehta's subservience, but he tolerated it for his daughter's sake.

'I have given you my commitment in legal ink. Once you fulfil your end of the deal, I will reciprocate with what I have promised. I hope the terms don't disappoint you.'

'Please, sir, don't embarrass me. We need not sign any of these future deals right now. I am already heavily indebted to you.'

'It's a two-way street, Nimesh. Even I will gain plenty from these tie-ups. Just see to it that Khambatta doesn't forsake the wagon in the last lap. I sincerely hope he won't be affronted by our decision to help Sunidhi win the title.'

'Don't worry, I will talk to him.'

'He has been stockpiling resentment ever since that incident at my house. Even today, he backed out of this meeting without an explanation and he didn't even answer my calls.'

'I will take care of Khambatta...'

Karmarkar cut him off with a raised eyebrow. 'In the most

delicate way possible.'

Nimesh qualified his previous statement. 'I won't antagonize him. Trust me, sir,' he added for good measure.

'Fine, I will leave you to it then. Report back to me once you speak to him and send the final agreement copies to me for my authorization.'

No sooner had Karmarkar set his foot outside the suite than Mehta called up Rohit.

Shikha's phone beeped with a message that read 'Room 5502. Reach in five minutes'. She shook with trepidation. Somewhere deep down, she knew that she was about to cross a line.

In Nimesh Mehta's bathroom, surging jets of water abraded his stocky calves as he sipped on a glass of wine and checked his phone. A pack of Marlboro Gold Advance rested on the platform, along with a platter of exotic cheeses, crackers and breads. Nimesh was getting impatient. He lifted his phone to his ear. 'Rohit, where the hell is she?'

'Go to the room immediately. Sir will be very displeased if you make him wait any longer.' Shikha's heart hammered into her ribcage as she read the message. She took shaky steps towards the elevator.

Meanwhile, Mehta downed the wine in his glass and headed to the bar for a refill. He paused momentarily as a thought flitted through his mind. He poured another glass for his guest. There was a sharp rap on the door. He quickly donned a bathrobe, dabbed some cologne on his chest and headed towards the door.

Mehta was nonplussed when he opened the door to find Karmarkar and Khambatta waiting on the other side. He managed to rearrange his face into a blank mask, but Karmarkar, who had left him just a while back, was forced to inquire if they were interrupting him. 'I hope you weren't expecting someone else, Nimesh.'

'No, not at all, Mr Karmarkar. I was quite exhausted, so I decided to unwind a little,' he replied smoothly and greeted Khambatta.

'I bumped into Khambatta in the lobby just when he called me. You should've seen the look on his face when I tapped him on his shoulder,' Karmarkar chuckled.

'Sorry, Nimesh. I was tied up in an important meeting with my all-India distribution head. We will be launching some new products soon, so we were considering some test marketing. In fact, I had called him to Marriott since our meeting was scheduled here. But then it took much longer than I had anticipated.'

'Anyway, I briefed Khambatta about our meeting and he is fine with it, barring a few things which we can discuss now.' Karmarkar wanted to settle everything at that instant, in person, but Nimesh's pallid face disconcerted Karmarkar. 'Are you alright?'

'Y...yeah, everything is fine. I will join you. Give me a minute.' Nimesh excused himself and hurried inside the bedroom. He called up Rohit frantically, but he was on another call. So Nimesh typed out a message furiously. 'Cancel the...' Before he finished typing, Rohit reverted his call. 'Rohit, cancel the girl immediately. I don't want to see her face anywhere close to the...' The doorbell rang before he could finish his instructions. Mehta ran out, but it was too late. Khambatta had already opened the door. His blood curdled.

'Hello. Aren't you a contestant from our pageant?' Khambatta recognized Shikha.

'Y...yes, sir.' Nervousness was clearly scrawled all over her face.

'How can I help you? I'm Ardeshir Khambatta of Belleza. We are the sponsors of this year's pageant. I hope you're aware of that!'

'Yes, sir, I... I know.'

'And this is Mr Karmarkar. He has been...'

'Y...yes, sir. I know who Mr Karmarkar is. His daughter, Sunidhi, is my roommate.'

Karmarkar briefly acknowledged Shikha. He was more interested in knowing what she was doing here and why Nimesh Mehta was sweating profusely.

'Who did you want to meet?' Khambatta asked Shikha.

'I... I came to meet Nimesh sir,' she replied hesitantly.

'Me? Why have you come to meet me? What could I possibly do for you?' Mehta squeaked, his voice shooting up with every passing word.

Shikha was jittery, but she tried to squelch her nerves down. *It's now or never.*

'Myself Shikha Azgaonkar, sir. I have come to c...c...confirm the title with you, sir.'

'Confirm the title? What made you think you could confirm the title?'

Shikha was stumped, but her conscience prodded her. *You came all this way for one thing. All three of them are here to have fun with you. Say whatever you need to and make sure you get what you came for.*

'Sir, I understand. I know what you want.'

'What nonsense! I don't even know you. How dare you come to my room without my permission?'

'B...but, sir, I am... I... I have...' Shikha spluttered.

'What are you up to? Who sent you over here? I will get you disqualified.' Mehta's façade couldn't have been more obvious. But neither of the other men interrupted, lest it snowballed into a bigger issue.

'No, sir! N...no, you can't disqualify me. I am from a very middle-class family, sir. I don't have my father also; he died. Sir, if you disqualify me, I will be nowhere. My mother...what will I tell my mother? And my two younger sisters? They have so much hope from me, sir.'

'Save your pity party for someone who buys it. You should have thought of all that before you came here. Your behaviour is unacceptable,' Mehta barked at her, outraged.

Shikha became hysterical. She bawled and beseeched for forgiveness.

'Who sent you here? Let me find out.' Mehta called up Rohit and gave him a piece of his mind. 'Who the fuck is this girl, Rohit? What's your name?'

'Sh... Shikha Azgaon... Azgaonkar.' She could barely utter decipherable syllables.

'This Shikha Azgaonkar, how did she get here? I want her disqualified at once.'

'No, sir!' Shikha shrieked. 'Please don't do that.' She fell at Mehta's feet and looked up at him with a tear-streaked face. 'Sir, see I got messages from that same Rohit you were talking to. How did I know you were in this room? Who could have given that information to me? He had messaged the room number to me.' She was shaking violently and fainted at the doorway.

Mehta was unmoved. He looked at Karmarkar and Khambatta impassively, maintaining his act. Karmarkar asked Nimesh to disconnect the phone. 'Cool it, Nimesh.'

Khambatta scooped Shikha up and deposited her on the sofa. He coaxed her to drink a glass of water and willed her to breathe regularly. He asked her to repeat that drill and joined Karmarkar and Mehta in a corner.

'It doesn't make any sense to disqualify her, Nimesh. The pageant's name will be dragged in the mud unnecessarily,' said Karmarkar. 'What do you say, Khambatta?'

'I agree. It won't do us any good,' Khambatta concurred, seeing through Mehta's foul play. A mutual consensus was reached that Mehta would give Shikha a stern warning and let her off the hook.

'Don't ever think of doing such a stupid thing again. I am letting you go this time. And nobody in this room will discuss this incident, just so your reputation isn't tarnished.' Mehta put up an over-the-top show.

Khambatta had a smirk on his face, unbearably smug that Mehta's veneer had finally cracked in front of Karmarkar. *What a moron! If he can play such games, I will show him who invented them.*

11

'What's wrong, Shikha? Speak up.' Sania took Shikha by her shoulders and shook her. 'Say something, anything.'

Sania began to panic. She had woken up in the middle of the night to use the washroom. It was three in the morning and Shikha was sitting as still as a statue on her bed. Even before going to bed, Sania had seen Shikha sitting motionless. She had tried to talk to Shikha, but let her be after she got no response. But now, it was beyond alarming. Sania rushed to the other room of the suite and gently nudged Simran, who woke up with a jump.

'What happened?' asked a startled Simran.

'Can you please come with me? It's urgent.' Sania whispered.

Simran rushed with Sania to check on Shikha. She immediately measured her pulse, felt her body temperature and pulled down her bottom eyelids. She tried to jerk Shikha out of her trance, but she didn't even bat an eyelid. 'Shikha, what happened? Look at me.' Simran forced Shikha to turn her head, but the latter had a hollow expression and her eyes had glazed over.

'She hasn't eaten or drunk anything since she came back last evening; not a drop of water,' Sania informed Simran who was thinking of a way to shake Shikha out of the daze.

'What time did you guys come back from the mall?' Simran asked Sania as she splashed water on Shikha's face. 'Get some more water, quickly.'

Sania handed Simran a bottle of drinking water. Simran poured half the bottle on Shikha's head. This did cause her to move but only to shake the water off.

'She left from there at four o'clock. She said she had to meet someone in Juhu.'

'Did she mention whom she had to meet?'

'No, not really. But she looked quite worked up even yesterday.

She finished her shopping in under half an hour and left in a hurry. I brought back her shopping bags to the hotel.'

'Shikha, can you talk? Can you tell me what happened? Have you taken something?' Simran bombarded her with questions, but Shikha remained immobile and mute. 'Does she do drugs or anything?' Simran asked Sania.

'Not that I know of.'

'Where is her mobile?' Simran's analytical mind deduced that her phone would give the next-best picture of what had really happened. She went through it methodically as soon as Sania handed it to her. There were calls and messages from an unknown number. She grew increasingly agitated as she read further. 'Who the fuck does this number belong to?' Simran wondered out loud. 'Do you have any clue?' she asked Sania, who replied in the negative.

'Her call log shows that she spoke to Rohit a bunch of times. There has to be a link there. Should we go and meet him?' Simran weighed the option of waking Rohit up.

'At this hour? Shouldn't we wait a little longer? Till morning, maybe?' Sania was cordial to a fault and she was horrified by the prospect of breaching the unsaid laws of decorum.

'You stay here. I will have a word with him.' Simran was determined to uncover the truth. 'That guy is a sleazy son of a bitch. I will have to use some shock therapy. Otherwise, he will have time to make up alibis.'

The corridors of the floor were expectedly deserted. Simran rang the doorbell to Rohit's room. There was no response. She rang it again and waited but to no avail. Then she rang it continuously till she heard the distinct sound of grumbling.

'Who is it?'

Simran banged her fist on the door. She could hear a pair of feet shuffling inside and a heavy-eyed Rohit finally opened the door. 'What do you want?' he demanded, his voice laced with irritation.

She simply stared at him. Rohit looked around to check if someone else was there with her. He had no clue as to why she was there. 'What do you want, Simran?'

'I want to squeeze your balls. Will you let me? Tell me. Please will you allow me?' Simran asked in a grotesquely infantile voice.

'Are you drunk?' Rohit was jolted. 'How dare you knock on my door at this outrageous hour?'

'What did you do to Shikha?' Simran asked him point-blank.

'What did I do? Where is she?' Rohit's voice had suddenly gone softer. Simran, who was great at picking up non-verbal cues, instantly knew that she had hammered the nail on its head. 'Where is Shikha?' he asked her again, his tail between his legs.

'She is dead.' Her cold, callous voice dropped like a bomb on Rohit's head.

'What? When did this happen? How did she? Don't tell me she killed herself!' Rohit broke into a cold sweat.

Simran brought back to mind all the techniques of interrogation she had learnt in journalism school. 'What did you do to her? Did you molest her or rape her after calling her to Marriott, Room No. 5502?'

'No, no. I only sent her to meet Nimesh sir because she was chewing my brains.'

Fuck me. I should have got my camera. Simran cursed herself. She couldn't go back to get it now. She didn't want to give Rohit any space to breathe or think. 'Oh, so you send all the girls who chew your brains to meet Nimesh sir?'

'Not that way, but she came to my room the other night, two days ago, and insisted that she wanted to win the title.'

'So Nimesh sir fucked her?'

'N...no. There was a fiasco, but I can't tell you much about it.'

'So you will tell it straight to the cops? Did Nimesh Mehta rape Shikha?'

'No, please try and understand...'

'Did you fuck her as well? Have all the title-winners been fucked by Nimesh Mehta all these years?'

'No...not at all,' Rohit fumbled, feeling his back against a wall.

'Not all?'

'No, I said not at all.'

'You seem to be jumbling up your words.'

'What exactly do you want to know? I have to talk to Nimesh sir. I'm going to be in deep shit.'

'I want to know the truth. What exactly happened there?'

'There was a huge fuck up. She went to meet Nimesh sir, but Karmarkar and Khambatta were also there. Things got really ugly.'

'So had they not been there, it would have been a smooth operation, is it? What is your modus operandi? How do you trap the girls? Do you prey on them when they are emotional?' Simran grilled him relentlessly.

'That's not true at all. Shikha had come on her own to talk to me.'

'So didn't you fuck her before sending her to Nimesh sir?'

'N… No. Why would I do anything like that?'

'Why? Don't you have a dick? Don't you like to fuck young girls? Or is it that you can't get it up?'

'You better watch your tone.'

'What are you going to do about it? Answer my question, you lech. Did you fuck her?'

Rohit stayed mum.

'So you did,' Simran looked at him with uncontained disgust.

'She did it of her own accord. Neither did I force her, nor did I emotionally blackmail her.' Rohit realized his plan had floundered miserably.

Simran simply stared at Rohit acrimoniously before storming off. Rohit collected his key card from its socket and hurried after her in his pyjamas.

Back in the room, Shikha had been sobbing inconsolably. Even Sunidhi had woken up but not knowing what to say or how to console Shikha, went back to bed. She was not used to being a caregiver.

Rohit was convinced Shikha was no more. He assumed that the turbulent wails coming from the room were that of the girls grieving over the loss of their friend. His heart sank in the clutches of dread and terror.

When he saw that Shikha was alive and kicking, he felt a huge burden lift off his shoulders. He tried not to look relieved, and feigned concern. Simran studied him intently, making him squirm internally. He did not dare to meet her gaze.

Rohit stretched out his arm to check Shikha's forehead, but she flinched away from his touch. Sania rushed to support Shikha.

Rohit backed away. 'Do we need to call a doctor?'

'There's no need,' Simran's clipped voice answered him from behind. Her glacial tone made Rohit fidget. 'Please let me know if you need anything,' he told Sania customarily and sprinted out.

Shikha's hands quaked as she dry-heaved harshly. Simran watched her histrionics and compelled herself to stay composed.

Sania came closer to Simran and whispered to her, 'I would rather that Shikha talks to her mother once. She will feel better.'

'As you wish. I'm going back to bed. I want to catch up on my sleep. You should try and rest for a while as well. We have a very hectic day ahead.' Simran's offhanded tone took Sania by surprise. She did not miss that there was no love lost for Shikha from her.

Early next morning, Prajakta was getting dressed for school when she saw Shikha's name flashing on her mother, Gurpreet's phone. 'Hi, Shikha di,' she answered brightly.

'Hi, Prajakta. It's me, Sania. Is your mom around?'

'How's it going, Sania didi? We watch you all on TV every day. It must be super fun?' an over-excited Prajakta babbled on the phone. 'I'm so jealous of all the clothes you get to wear...'

'I'm sorry to cut you short, but can I talk to your mother straightaway? It's a matter of urgency.' Sania was in severe need of sleep and in no mood to entertain Prajakta's banter.

'Hello, Sania. Is everything alright, Beta?' Gurpreet asked her kindly.

'Yes, Auntyji, everything is alright.' She stepped away from Shikha and continued. 'It's just that Shikha has been a little nervous since last night, so if you could please talk to her. There's a tremendous amount of pressure here, Aunty.'

'Sure, Beta. Give the phone to her. Is she close by?'

'Yes, Aunty. Just a moment.'

'Your mom,' Sania urged Shikha to talk, but she remained unresponsive. 'Talk to her or she will be even more worried.' Sania pushed the phone into Shikha's hands, but she didn't even hold it. Sania wrapped her fingers around Shikha's hand and lifted it to her ear, coaxing her to speak up.

'Haan, Mummyji. I am fine,' Shikha finally broke her silence.

'What happened, Beta? Why have you become so nervous? Even if you don't win, I will not feel bad. You are trying your best, aren't you?'

Tears tumbled down from Shikha's eyes. The happenings of the last few days flashed in her mind. She was mortified beyond words. She couldn't even share her humiliation with anyone, especially not her mother.

'Take good care of yourself. If you cannot do it, come back. There is no compulsion. Your well-being is more important.'

'Okay, Mummyji,' Shikha choked with guilt.

'Do you want to come back?'

'No, Mummyji. I will be alright.'

Simran was trying desperately to sleep in the other room of the suite, but the melodrama kept her awake. She looked on as Sania sat beside Shikha and caressed her hair tenderly in an attempt to put her to sleep. Shikha hugged her tightly. Sania's warmth melted Simran and her heart went out to Sania.

'I hope you remember that tomorrow is the pre-judging round,' Sania told Shikha, who responded with a meek nod. 'You better pull yourself together.'

'Thank you, Sania, for everything.' Shikha's lips quivered and she burst into tears again.

Simran got up from her bed and collected her purse from the table, which had been recording everything. She plugged a cable in her laptop and slipped her headphones on. Weary to the bone after the previous night's fracas, she drifted off into a deep slumber, with her headphones on.

12

If there was one thing Nimesh Mehta was terribly good at, it was manipulating his way out of tight corners. He called Rohit to the office and together the two of them went through a list of the girls who had been shortlisted for various sub-contests. 'What can we give Shikha?' he asked Rohit bluntly.

After much deliberation, they came to the conclusion that Shikha could be adjusted in two categories. 'But, sir, before we finalize this, we will have to get the approval of the respective co-sponsors. It was clearly mentioned in the co-sponsorship deal contracts that the winners of sub-categories would be chosen by their representatives,' Rohit regurgitated the terms.

'In that case, you have a massive task on hand. You will have to influence these brand buggers to choose Shikha. I cannot be seen getting involved in any of these decisions. I hope that is absolutely clear to you?'

'Yes, sir, crystal clear. So I should name her for both the categories, Miss Daring and Miss Voluptuous, right?'

'Yes, both of them. Invent a new category if you have to. But see to it that her mouth remains shut. That dumb whore has burnt a huge hole in my image.'

'Why have you suggested this girl's name for Miss Daring, Rohit?' asked Dinesh, the brand manager of one of the sponsors.

'Because she is quite daring, very adventurous and fun loving.' Rohit used all the honesty and sincerity that he could draw upon to sell his answer, but Dinesh did not buy it.

'You talk as if you have already had your share of fun with her,' Dinesh guffawed loudly.

Rohit, who was initially intimidated by the prospect of

interacting with Dinesh, realized that he was a fellow lech. Together, they discussed all sorts of slimy and seedy things under the sun and more.

Dinesh agreed to choose Shikha for the Miss Daring award. 'People have an impression these awards are decided after a lot of give and take with the girls, that they are free to get physical with anyone. But it is only when you come inside that you get to know that these are just rumours.'

Poor bastard doesn't know how to play the game. These girls spread out like a bedsheet to get these awards, Rohit thought to himself, while saying out loud, 'Dinesh, these girls are the true symbols of tradition and modernism. They represent a vibrant young India of tomorrow.'

'Three of our company officials will be coming for the award ceremony tomorrow. See you then,' said Dinesh as he collected his bags and got ready to leave.

Rohit heaved a sigh of relief once he was alone, and immediately called up Nimesh. 'Sir, Miss Daring is confirmed for Shikha. I will be meeting the Desirous brand people for Miss Voluptuous now.'

'Hold it. There's no need for that. One award is more than enough for that slut. For Miss Voluptuous, I have Harsha in mind. What do you think of her?'

'Yeah, she has fantastic assets. I think the brand will also prefer someone like her.' Rohit walked towards his room while he spoke to Nimesh.

'That was easy. I didn't even have to convince you to agree with it. Have you been shagging her as well?'

'No, sir,' Rohit squeaked.

Nimesh chortled at his pathetic joke. 'I was pulling your leg. But I am curious to know how you convinced Shikha to meet me. Did she approach you or did you dangle something at her?'

Rohit had dangled something at her alright, but he wasn't stupid enough to tell his boss about it. 'She approached me, sir. She told me she wanted to meet you and confirm the title.'

'And you asked her to connect with me straightaway? Did you

brief her that she would have to service me to confirm the title?'

'Obviously, sir. This is not my first time. I explicitly asked her what she wanted to meet you for. And she told me that she would do anything to win the title. I told her that she had to be cent percent sure because if you are willing to help her, it shouldn't happen that she isn't willing to help you.'

'Help? We should register ourselves as an NGO.' Nimesh roared with laughter. 'So anyone who approaches you to meet me is asked to help me in return for my help? You are one corny rascal.'

'Sir, this was just the sixth or seventh time in all these years. You have always managed to talk to them directly otherwise.'

'Approaching them directly was becoming risky. It's easy to pick them up when they get sloshed at parties, but otherwise, it is a very tricky thing. To be honest, I love the thrill. Anyway... I'll call you later.' Nimesh had hung up before Rohit could react.

Rohit simply shook his head and reached for his room's door knob. He was about to step in, when he saw Simran. He jumped inside and tried to slam the door shut. Alas, Simran had managed to stick her foot in the door.

'What kind of behaviour is this? What the hell do you want? You can't barge into my room like this,' Rohit warned a belligerent Simran.

'I need to talk to you.' If Simran could burn a hole by glaring at someone, Rohit would've been mush by then.

'What about? You spoke to me at length yesterday. There isn't anything else I want to talk to you about. You lied to me about Shikha.' Rohit peered out of a half-open door as Simran refused to back out.

'Listen up, vile pervert. I swear to everything holy I will ruin you.'

'Don't give me such empty threats. We are running a perfectly legitimate business.'

'You think it's legitimate to create a den where you prey on young gullible girls and sleep with them in exchange for promises of titles?'

'People use sex as a currency everywhere; be it offices, colleges and even schools. You name it. What's the big deal anyway? It's not like someone is getting raped.'

'What if I file a case of molestation against you?' Simran couldn't believe her own ears as those words tumbled from her mouth.

'What? You are insane.'

'As a matter of fact, I am. Are you going to let me in or not?'

'Only if you watch that loose tongue of yours.' Rohit let her in reluctantly. 'Using such hostility will not get us anywhere.' Simran exhaled inaudibly and stepped in.

Rohit offered her a chair and settled down on a sofa facing her. 'Will you have some tea or coffee? Or, some fruit juice?' Rohit asked her under the pretext of polite courtesy, but he was simply getting his thoughts together.

'Can you make me meet Nimesh Mehta? I am willing to do anything.'

'No, I cannot.'

'But why not?'

'You don't qualify.'

Simran cackled at him disdainfully. 'In what sense do I not qualify? How would you even know? You haven't even tried me yet. I guess I will have to give the audition with you first before you okay me for the big boss, right?'

'I think you are being unnecessarily crude and nasty.'

'You exploit young girls and then have the audacity to call me crude? You whoring hypocrite,' she lashed out.

'It's better if you leave right away.'

'I will not and you cannot make me. I want to know how your entire racket works.'

'Are you doing a journalistic stint here? If you think you are some activist who has come to clean the system, then you are fooling yourself. For your information, out of these twenty-five girls, twenty are willing to participate in an orgy to win the title; they are that desperate. So save your reformist agenda for some other time.'

'How can you be so sure that most of them are willing to sleep for a trophy?'

'Just like a goldsmith knows his gold from other metals, a girlsmith, like me or Nimesh, knows how to assess girls inside out.'

'What is the meaning of fillers, Mr Girlsmith?' Simran wanted to gag at his sickening terminology, but she stayed strong.

'You still haven't figured that out from the time you interviewed Nimesh sir?'

Simran gave him a tight-lipped death stare.

'It is something that will disturb you, so it is better left unsaid.'

'I don't care if I find it disturbing. Tell me what it means,' Simran demanded.

'It is a simple term. You fill in the blanks with fillers.'

'What do you mean?'

'In your channel, when you have to fill a slot which does not have a high viewership, what do you do?'

'We get a show from the past or some low-priced programme to fill that slot.'

'Exactly! That is what a filler is, to fill the slots.'

'So most of the girls you get are fillers? But how is it a game of fillers?'

'You're a smart cookie. You will figure it out.'

A few of them had wrapped themselves in sarongs and kaftans, but most of the girls were strutting in their swimwear when Rohit stepped into the banquet hall. He was doing a cursory headcount. When he passed in front of Shikha, he could feel the anger radiating off her and apparently, so could Simran and Sania. Simran was apathetic to it, but Sania held Shikha's hand and gave it a reassuring squeeze, willing her to calm down. Rohit moved along, stopped to have a discussion with Neelam and handed a list to her. She stepped forward to address the contestants. 'We will be heading for the finale venue in about an hour and a half, for a basic stage rehearsal.'

The girls scampered off to their rooms to pack and get dressed. Within no time, they were out carrying their bags, rushing towards the lobby and on to the driveway.

Even while they were waiting in the driveway, some of the girls, including Shikha and Sania, were practising their choreography. Shikha paused the song and took off her headphones when Simran approached her and gestured that she wanted to talk to her.

'What are you talking about?' asked Shikha, clueless.

'You told Harsha that Sunidhi will categorically win the title. You specifically mentioned that they will ensure that Sunidhi wins. You were referring to her dad and Nimesh Mehta, weren't you?' Shikha was taken aback by Simran's knowledge of this and looked at her suspiciously. Shikha was sure that when she had spoken to Harsha, there had been no one else in the suite, so she wondered if Simran had been hiding somewhere and eavesdropping.

'Don't play coy with me. Harsha has told me all about it.' Simran's explanation comforted Shikha slightly.

'I got to know from Khambatta that Sunidhi has been blackmailing her dad to pull the strings to make her win. It seems like from the day she made that bet with you, she decided to win by hook or by crook.' Shikha's revelation did not surprise Simran even a little bit. She had expected this would happen all along.

'But I am not going to let her win. I have my own plans.' Shikha's bumptious tone reflected her unforgiving mood.

'Like what?'

'Why should I share them with you? So you can win the title? You have to hunt for your survival.' With that Shikha gave a haughty flick of her wavy hair and sauntered off to the luxury coach that had entered the driveway.

Simran discreetly switched off the camera.

13

The who's who of the glitterati were present at the final event of the pageant. Twenty-five bewitching girls marched to rousing music and formed a semi-circular arc on the stage. A spotlight illuminated the host of the show, Karan Dhillon, who walked briskly with a mike in his hand and waved jauntily at the crowd. He announced the names of the ten semi-finalists. Sania, Shikha, Sunidhi and Simran, all four of them were selected. They were happy about it, but Shikha was ecstatic. She gave Simran an 'I told you so' look from across the stage. The top ten finalists smiled and held their stance as the crowd cheered for them. Then they rushed backstage, with poise, of course, to tog out in their next ensemble.

Away from the glitzy finery and foofaraw, a perturbing picture greeted one's eyes. The girls who had been rejected tore at their hair and mourned their loss.

The ten semi-finalists had a one-on-one with celebrity judges of their choice, who, in turn, asked them the most hackneyed questions. The objective was to gauge their conversational skills, clarity of thought and poise. Five of the ten semi-finalists would be eliminated based on this question-answer round.

Lacing it with as much drama as he could, the host announced with great aplomb the names of the top five finalists—Ankita, Dhwani, Sania, Simran and Sunidhi. A booming ovation resounded in the auditorium as the five finalists made a lap of the stage. Karmarkar's wife grabbed his arm with glee as he subtly nodded at Mehta.

Shikha felt like someone had stuck a knife in her gut and pulled her insides out. Soon everything in her mind's eye was enveloped in a red haze. Sania was very pleased with her victory but felt sorry for her friend's loss. Sunidhi simply had a look of arrogance on her face. But Simran was in a complete daze. She imagined being crowned Miss India and visualized the baffled reactions of people around her. Photographers and media people were clamouring to get her shots.

'Simran!' Sania called out to her and shook her out of her reverie. 'Where are you lost? We have to get ready. Hurry!'

Simran took a detour on the way and found a secluded corner. She called up the one person she could count on. 'I'm in a huge dilemma, Rudy.' She updated him about the recent developments and her current predicament.

'I would say it's a once-in-a-lifetime opportunity, babe,' Anirudh encouraged her. He was seated in the audience next to Gul who gestured at him to hand over the phone. 'Gul Sir wants to talk to you.'

'Go for it, Simran. You will kill it.' Gul sounded fiercely excited.

'I am not so sure, sir.'

'You might not have expected this to happen, but life is unpredictable. Things happen when you least expect them to. You have to be fearless, Simran. Here, talk to Anirudh.' Gul returned the phone to Anirudh.

'What have you decided, babe?'

'I don't think it will be right, Rudy.' Simran's forehead was creased with strain.

'Why do you say that? If you win, you can make people listen to whatever you have to say,' Anirudh tried his best to wangle her, but a hint of exasperation in his voice betrayed him.

'You know that I have been against beauty pageants in principle. My objective was to expose the pageant, not win it. If by some strange coincidence I win it, I will be a big hypocrite.'

'I am sorry, I don't agree.'

'I would rather be a filler.' Simran was surprised to hear herself using that term.

'What do you mean?' Anirudh asker her, baffled.

'It means you are a scheming chameleon. Because I am doing well now, you feel I should go ahead and change my priorities and beliefs. How do you think it will pan out? Do you want me to create a ruckus when they are about to crown me? Or better yet, tomorrow when I become the Beauty Queen, I could shout slogans against them during the press conference.'

'We could think of ways to do this. If you are an insider, you will be privy to a lot of grimy things. I would say you shouldn't back out.'

'I would like to prove, as an outsider, that this beauty business is ugly, rather than work from within it and get caught in a "sour grapes" situation if I don't win it.'

Anirudh walked towards the backstage while talking to Simran. 'Listen, I have got to go now. This is entirely your call, Sims.'

Meanwhile, Shikha had created quite a scene backstage. She shook with fury as she shouted expletives at the organizers. Her theatrics caught Simran's attention and she instinctively recorded it all. 'That bastard Nimesh Mehta is running a huge racket with the help of his pimp Rohit,' she screamed, outraged. 'This is just a show to fool people. The winner has been decided. Take it in writing that Karmarkar's daughter, Sunidhi, will win. That obnoxious bitch even made a bet!'

Rohit, who felt humiliated to the hilt, did not dare to shut Shikha up. Unable to locate Simran in the green room, he snapped. 'Where the hell is Simran? Find her immediately.'

Some of the young volunteers backstage scrambled to locate Simran. One of them found her lying on the floor, unconscious, near the backstage wings and shrieked for help. Neelam reached the spot and asked for someone to give her a bottle of water. She splashed some water on Simran's face and shook her as gently as she could.

With what seemed like gargantuan effort, Simran opened her eyelids sluggishly and registered her surrounding with a glazed look in her eyes. 'I... I suddenly felt v...very giddy. I don't remember what happened.' Simran's pretence was convincing.

'Can you please get up and get ready as soon as possible? We are running ridiculously late.' Neelam had an uncontained sense of urgency in her voice.

'I don't think I will be able to continue, ma'am.' Simran sounded so crestfallen that Neelam didn't have the heart to push her, lest she goofed up on stage.

Neelam was having a heated discussion with Rohit who stopped her to answer his phone. 'Give me a moment. It's Nimesh sir.'

She was getting increasingly agitated. 'We don't have much time,' Neelam snapped at Rohit. 'Tell Sir we need to finalize the fifth girl right now.' Rohit indicated to her to simmer down.

'Yes, sir. Okay, sir! We will take Harsha.' Rohit's statement irked Neelam who thrust a stack of papers under his nose and pointed at a list vehemently. 'I will call you back in exactly five minutes. I will brief Neelam to get Harsha ready.'

No sooner had Rohit disconnected the call than Neelam launched into an apoplectic rant. 'What on earth is happening? Why the hell do we have this list if you're randomly picking somebody? The scores are clearly in favour of Anusuya. Not to mention, Harsha is at the bottom-most spot on the list; even Shikha has a better score than her.'

'We cannot go against the boss' orders,' Rohit told her in a matter-of-fact tone, categorically dodging her eyes.

Neelam was appalled when she had an inkling of what was happening, but it was too late to pick an argument with him.

'The judges will know that the scores have been tampered with.' Neelam tried one last feeble attempt to reason with Rohit.

'The judges don't know the cumulative scores. Each of them only knows the points that they individually awarded to the girls. They will not know what marks the others have given them.'

Neelam was stumped. She couldn't argue with his logic. 'Let me get Harsha ready,' she said sulkily and left in a huff.

The volunteers stopped Shikha from getting inside the green room. Her hysterical outburst just moments ago had scared the organizers and they did not want a repeat of that.

'I have to meet her. It's urgent.' Shikha was fuming. The make-up on her face was smeared by tears and sweat.

'We have been instructed to not let you go inside, ma'am,' a young volunteer pleaded.

'Buy why? You think I will kill someone? Just because I had the balls to speak about the bitter truth, I'm suddenly a mad woman?'

Inside, Sania was being helped by two assistants to get ready. She was wearing a deep crimson floor-length gown, which had a high slit and was encrusted with dull, sparkling stones in the bodice. The deep neck revealed a creamy expanse of skin and angular collar bones. She wore her long, straight hair naturally. A wide gold wrist-cuff was her choice of accessory. She looked like a warrior. When she found out that Shikha wanted to meet her and she wasn't being allowed entry, Sania went out to meet Shikha.

'She is in a foul mood. Don't give her too much importance. She will upset you as well.' Dhwani, who was in the adjacent make-up cubicle, cautioned Sania, who gave her a curt nod of acknowledgement.

Seeing Shikha's dishevelled state, both physical and mental, Sania was deeply stirred. She immediately broke through the cordon of volunteers who were stopping Shikha and hugged her affectionately. Sometimes, all it takes is one word, or one gesture to make a person crumble. Shikha sobbed profusely when Sania embraced her and out flowed her tears, resentment, disappointment and despair. 'I thought I could win, I so wanted to. Now there's no hope for me. I am finished. This was the *only* chance I had of becoming something.'

Sania blinked back her tears. 'This is not the end of the world, Shikhu. In fact, this is just the beginning. You have a lot more going for you than this. Just hold yourself, take a deep breath and let go of all your anger.'

Shikha stopped hiccupping and wiped her eyes dry. 'I want to tell you something very confidential, Sania.' Shikha dragged her to a relatively secluded corner.

'What is it? Can't we talk about it after the final round, please?' Sania was a bundle of nerves, but she wanted to ameliorate Shikha's pain as well. Shikha jumped as two people crossed them. Unhappy with the atmosphere, she tugged a half-willing Sania to the washrooms.

Simran noticed them but could not chase the two as her motives would become glaringly obvious. All the same, a few moments later, she entered the loo as well. 'Just don't mention it to anyone, please, Sanoo,' she heard Shikha tell Sania.

'Hey!' Simran surprised the two.

'Hi, Simran. I heard you dropped out of the competition. I hope you're feeling better now,' Sania said sympathetically.

'I was terribly giddy all of a sudden, but I can feel myself recuperating. What are you guys doing here? Don't you have to be on the stage in a couple of minutes?' she asked Sania.

'I do, but she was very upset. So I was trying to boost her morale,' Sania said, looking at Shikha.

'Yup, she is trying to boost my morale,' Shikha's mindless regurgitation of Sania's words was enough to ring alarm bells in Simran's mind. She sensed something was off but didn't push it.

'I really need to get back to the green room and finish my make-up.' Sania left in a dash, with a faint rustle of her gown.

Simran was just about to walk out with Shikha when Shikha stopped in her tracks.

'Didn't you come here to use the loo?' Shikha asked Simran.

'Oh yes, I completely forgot,' Simran laughed unconvincingly as she turned back to use the washroom.

'I wanted to ask you something.' Shikha had a slight doubt about Simran in her mind.

'Even I wanted to talk to you. Give me a second.' Simran shut the cubicle door, sat on the toilet seat for a few seconds, out of compulsion, flushed and stepped out. But Shikha was nowhere to be found.

14

Garbed in ornate couture floor-length gowns, the five finalists lined up on the stage, each in front of a mini workstation which had an electronic notepad, and awaited further instructions.

'One question will be posed to all of you. You have to deliberate your answer and jot it down on the electronic notepad. You will have exactly ninety seconds. You have to then recite your answer, word for word, so that the judges and audience can give their verdict,' the host, Karan Dhillon, explained to them. He then circled the contestants slowly to confirm that they were ready and to remind them that this was the last and the most crucial lap of the pageant.

'And the final question for our gorgeous young ladies is: In the glamour industry, what according to you is more important—beauty or character?'

The girls thought hard for a moment before scribbling their answers on the tab. They were fraught with nerves and nit-picked on their answers as they wrote. Every passing second seemed to tick by faster and the pressure mounted. The blaring sound of the buzzer told them their time was up.

'That's all the time you'll get, ladies. Please put down your stylus.'

The girls heaved a sigh of disappointment. They stepped on stage, one by one, as their names were called out, to reveal their answers.

Ankita was the first one to be summoned. 'Even if beauty is skin deep, in today's superficial world, beauty alone can take you places. No one is bothered about character.' Ankita's answer evoked a lukewarm response, and she sensed that her viewpoint was perhaps not welcomed.

When Harsha took centre stage, Rohit's beady eyes instinctively sought Nimesh Mehta, who was seated in the crowd, close to the judges, and just a few seats away from Karmarkar.

'Your character is what you have when you have lost your beauty. So, according to me, both are equally important.' Harsha got a tepid response from the audience as well.

On such platforms, diplomacy didn't score points.

'Beauty is what you have, character is what you are, and happiness comes from what you are.' Dhwani's answer impressed the audience and there was a thunderous applause.

Sania was next. She held herself high and with a confidence that could impress even her detractors. She had a steady voice and a serene smile as she answered. 'Youth and beauty fade away, but character endures forever.' Sania got an electric response from the audience.

The last contestant to give her answer was Sunidhi. All eyes were glued on her as she took centre stage. She looked statuesque in a risqué gold lurex gown which accentuated her toned form and complemented the warm undertones of her skin. Nimesh Mehta briefly exchanged looks with Karmarkar and both their faces were wrought with unease. *Would Sunidhi manage to sweep the audience and the judges' ruling?* Everyone eagerly awaited her response. But the silence stretched and the clock kept ticking.

A twitch of discomfiture jolted through Nimesh's body. His vision located Rohit, who looked equally anxious. Both of them exchanged an agitated look. Mehta's stomach did a backflip as he realized something had gone awry.

Sunidhi had still not spoken her answer and the audience had started whispering.

'Hello, we have to go home,' a voice from the audience broke the silence and they all started jeering at her till Karan had to command them to mellow down and maintain decorum. He then called out to Sunidhi, but she didn't respond. She stood like a statue, with a glazed look in her eyes. The host looked at Rohit, who was staring at Nimesh, who in turn was surveying Karmarkar for an indication. They were clueless. Mehta finally nodded his head and suggested that they should move on.

As Karan approached Sunidhi, she gazed at him vacantly.

'Sunidhi, I am extremely sorry, but we cannot give you any more time. Judges, I request you to prepare the final list of winners.'

The judges had a lengthy discussion, while the volunteers chaotically ran to and fro, taking and handing papers.

An envelope was handed over to the host. Mehta faked an expression of polite curiosity that indicated he was not involved in the decision-making process. But in reality, nothing happened on the ground without his knowledge. Rohit had already sent him a text with the names of the winner and the runners-up as soon as the scores had been tallied. Mehta was not at all happy with the results, but he was helpless.

'The girls whose names I will announce now are going to be in a different orbit altogether after this moment. They will become the new stars, the new faces to launch a thousand brands and to inspire young girls across the nation. The first person I want to call on stage is the second runner-up, Miss Harsha Mehra.' The audience cheered on as Harsha walked towards the stage.

'The first runner-up is Miss Dhwani Majithia.' Dhwani started crying as soon as her name was announced. She walked to the stage, giddy with happiness.

'And now, ladies and gentlemen, the name we have been waiting to hear. The winner of the seventh India Beauty Queen pageant is Miss Sania Ahmed!' There was an ear-splitting cheer as the crowd hooted for her victory. Sania thought her ears had deceived her. She covered her face with both her hands and did not budge for a couple of seconds. 'Miss Sania, I hope you are alive,' Karan jested.

Sania laughed uninhibitedly and strode on stage. The winner from the previous year's pageant congratulated her and slipped a sash over her head and placed it diagonally across her body. She then crowned Sania with an exquisite crown made of prismatic crystals interspersed with massive garnet drops.

Emotions were running high as Sania waved at the crowd, her vision blurred by happy tears brimming in her eyes. When she made her way towards the backstage, Shikha was still drying her tears. She beamed at her friend, sincerely ecstatic for her win.

Simran, who stood besides Shikha, punched the air to cheer Sania and whistled loudly. The three of them hugged tightly, grateful for each other. But Sunidhi, who was still in a state of bewilderment, looked at Sania in disbelief. She fumed at the three of them, as she was proved wrong.

Shiraz, who was seated in the audience, finally managed to make his way backstage and locate Sania. She saw tears of pride welling in his eyes as she spoke to her mother on the cell phone. Sania was collected and composed all this while but talking to her ammi burst a dam within her. She wept as she hugged her father, grateful for having such supportive parents.

'Thank you, Abbu,' she said, realizing that those two words fell short of conveying the surge of gratitude she felt for her parents, and kissed her father's cheek.

After

15

The after-party of the IBQ pageant was an extravagant affair. Wine flowed abundantly, exotic gourmet food was lined up on the buffet table and the people were ready for revelry.

The contestants were looking forward to the party, as they could finally let their hair down. But a significant number of contestants had chosen to return home instead. After three gruelling weeks, they couldn't wait to get back to the familiar comfort of their own beds.

Sunidhi was one of the absentees but for a different reason. She didn't want to meet anyone after the fiasco in the finale. Karmarkar had gone backstage to talk to Sunidhi after the show, but she was nowhere to be found. She didn't want to see anyone, especially her father. She was inexplicably upset with him for having let her down. She took off with Jai and was unreachable ever since.

Shikha's emotional rollercoaster ride had left her too jaded to enjoy the party. But since Sania had won, she felt like a small part of her had too. She tagged along with Sania in the hopes that she would meet someone worthwhile who could change her fortune.

Simran was also there for the party, but she was on a mission. She wanted to get to the bottom of what had happened in the finale. She marked Nimesh Mehta, Karmarkar, Khambatta and Shikha as targets for information to solve the entire jigsaw.

Mehta, who was in high spirits, was surrounded by a bevy of beauties. After the pageant, he had a bigger role in their lives. Like bees to a honeypot, the girls besieged Mehta, knowing well that he possessed the magic wand. His talent management outfit was the most prolific one in the industry and being in his good books could change the girls' destinies.

But Mehta's exterior was a façade for the tempestuous storm brewing inside. He had failed to fulfil one small demand that Karmarkar had made of him. He had unleashed his pent-up anger on his team after the pageant got over. 'What the fuck were you doing? Sleeping? I am the owner of this bloody pageant and even I don't know who stole the thunder from right under my ass. What will I tell Karmarkar?'

His team knew better than to respond to him when he was so waspish.

Mehta was making small talk with one of the overeager contestants when his phone rang. He excused himself. 'Yes, sir. I am at the party itself. Where are you? I will be there right away, sir.'

Karmarkar was nibbling on a small portion of smoked lobster salad and a slice of garlic bread brushed with rosemary oil. He was impeccably dressed in a bespoke charcoal single-breasted dinner jacket with notch lapels, a crisp arctic-white dress shirt open at the collar, formal slacks and hand-stitched Oxfords. Despite his air of sprezzatura, Karmarkar radiated an aura of dangerous power. His onyx eyes glittered in the aureate lighting. He acknowledged Mehta with a curt nod as the latter seated himself opposite him.

'Aren't you going to eat something?' Karmarkar asked Mehta out of ingrained courtesy.

'No, I am good. I will have another drink though, and then eat with my team later,' Mehta beckoned the waiter as he replied and placed his order of a large Glenmorangie Signet with four ice cubes.

'Did you make any progress in finding out what happened?' Karmarkar was referring to the debacle that had happened in the finale, when Sunidhi went completely blank.

'To be honest, there has been some disturbing news about Sunidhi all along. I did not want to bother you earlier, but I feel that could be what triggered this particular incident.' Mehta's pejorative tone grabbed Karmarkar's undivided attention. 'See, Sunidhi has been seen taking some stuff, you know. Hope you understand.' Mehta tried to avoid putting the reality explicitly.

'I am sorry, I don't,' Karmarkar replied brusquely. He knew what Mehta implied, but he wanted Mehta to utter those words out loud.

'She has been doing hard drugs...cocaine, ecstasy and meth.'

'How do you know that?' Karmarkar felt like the world

had slipped from under his feet, but he maintained a collected demeanour.

'People from my team have seen her do it. She had some friends visiting her at the hotel who were heavily into it.'

'Why didn't you tell me earlier?'

'I was not sure if I should have. Most of the kids today indulge in these things recreationally. Barring a few, most of them get out at the right time,' shrugged Nimesh.

'And you are saying Sunidhi will not be like one of those few?' Contempt dripped off every word Karmarkar articulated. He disliked how casual and nonchalant Mehta's attitude was.

'I hope not. Please don't hold it against me because I didn't want to be a cheap shot. I was just keeping a watch on her.'

'No grudges. Thanks for keeping me in the loop. I need to make a move.' Karmarkar shook hands with Nimesh and was ready to leave. One of his security personnel called up the driver and informed him to keep the car ready.

Mehta looked on as Karmarkar strode out, oozing a sense of purpose—as always. Rohit, who had been on the fringes, approached his boss. He handed some documents to Mehta and whispered something in his ear. Mehta's eyes enlarged when Rohit delivered him a whammy as he skimmed through the printouts. 'Are you sure?' he asked Rohit.

'Very sure, sir. Look over there, to your right. See how unreservedly Khambatta is chatting up Simran Thapar. It looks like they have known each other from before. Gul Mohammad is the head of Simran's channel and his assistant looks like he's mooning over Simran,' Rohit said ominously.

'But Simran withdrew herself from the top five. How can there be a connection?' A bewildered Nimesh looked at Rohit for answers.

16

'Every fucking step in the game was planned out for me. I still don't understand how it went to shit. Someone screwed me over big time.' Scads of cigarette stubs dotted the ashtray. Sunidhi had been smoking like a chimney. She puffed away as she spoke to Jai on the phone.

'You go easy, Sunidhi. Let your dad find that out. If you try to poke your nose in mud, you'll get muck on your face.'

'Sunidhi! Sunidhi!' Karmarkar's voice thundered from outside the room.

'Jai, I have to go. My father is here,' she whispered hurriedly and disconnected the call. She promptly cleared the cigarette stubs, sprayed some room freshener, popped a chewing gum and answered her father. 'I'm here in the room, Pops. Just give me a minute, I'm on a call.' Sunidhi dashed to the washroom and spritzed herself with a zesty body mist. She saw her reflection in the mirror and flipped herself off.

Karmarkar was in a perceivably grim mood. He sat in front of Sunidhi who made a show of being too occupied chewing gum and categorically avoided his eyes.

'Where were you last night?' Karmarkar asked Sunidhi once she had settled down across him in the living room.

'I had gone out with Jai and some other friends.' Sunidhi didn't feel an iota of contrition for not meeting her father after the pageant.

'I heard some very alarming news; something I would have never expected to hear,' Karmarkar continued in a relentlessly severe manner.

'What is it? Did you find out who was responsible?' Sunidhi was anxious to know if there had been any developments regarding last evening's catastrophe.

'Yes, I have. I found out that you are heavily into drugs. Is it true?' Karmarkar asked her without any prevarication, blocking all her exit routes.

'N...no, no, Pops. Who told you? It's an utter lie,' Sunidhi gathered her wits about her.

'Look at me straight in the eye when you are addressing me, Sunidhi,' Karmarkar told her with a chilling calmness.

'I do s...smoke sometimes, Pops. But that's all.'

'I know that very well. Two years ago, you weren't willing to admit that either. The one thing that I have always told you is to own up to anything you do. I want to know why you went blank on stage. Was it due to something someone had mixed in your food or drink, or some stuff you had taken? Had you doped too much?' Every question Karmarkar hurled at Sunidhi felt like a punch in her gut.

'You are jumping to conclusions, Pops,' Sunidhi started to bawl. 'Someone has brainwashed you. You have no idea what happened last evening. You must have very little trust in me if you're condemning me on the basis of a speculation. Yes, I may have taken a lot of liberties, but I have never been irresponsible. You are accusing me of being grossly unreliable.'

Hearing her daughter sob, Sunidhi's mother rushed to the living room. 'What's the matter? Why this ruckus?'

'Your daughter is living in denial. I gave her the chance to confess and come clean, but she doesn't want to admit anything.'

'Did you even ask Nimesh Mehta how the fiasco happened? Why I blanked out?' Sunidhi asked her father in between whimpers.

'I did; he was the first person I spoke with. He alluded it to something you had tried several times before. He said his team had given him a low-down on your activities. According to their reports, you have been crossing the line often, rather snorting it often.'

'I can't believe you would label me as a junkie simply because you have failed to find the actual reason behind the botch-up.' Sunidhi was done crying. 'I don't think I would like to be insulted any more. You are palming off your failure on to me. I don't want to continue living here.'

'What do you mean? What are you going to do?' Sunidhi's mother asked her. A sense of foreboding settled in the pit of her stomach.

'I want to be on my own.' Sunidhi looked at her dad and declared it with a finality that shook him.

But he didn't back down. 'You are free to do as you please. I just wanted you to be honest and have the courage to fess up your follies.'

'Don't be stubborn, both of you. Please don't fight! Whatever happened has happened; there's no point fighting over spilt milk. Why do you have to be so obstinate, Yogesh?' Sunidhi's mom tried her best to play the peacekeeper.

'She is the one being obstinate, not me.'

'I am leaving this house.' Sunidhi had had enough of this and she walked away in a huff. She went to her room and immediately started tossing her belongings into a suitcase. She called up Jai as she bundled additional clothes and shoes in a haversack. 'I am coming over to your house, Jai. I will be staying there for a few days.'

'What happened? Did you have a row with your dad?' Jai asked her in all anxiousness.

'I will come over and talk.' With that, Sunidhi hung up and hauled her bags to the living room.

Her mother was hysterical. 'What are you doing, my child? Don't be stupid! This is not such a serious issue. Yogesh, please tell her not to be impulsive and behave childishly,' her mother urged her father, breaking down utterly.

'She is not a kid any more. She needs to grow up. She made me do things that were completely against my principles. As if that wasn't enough, she has done something that is far beyond my level of tolerance,' he said furiously.

'So be it.' Sunidhi picked up the car keys.

'Stop her, Yogesh. Stop her! I beg you, please stop her. You can't let our only child walk out of our lives.'

'I want her to know life is not a joyride. I have given her such a cushy existence that she has forgotten that underneath the privilege she takes for granted are the thorns that I have treaded on.'

'Sunidhi, at least you be a little more sensible, my dear. Don't take a step that will create a permanent rift between us,' her mother implored.

'No, as your husband keeps telling me, I need to experience how tough life is outside.'

'Leave the car keys and credit cards.' Karmarkar's pitiless remark cut Sunidhi like a knife. There was no way she could yield now. She fished out the car keys and credit cards from her tote and flung them onto the floor. Karmarkar winced and Sunidhi left.

Simran was at home, engrossed in the footage playing on her laptop.

Sania and Shikha were fooling around in this part of the recording, making faces and passing silly comments. Shikha was particularly nasty as far as Sunidhi was concerned.

Simran fast-forwarded it.

Shikha was using Sunidhi's expensive make-up when she wasn't around. Sania, who usually did not participate in such pranks, was keeping an eye on the door. As soon as she saw Sunidhi coming in, Sania gave Shikha a signal. In a state of panic, instead of running towards her own room, Shikha went straight towards the entrance and bumped into Sunidhi. The excessive and bizarre make-up on her face actually made Sunidhi laugh.

Simran paused the footage. She reflected on a few things and made a mental note of them before fast-forwarding it and playing the video.

'That bet was quite an ego trip she was on,' Sania was telling Simran and Shikha.

'But she is doing whatever she can to win the bet.' Shikha replied.

Simran fast-forwarded the tape again. It was the day of the final round when she had feigned unconsciousness. She had deliberately kept the camera rolling when she had pretended to be grievously unwell. She spotted Anirudh in the footage. He was interacting with Shikha. *That's very strange*, she thought to herself.

Simran instantly called up Anirudh. 'Hey, what time are you

coming back? I had to talk to you. No, no, let's talk once you're back.' Simran shut down her laptop, disconnected the hard disk and put them both back in her bag. *Why would Anirudh come backstage?* she wondered.

Shikha was back home in Pune, sulking futilely.

'Ta da! Here, take this, from me to you.' Shilpi handed a small, cardboard Miss India crown to Shikha.

Sensing her bad mood, Prajakta, who was trying on one of Shikha's dresses, intentionally tried to get a rise from her sister. 'Oh shit! It tore.'

Shikha looked at Prajakta angrily. She made Prajakta take the dress off and went back to sitting sullenly in a corner. Seeing her daughter so down in the dumps, Gurpreet decided to cheer her up. 'Let's go for a movie, just the two of us,' she told Shikha.

'Even I want to come along,' Shilpi interjected.

'Do you want to go, Beta?' Gurpreet asked Shikha again.

'I don't like being treated as a loser. Please spare me your sympathy,' snapped Shikha at her mom. 'For God's sake, leave me alone.' She stomped off to her room and locked herself in.

After some time, Gurpreet, who had made delicious, steaming hot soup for Shikha, rapped on her door. But there was no answer. 'Shikha, open the door, I have made your favourite carrot soup. Shikha, open the door.' Her mother continued to knock on the door. One by one, Gurpreet, Prajakta and Shilpi kept getting things to bribe Shikha with, but there was no response whatsoever.

Soon, the seconds stretched to minutes, and the minutes to hours. It had been two hours and Shikha still hadn't answered the door. Gurpreet began to panic. She started hammering her fist on the door, fearing the worst. 'Don't get so upset, Shikha. I don't have anyone but you to carry the burden of these two,' she cried.

Seeing their mother so distressed, Prajakta and Shilpi started hollering away as well.

'Open the door, Didi!'

'Please open the door!'
'Mummy is worried!'
Their shouts of concern were only met with silence.

On her mother's instruction, Prajakta pulled up a chair in front of the door and clambered onto it. She swivelled open the *roshandan*, or blinds, and peered inside. What she saw made the walls of her throat close in. Shikha was lying insentient on the bed and her hand hung limply off its edge. 'DIDI!' she screamed with insurmountable anguish and fell into a heap on the chair. Her vision blurred as a big swell of tears threatened to spill out. Seeing her so, Gurpreet felt like someone had reached inside her and was tearing her gut out. 'What did you see?' Gurpreet grasped Prajakta's shoulders and joggled her, but she wordlessly shook her head in denial.

Just then the door opened and a muzzy-eyed Shikha emerged out of the room. 'What happened? Why are you guys creating such a scene?' Shikha asked.

Gurpreet, who was still in a daze, couldn't form a coherent sentence because of the overwhelming relief that washed over her. 'You were not resp... Why didn't you open the... I was so scared.'

'Mummyji, I fell asleep,' Shikha replied irritably, still drowsy from her siesta.

Gurpreet tightly hugged her daughter; Prajakta and Shilpi joined in as well.

17

'Are there any global issues that you plan to take up, like the earlier winners of the pageant did?'

'Yes, I would like to voice my support for those protesting against crimes towards women,' Sania was composed. She had conducted herself reasonably well so far at the press conference held at the Aurangabad airport.

The entire media of Aurangabad had descended upon the airport to welcome their local hero. The photographers were falling over each other to get the best shot of the new India Beauty Queen. Luckily, she had been briefed about such a response in advance and the local administration had made proper arrangements. A makeshift pandal had been created. A local MLA, Mr Dandekar, and one of the leading publishers of Aurangabad, shared the dais with Sania.

'Will you be trying for Bollywood, like most of the earlier winners did?' another media guy asked Sania.

'Frankly, I don't know. At this point, Bollywood is a far cry.'

'So if Ranbir Kapoor or Ranveer Singh offered you a film opposite them, you would refuse?'

'I never said that,' Sania chuckled. 'Anyway, there is no point discussing a hypothetical situation. I would like to concentrate on my career. Don't ask me about my career choices, as I am absolutely clueless now. I guess I'll just play it by ear.' Sania's insouciance regaled the reporters.

'Aishwarya Rai, Sushmita Sen, Lara Dutta, Priyanka Chopra and many others have used beauty pageants to get a break in Bollywood. Don't you think pageant contestants are becoming more and more artful? You try to hoodwink the media and the world by pretending to sympathize with social causes when actually all you are thinking about is a break opposite some big film star.'

'That's a rather simplistic understanding of a situation. When you participate in a pageant, it is a devastatingly excruciating time. There is tremendous pressure; you don't know if you will even get chosen for the top twenty-five, let alone win the pageant. So this Bollywood agenda that the media is accusing us of is completely unfair.'

'If you get a break in Bollywood, will you be willing to expose?' a sleazy reporter asked her.

There was an instant murmur in the crowd; talks of sex and nudity usually generated a lot of hype and interest in reporters because that's what sold.

'I don't want to waste my breath answering such worthless questions.' Sania was extremely offended by the question and it showed.

'Don't you think you are misleading the young girls in our community?' one of the reporters asked her authoritatively. Everyone turned around to see who the voice belonged to. The young Muslim man with a Dutch beard got so many stares that he was forced to look at the people around him. He had a defiant look on his countenance. 'Haven't you sinned by showing yourself to people outside your immediate family?'

A few others who were a part of his posse began to get vocal as well.

'Don't you have any shame?'

'How can you indulge in such sinful acts, being a Muslim girl yourself?'

'I haven't done anything to be ashamed of. All I have done is participated in a beauty pageant. If there is anything to be ashamed of, it's you and your bigotry,' Sania snapped at him aggressively, very unlike her.

'Is this what you are teaching young Muslim girls? To parade around half-naked for money?'

'What do you know about young Muslim girls in India? Do you know how oppressed and discriminated against they are? Young Muslim boys are enjoying the best of both the worlds, whereas...'

'Keep your tongue in check. Don't make baseless arguments,' the ring leader warned her.

'You should be publicly flogged; only then you will understand,' one of his cronies shouted.

'How dare you go against our community's values and beliefs?' another one chimed in.

'Can you answer a question of mine?' Sania asked in a steady voice on the microphone, her voice ringing in the pandal.

The bearded man hushed the others and gesticulated her to proceed.

'Can you tell me why haven't the Khans of Bollywood—Shah Rukh, Saif, Aamir, Arbaaz and Fardeen—married Muslim girls? Saif and Aamir Khan got married twice, but even then not to Muslim girls. There are hundreds of young "liberated" Muslim men who don't even want to date girls from our community—let alone get married to us. Answer me! Do you know how that makes us feel?'

'Shut up, you whore! You think you can say such things and get away with it?' Furious, the group of men started hurling curses, chappals and bouquets at her. One of the bouquets hit Sania on her head.

'Your threats will *not* silence me. Why do the so-called "modern" Muslim men no longer find girls from their own community attractive?' she yelled at them.

Things went completely out of hand. The fundamentalists who had masqueraded as journalists began to get extremely violent, even as the police and the security tried to overpower them. The dais was cordoned off and Sania was whisked away by the policemen. The news channels had a field day.

At Sania's home, Shamim, Sakina and Ayub were very upset. A celebratory moment had turned sour. The showdown that had happened just an hour ago was being blazoned as breaking news on all major news channels.

'Newly crowned Beauty Queen, Sania Ahmed, had to face the music of fundamentalists when she reached Aurangabad, her hometown. Reminiscent of the infamous Taslima Nasrin incident in Hyderabad a few years back, this episode of Beauty Queen Sania Ahmed will further fuel the discord between moderate and radical Muslims.' The report from NDTV then aired Sania's outburst where she questioned the proclivity of well-known Muslim stars of Bollywood.

'You should not have spoken to them so aggressively. It doesn't take time for things to flare up.' Despite Shamim's admonitions, Sania knew her mother tacitly supported her.

'I made *shikanji* for you. Drink it; it will cool your nerves,' Sakina told Sania as she handed a glass of lemonade to her. She showed her solidarity with Sania in a very subtle but firm manner. Having been at the receiving end of injustice and unable to forge a way for herself as far as her career and life were concerned, Sakina had plenty of pent-up aggression.

Ayub, the youngest amongst Sania's siblings, was a good peach but an extremely flippant one. He supported the winning side and in his view, even though Sania had won the pageant, she was definitely not going to win the war. Moreover, the fallout of her win had proved to be adverse on him and Sajid. They had been dismissed from the family business by their beloved mamujaan. As a result, Ayub didn't even offer a smile to his sister.

Sajid walked into the room with his wife and daughter. He wore a traditional *Pathani* kurta, along with a pronounced grimace. As his three-year-old tried to run towards her phupho, or aunt, he hoisted her in his arms, handed the bundle to his wife and gave them a directive to head towards their bedroom.

'So, what have you achieved?' Sajid addressed Sania and broke the uncomfortable silence with an even more uncomfortable question.

Sania stayed mum and refused to take the bait.

'I asked you something. What earth-shattering achievement have you made by winning this godforsaken Beauty Queen title? You have made us enemies of our own people. Do you even realize that because of you we will have to burn in hell?' Sajid vociferated.

As if his words were a premonition, slogans of her name started being chanted in the street. 'Sania! Sania! Sania!'

Their voices grew louder and louder.

Sania's family was terrified. Shamim instinctively wrapped her arms around her daughter and drew her close. Sania's fear took over her and she started crying. She couldn't process the turn of events in the last few hours. Just a little while back, she was flying First Class, feeling on top of the world. She could never have imagined such a steep slide would happen.

'See, I had told you. We will all burn in hell. Our lives will become a curse for us. They will torch our house. They will set us all ablaze.' Sajid was foaming at the mouth. He wrenched Sania away from Shamim's embrace and yanked her towards the balcony. 'Go face them now, you disgrace. You deserve their wrath.'

Sania tried to resist Sajid with all her might but to no avail. What she saw outside her house made her head spin.

A huge crowd had gathered in the street. They were holding placards and banners, and chanting Sania's name. 'Welcome home, Sania', 'We love you, Beauty Queen of India', 'We are proud of you', the placards read.

It gave Sania goosebumps. All the fear, fright and panic that had built up in her mind vanished in a second. She looked at them with bright eyes and then went inside. She pulled her mother out wordlessly to make her see what she had just witnessed. Shamim was so elated that she clasped Sania in a bear hug and called out to Sakina, Ayub and Sajid, asking them to come and see the turnout.

As all of them gathered in the balcony, Sania looked at Sajid with hurt and injury explicitly written on her visage. She mustered the courage to voice her mind. 'This is what I have achieved... love and compassion from these people. And this is enough to last me a lifetime.' Tears streamed down her cheeks as she waved out to the crowd. This moment easily surpassed the one when she was crowned. The people from her colony, some of her school and college friends, young Aurangabadis, kids, teenagers, uncles and aunties, everyone wanted to meet her. Unable to restrain the overwhelming swell of emotions raging inside her, Sania ran inside. Sajid was dumbfounded by the scene that unfolded before him.

18

'Where are you?' Simran asked Anirudh on the phone.
'Under the building. I'm just parking my car.'

'Rudy, hurry up,' Simran called out to him from the bedroom when she heard him turn the keys and open the main door. The sound of her TV playing in the bedroom could be heard blaring outside in the living room.

'Just give me a moment,' Anirudh responded and stepped into the washroom.

'First come here, Dodo. There is something important you need to see,' Simran shouted from the bedroom but in vain.

'A statement like this is a very provocative response but a pertinent one. She is putting forth a view which she is affected by too. Girls in the Muslim community have never had a voice or a platform to express their true feelings.' An eminent social activist commented on Sania's outburst in a debate on Times Now.

Simran was galvanized. She ran out to see what was taking Anirudh so long. She knocked on the bathroom door fervently. 'What are you doing inside?'

'Playing badminton. Saina Nehwal insists that she will only marry a guy who can beat her.'

'Forget Saina, Sania, our beauty queen, has given the media a swift kick on their butts. They are all congregated outside her house in Aurangabad.'

'What has she done?' Anirudh's curiosity was piqued.

Sunidhi was drawing a line of coke at Jai's house, a cramped ground-floor flat in a dilapidated building in Mahim. Jai's room had a separate entrance from the back gate of the building. He lived with his greying mother and a younger brother who was in junior college. Jai was the sole breadwinner in the family, but he barely earned enough to make ends meet. His fulltime job was to cling to Sunidhi and linger around her. As a result, his family was living in abject financial paucity. Whatever meagre savings his mother had, were being depleted by running the house with it.

Jai had been an exceptional student in school and college. With great difficulty, he had managed to pay the fees for his seat in IIM Bangalore that his partial scholarship did not cover. It was during his annual cultural festival that he had met Sunidhi. The two had connected amidst disorienting laser lights, a painful clamour emanating from the mosh pit and indecipherable growling exploding from the stage. So deep grew their bond that Jai quit his management school to be with Sunidhi.

Initially, Sunidhi would go out of her way to be with Jai but lately, she seemed to have grown distant. But he continued to worship her with equal ardour. He showered her with attention and compliments. Being sharp and quick-witted, he tugged at her strings in more ways than one. He was fully aware that Sunidhi's conceit ran deep and thick. But whenever she was in a dilemma or she needed lifting up, she depended on Jai implicitly. He was her emotional crutch.

'Please wait outside. I will get the cash,' Jai instructed Usman, his supplier. Usman was a towering young man, with a formidable scar across his left cheek. He had set up base near a dargah in Mahim. He was born in the streets and raised by the local mafia. Later, he decided to part ways and start off on his own. He was now the capo of a small but notorious squad, and had made a reputation for himself as the indisputable, upcoming dealer in that locality. He had been trying to establish a high-profile clientele, but there were limitations in this neighbourhood; the people who lived here were not well-heeled. His assistant, Munna, was a gangly nineteen-year-old boy who had engaged in so many unspeakable acts that even Usman felt unnerved around him at times.

Jai latched the door chain and looked for Sunidhi's purse. She was completely wasted and lying on Jai's bed, knocked out cold. She was barely covered in her flimsy underwear. Jai suppressed a groan as he hardened. It had been over a year since Sunidhi had denied him entry inside her because she was repulsed by him in that sense. Jai cleared his head and got onto the task at hand.

He found her purse lying on the floor, near his bed. He fished out a couple of thousand bucks. Little did he realize that Usman was peeping in from the window, getting a full view of Sunidhi's semi-nude body. The sight made him dribble. Munna too squeezed himself into the viewing space to have a *dekko* at the live porn, irrespective of how lifeless it was.

Jai undid the security chain and stepped out to pay Usman who sprang back from the window as soon he heard the grating sound of the lock.

'I can give you stuff on credit also, if you want. I have this fresh stock of coke, top quality.' Usman opened a pouch of cocaine for Jai to have a look. Jai tasted a pinch of it to verify its authenticity. He was satisfied.

Usman offered him a small glass tray and drew up a line for him. Jai snorted it greedily. In a few moments, he felt alive. All the synapses in his body sparked with awareness. Breathing was a pleasure, as if the air surrounding him was suddenly saturated with oxygen and he was inhaling crisp, pristine mountain air.

'How much?' Jai asked Usman.

'4.5K for a gram.'

'That's a lot. We're regular customers.' Jai knew the prices in the white market were highly competitive, but he still tried to bargain.

'If you promise to take at least ten packets a month, I will give it for 3.5K.'

'What's happening, Jai? Who are these guys?' a stumbling Sunidhi mumbled to Jai. She had woken up, and walked up to the door, not caring for her attire or rather, the lack of it.

'Replenishing our stock.' Jai nudged her to go inside, but she didn't budge. So, he grabbed her arm and prepared to drag her in. But Usman was too quick for him. He flung the door open. He followed them into the room with an air of entitlement.

Usman looked at Sunidhi in such a lascivious manner that

even she was taken aback. 'What is your name, hungry boy?' she purred, unintimidated.

'Usman Drug Dealer.'

'You have "drug dealer" in your name itself?' Sunidhi chuckled.

'I will call you when I need anything. You may go now,' Jai told him firmly. He grew even more uncomfortable with Usman when his lackey followed his boss' footsteps. Jai cornered Usman and drew himself up to his full height. Usman didn't even bat an eyelid.

'Madam, this is my card,' Usman told Sunidhi, chucking his card at her, and began walking towards the door. 'Call me any time. I will give you credit because Madam is nice person.'

After Usman and Munna left, Jai latched the door from inside and let out a sigh of relief. He made Sunidhi sit down with him, a grave look on his face. 'These are not nice guys, Su. They are trouble in uppercase,' he explained to her.

'Ok, Father! Now, what's on the menu? Your baby is craving for some more nose candy.'

'You've had enough for one day! I don't understand what has happened to you all of a sudden. I need to talk to your dad at once.'

'I don't want to go back home. I will find another place. But for the love of God, don't get preachy with me.'

'Didn't your mom call you in the evening?'

'Yeah, she was telling me to move to the Worli flat…it's vacant.'

'Why don't you do that? My place is a shit-hole. You deserve better. Why don't you move to that Worli apartment?'

'No, it belongs to my dad,' she replied vehemently. 'And I don't want anything that belongs to him. I want to make it on my own. You will be my partner, manager and man Friday, all in one. Ok?' Sunidhi's voice reverberated with gumption.

'Do I have a choice? Have I ever had a choice? You have always called the shots. Partner and manager sound too glorified, man Friday is the right term for me. You'll reduce anyone who is with you for long to a servant,' Jai said, his voice laced with self-pity.

'But, Sims, we have made a commitment to the channel,' Anirudh reasoned with her as he pulled on a pair of checked boxers.

'I have absolutely nothing worthwhile to show.' Clad in Anirudh's oversized t-shirt, Simran sauntered to the loo to brush her teeth before going to bed.

'You're being too harsh on yourself. I think that the footage you have is excellent. We can make a killing off it,' Anirudh told her as he joined her at the wash-basin.

'Killing? What killing can we make by trumpeting personal moments of these girls? It's no sting-op,' said Simran firmly.

'Sims, I got you this assignment with a lot of difficulty. I had to constantly pester and goad Gul. We have enough footage to showcase a riveting story.'

'There is no story, Rudy. We cannot force ourselves to do this, just for the sake of it. If we knew why Sunidhi had gone blank in the finale would be a story worth sharing. The rest is routine stuff.'

'You captured Sunidhi snorting coke on camera. Is that routine?'

'So what's the big deal? Half the bloody world is doing drugs and getting hopped up on God knows what. What I have is not an exposé but a clichéd story of a rich girl being a brat.'

'Dude, she is Karmarkar's daughter.'

'Karmarkar's daughter simply did an ordinary thing. There is nothing extraordinary or exclusive about that.' Simran was beginning to lose her composure.

'It is a big deal because she is Karmarkar's daughter.'

'You are getting a tad bit too personal, aren't you?'

'No, Sims. What vendetta could I have against Sunidhi or Karmarkar or anyone for that matter?'

'Maybe Gul has some agenda which you are unaware of. He could easily be playing you.' Simran's shrewd counterpoints put Anirudh on the back foot.

'Riddle me this, Rudy. What was Gul doing the night before I was supposed to leave for the pageant? Why had he kept me on hold till the last moment as far as this operation was concerned?' Simran contemplated out loud.

'How would I know, babe? He was probably waiting for a go-ahead from the channel owners.'

'As far as I know, he was at Karmarkar's party so he could acquire telecast rights for the pageant. He was hopeful because Khambatta had stepped in as the sponsor. And Khambatta is a devotee of our channel because it caters to his target market segment.'

'When did you find this out?' Anirudh's interest in the conversation had piqued again.

'I extricated this information from Rohit. He told me that Gul was responsible for the showdown between Mehta and Khambatta. He offered some degrading sops in the name of free commercial time to swing the deal with Khambatta. Mehta and Karmarkar refused him flatly; to an extent where Mehta insulted Gul to his face.' Simran was mindful of what had happened. 'Gul hasn't made any mention of this to you, has he?' Simran questioned Anirudh, curious to know if Anirudh was complicit in this plan.

'No, never.' Anirudh's pensive mood convinced Simran that what she had revealed was a massive revelation. She hugged him from behind and rested her cheek on the angular planes of his back.

But Anirudh was clearly not done talking. He disentangled himself out of her embrace and faced her. 'Suppose, for a moment, I buy your point of view that Gul had a tiff with Karmarkar or Nimesh Mehta or whosoever, what do we lose in the bargain? We are simply doing our job.'

'I am sorry, Rudy, but I am not going to be party to a dick-measuring contest. I took up this sting-op with an objective in mind and this is not it.'

'Which objective are you harping about?'

'Go screw yourself. Of all people, I can't believe you are asking me this question. I made it amply clear to you before that my sole purpose of taking up this assignment was to expose the ugly face of the beauty business.'

'What would you know about purpose? You still endure being the host on that stupid chat show, even though it is like "slow poison" to you.'

'Anirudh, I have to earn my living, pay my rent. It's not as if I am doing something scandalous!'

'You sound like a fickle ideologist to me, picking whichever side suits you.'

Anirudh's acerbic words provoked Simran immediately.

'Sod off, Mr I'll-sell-my-soul-for-a-*vadapav*.' Simran lashed out at Anirudh. 'If that sting-op is telecasted, it will be the very last thing you ever see.'

'Okay fine, we won't telecast it,' Anirudh backed down in an attempt to pacify her. 'But what will I tell Gul?'

'I will handle Gul.'

'Simran, I hope you are taking into account that my position could get really awkward in this face-off.'

'I am looking at this issue objectively. I will not let you suffer because of my botch up. Promise! Let's talk tomorrow.' Simran flopped on the bed and pulled up her soft bedsheet.

'I have a feeling you are suffering from guilt syndrome,' Anirudh pursued.

'I know you think I'm backing down, but if you look at it from my viewpoint, I am saving myself from getting entangled in a much bigger predicament. All the twenty-four contestants trusted and confided in me. I can't betray their trust,' Simran spoke with finality.

He was so attuned with her emotions that he saw through her adamantine exterior and detected her torment. He took her hand in his and gently brushed his lips against her knuckles. Simran's eyes shimmered with unshed tears. He clasped her in his arms and kissed her head. 'I understand, Sims. I am with you.'

19

The confrontation at the press conference was headlined so extensively that Sania became a celebrity overnight. News channels were clamouring to interview her, to know about her opinions on gender biases. A huge media contingent with OB vans set up camp outside Sania's house in the shroud of night. They were strictly forbidden from setting foot inside her bungalow premises. The scene was a rare sight for Aurangabad.

Sania was not even remotely aware of the magnitude of ripples she had caused across the country and subcontinent too. Her social media accounts were being flooded with messages; some of which lauded her honesty and courage, while others backed patriarchal norms.

It was half past eight in the morning when the screen on Sania's phone flashed—eighty-seven missed calls. In an attempt to categorically avoid calls from the media and the press, she had put her phone on silent mode and was submerged in a photoshoot of a different kind. The entire neighbourhood had turned up at her doorstep to get pictures and selfies clicked with the new Beauty Queen.

In a city like Aurangabad, glamour was as rare as a spotless street in Mumbai, and media celebrities as scarce as unpolluted air in Delhi. So Sania's victory was celebrated with great enthusiasm across the town. Locals had been queuing up outside her house since seven in the morning to shower her with flowers, gifts and cards. Her family members were excited to help and each of them was assigned a task. Sakina was in charge of taking pictures and videos, Ayub and Shamim were managing the crowd and Zubeida, the house help, served refreshments to the fans. Ayub had completely switched sides after he summed up Sania's popularity.

Yet, there was one person in the family who was extremely

unhappy with the proceedings and refused to participate in it. Sajid was convinced Sania had invited trouble for the entire family. 'All this will evaporate in no time. This is all just a fake show, so don't get carried away,' he told his wife Zeenat, loudly. The jibe was meant for Sania who was close enough to hear her brother's barb.

Sajid had given strict instructions to his wife and daughter to stay away from Sania. He was so uncouth that he snubbed one of the neighbours when she asked him to click her picture with Sania. He even clouted his three-year-old daughter for being stubborn about getting photos clicked with Sania. Despite everything, neither Zeenat nor Sajid was able to keep the little one away from Sania.

When the crowd of visitors finally thinned down, there was a collective sigh of relief in the Ahmed household. But screams and shouts still erupted outside their home as the police force tussled with the media. Sania was too tired to be bothered by it. As long as the paparazzi was kept at bay, she didn't care.

She was astonished to see 278 missed calls on her phone, along with an obscene number of messages. Among a bevy of unknown numbers, she spotted calls from Rohit, Simran, Shikha and Nimesh Mehta. She didn't know where to start. It finally began to sink in that something spectacular had happened to her.

Her phone's screen began to flash again and she answered it in a heartbeat this time. 'Hi, Simran. I'm sorry I was unavailable earlier.'

'You really gobsmacked the whole country yesterday. You were spitting fire, man. Do you realize what you've done?'

'I just said what I felt and experienced, Simran.'

'It's very rare for a Muslim girl to speak out against the shackles imposed on her by her community, Sania. And when she does, this is what happens; everybody sits up and pays attention.'

'So much for protecting my honour,' Sania said miserably.

'*Au contraire mon ami.* On the contrary, my friend, from what I see, you are on your way to becoming a champion.'

'I am no champion. I'm still struggling to find a firm foothold in the industry. I just want a good career, that's all.'

'I am afraid the world is too convoluted for someone as humble and guileless as you. And don't worry, I am confident you will come through,' Simran motivated her.

'Thanks, you don't know how much those words mean coming from you.'

'Don't forget that you're a hero, an inspiration to countless girls nationwide. Bask in the glory of this new-found success and choose your assignments wisely. You will have a magnificent career.'

The two said their goodbyes to each other and Sania started going through the messages on her phone. It would take hours for her to read them all, so she prioritized the familiar names.

'You are a rock star, Sania! Everyone is talking about your bold speech. Bravo! And don't forget that you have to give me a treat for all that I have done for you.' Shikha's message ended with a p-faced emoticon, but Sania knew she wasn't kidding about the treat.

'Sania, we have got some excellent assignments for you. Call me.' 'Still waiting for your call.' 'Call me ASAP.' Rohit had sent her numerous messages, each more urgent than the preceding one. Sania was typing out a reply to him when Ayub came skipping into her room with a twinkle in his eye.

'Sania aapa, I have a surprise for you.' Ayub grinned from ear to ear.

'What surprise do you have now?' Her eyes were glued to her phone as she typed out a response to Rohit and hit 'send'. When she lifted her gaze, Sania saw Rashid entering the room with his sisters, Noor and Shagufta. They ran towards her and sandwiched her in hugs. She was thrilled to meet her cousins. The three of them had grown up together but recent circumstances rarely allowed them to meet up. Even though Sania was displeased to see Rashid, especially after what he did to her before the pageant, she masked it well. She knew the situation required to be handled tactfully.

'Sania aapa, Rashid came here on his own to meet you. He wants to talk to you,' Ayub communicated on behalf of Rashid.

'Okay, you two wait outside in the hall. I will join you in five minutes.' Sania hoped that her younger brother understood the subtext of what she said. She didn't want Rashid in her room. Ayub took his cousin out, while Shagufta and Noor bombarded Sania with questions about the pageant.

In the hall, Rashid munched on tea-dunked jeera biscuits while waiting for Sania. Ayub sat next to Rashid and made small talk with him. He was running out of topics to banter about when Sania walked in, holding a Moroccan pattern mug. She sat opposite Ayub and sipped on her lemon tea. She was dressed in an Ecru kurta with cloud-white chikankari, or traditional embroidery, work. Rashid was transfixed by her ethereal allure and wondered if she had always been this exquisite. He tried to break the awkward silence, but words failed him. Instead, he ended up opening and closing his mouth idiotically—like a fish.

'Did you take Mamujaan's permission before coming here to meet me?' Sania finally spoke up.

'Yes. I mean, no,' Rashid fumbled for the right thing to say. He was confused whether or not to project himself as an independent, thinking person.

Ayub held back a chuckle and Sania struggled to maintain a straight face.

'Won't Mamujaan be mad at you?' Rashid found himself contemplating Sania's question, failing to detect the ridicule in her tone.

'Abbu hates anything that is modern,' Rashid said, proud of his answer. *That would be enough to impress the girl who is suddenly the toast of the nation*, he thought to himself.

'So, I'm a modern thing that your father hates.' Sania surprised everyone, including herself, with her mordacity.

'No, I didn't mean it in that sense. I meant that at least I can be modern, even if Abbu isn't.'

'Of course, you can be ultra-modern,' she patronized him. 'You can take you first step towards modernity by shaving off this *mullahji* beard of yours.'

Rashid touched his beard reflexively, feeling the heat of Sania's digs. He straightened his back, cleared his throat and said what he had really come there to say. 'I came to meet you with just one mission in mind. I had proposed to you earlier, but you spurned me. I want to renew my offer. I would like to marry you, in spite of your Beauty Queen title,' Rashid said earnestly.

'Oh, Rashid miyaan, you are so generous and kind-hearted. I can't believe how blessed I am. How can I ever repay my gratitude to you for even considering me?' Sania's straight-faced talk was so deceptive that Rashid found it difficult to ascertain whether she really meant what she said or if she was simply sneering him.

Ayub chuckled openly this time.

Rashid was offended, but he maintained his composure. 'Just one more thing,' Rashid continued. 'Before we get married, I would like you to renounce the Beauty Queen title.'

'Can I ask you a question? After we get married, will I have to wear a burqa?'

'Whom do you want to show your face to, your husband or the whole world?'

'I can ask you the same question, Rashid miyaan. You are mind-numbingly handsome. Is your sexiness for your wife or for other women who might eye you? Will you also wear a burqa?'

'My sexiness is for you, my wife-to-be.'

Sania was so put off by Rashid's sly leer that she dropped all pretence at once. 'Are you suffering from a concussion or are you generally this deluded? I will never get married to you, even if you are the last man on earth, Rashid miyaan.'

'Do you realize that if you say yes to me, Abbu will take Sajid bhai and Ayub back in the business? Are you so selfish that you will forsake their well-being for your stubbornness?' Rashid got down to brass tacks.

Sajid, who had just walked into the room, overheard the conversation. He waited for Sania to respond and stood right in front of her. She was unnerved by his peremptory conduct. Sania was saved by the bell. 'I have to take this call, please excu...'

'We have everything that you could want, all the luxuries that you could ask for. Besides living a royal life with me, your brothers will also be back in the business,' Rashid interrupted.

Sania felt pressured against her choice with Ayub and Sajid present. She could sense their expectations and hope. Her phone continued to vibrate persistently in her hand. She couldn't react insolently, but she also couldn't bear to hear another word of Rashid's spiel. 'Please, Rashid miyaan, I have no interest in getting married to you or anyone else at this juncture in my life. It's probably futile to say this, but I sincerely hope you understand.' Her phone began to ring again. It was Rohit calling yet again. 'Now, if you'll please excuse me.' She quickly dashed out of the room and received the call. 'Yes, Rohit, tell me.'

Rashid stared at Ayub in disbelief, unable to process the rebuff.

'Rashid miyaan, don't worry. I will talk to Sania aapa,' Ayub told him in a conciliatory tone.

Sajid walked over to Rashid and squeezed his shoulder reassuringly. Rashid shrugged it off brusquely and stormed out without a word.

'Fine!' Sania spoke into the phone. 'Just send me the ticket details.'

20

When Sunidhi had turned five, Karmarkar had gifted her a bicycle. It had a bubble-gum-pink body, alabaster-white seat and pedals, and a bamboo basket in the front where Sunidhi loved to carry her favourite stuffed toy, Mr Fluffles—an obese, fuzzy brontosaurus. The bicycle came with a matching helmet and rainbow ribbons which fluttered around the handles. Every day, Karmarkar would unfailingly take out time in the evening to teach Sunidhi how to ride it. Initially, he would hold the bike from behind while she pedalled vigorously with unwavering focus. Karmarkar would wait the whole day to hear her laugh with unbridled joy. After several cuts, scrapes, bruises and cries, Sunidhi was ready. Karmarkar ran along with the bicycle as Sunidhi pedalled resolutely. At some point, he stopped, but off she went, unwavering and determined. Karmarkar had felt a twinge of sadness as she hurtled ahead, realizing that she would need him a little less from that day onwards. And now, it seemed like she didn't need him at all.

'Ever since Sunidhi has left, you have been moping around. And don't you dare pretend like you haven't,' Karmarkar's wife threatened him. 'Might I ask, what is the point of this behaviour? It's not like you're going to ask her to come back. Your ego is too big for that. Mark my words, you will repent this.'

'Any father in my place would have reacted exactly the way I did,' Karmarkar defended himself.

'No! No father would have let his only daughter leave the house like this.'

'So, I should have just let her continue with her wayward ways? This is not how we raised her to be, Suhasini.' Karmarkar told his wife.

'You could have tried a softer route! I don't understand why you get so despotic when it comes to dealing with your children. Your son barely talks to you; a Stanford graduate, who could be an excellent asset to your own company, is languishing away in the U.S. And your...'

'I won't take that,' Karmarkar interrupted her. 'Vivaan is doing extremely well for himself. I would rather that he gets experience in some of the top multinational companies before he joins me. It doesn't matter if he resents me right now; sooner than later, he will realize that I only did what I did for his growth.' Karmarkar parked himself on the dining table to eat his morning fruit, which was usually either a pomegranate or a papaya. That day, it was papaya.

'And what about Sunidhi? You think she will also realize it soon? I don't want you talking about how this will help her professionally. I want to know how you intend to make her feel secure again in this family. She has been uprooted from her home by her darling pops.'

'I got a call from Nimesh late last night. He was apologizing about the fiasco that happened with Sunidhi. He said that Sunidhi was not at fault. In fact, she saved them from a serious embarrassment. They wanted to thank her.'

'So that is why you have been shuffling around the house since morning with such a guilt-ridden face,' Suhasini remarked, giving him a see-what-you-have-done-now glare.

'Suhasini, I feel horrible for having doubted our daughter. I didn't even give her a chance to explain herself. It's no wonder she was so offended by my distrust.'

'So are you waiting to print invites before you call her?'

'I have been trying her number since last night, but it is still switched off.'

'So why didn't you tell me? I have been in touch with her. It's a different matter that she does not look up to me as much as she looks up to you.'

'She is in Jai's house, right?'

'Yes. He has been taking very good care of her and making sure she doesn't overstep the line.'

'What rubbish! Jai himself is a junkie. He's the reason why Sunidhi got exposed to drugs in the first place. He is just living off her.'

'He loves her. He gave up his studies for her.'

'Fat good that will do! That is sheer foolishness, not love. What will he do in life for a living? Bloody bumbling buffoon.'

'And still she left you to go live with that buffoon. In spite of you having brought her up, she prefers him over you.' Suhasini was quick to pounce on Karmarkar.

'It's not as if she has moved there permanently. She will come back.' Karmarkar sounded like he was trying to convince himself of that, more than his wife.

'Try your luck. As far as I know, your daughter is more stubborn than you,' Suhasini said bleakly.

Karmarkar rose from the table as a house help came out to clear the plates.

'Do you know where she is? I want to go and meet her,' Karmarkar asked his wife, his concern for his daughter glaringly obvious now.

Jai's house had never been so speckless before. Every surface had been scrubbed squeaky clean. It was a momentous day for him. 'I have always thought very highly of your dad,' Jai told Sunidhi.

'Then he is all yours. I have absolutely no problem if I don't see him for the rest of my life,' Sunidhi replied.

'Don't be ridiculous, Sunidhi. You can't condemn him for life over such a piddly little fight. You should be grateful for what your dad has achieved in life and take the baton further if you can.'

'You should become a priest, man.' Sunidhi removed a cigarette and was just about to light it when Jai snagged it from of her mouth.

'Go jerk off, loser! Are you my dad's PR rep?' Sunidhi needed a hit of nicotine in her system to deal with her father, but Jai had denied her that.

A carbon-black Rolls-Royce Phantom pulled up outside. It looked completely out of place in the squalid street. Karmarkar stepped out, looking formidable in a three-piece suit. Jai observed him, admiringly, from a corner window.

'Your dad is here, Sunidhi. Wait, your mom has also come along.' Jai was anxious now.

'So, big fucking deal! Wait, wait, wait, listen,' Sunidhi held Jai back desperately. 'Don't fall prey to their emotional blackmail. I am staying here with you forever.' When Jai gave her a dismissive glance and was about to make his way outside, Sunidhi grabbed his crotch. 'I will give you a nice treat later.' Jai got tickled instead of getting aroused and he burst out laughing. He freed himself from her python-like grasp and stepped out of the back door to receive the Karmarkars.

Karmarkar looked lost in the little compound. He was walking around the building hopelessly, in circles, when Jai rescued him.

'Hi, sir,' Jai greeted Karmarkar and offered him his hand.

Karmarkar shook it. 'Hello, Jai. We weren't sure about the right entrance.'

'It's a common confusion. We have two separate entries to the house. Please follow me, and watch your step here,' Jai cautioned them about a sewage pipe with a protruding lid as he guided them to the rear doorway. 'It causes quite a few people to trip over,' he explained.

Mrs Karmarkar thanked him. She had always had a soft spot for the boy and his caring attitude.

Inside, Sunidhi was waiting for them, cross-legged, on the bed opposite the door. She looked past her parents, like they were invisible. Karmarkar was ticked off by her blatant indifference and disrespect but didn't show it. Suhasini walked towards her daughter and tried to hug her, but Sunidhi stopped her, and proffered her a hand instead. Suhasini accepted her stiff arm and sat down next to her.

'Hi, Mom. How are you?' Sunidhi murmured softly to her mother, as if she didn't want her to find out the longing in her voice.

'How do you think I will be? I spend all my days and nights worrying about you, dear.' Suhasini's eyes welled up as she observed how gaunt her daughter looked. The shadows under Sunidhi's eyes and cheekbones made her look very haggard.

Meanwhile, Karmarkar accepted a bottle of packaged mineral water from Jai while eyeing the house. The place was small, dingy and overstuffed with worn-out furniture. An open door led to the living room which resembled a godown. The room that they were sitting in was not even half the size of Karmarkar's washroom, but he did not make his distaste apparent.

'I would like to talk to you alone, Sunidhi,' Karmarkar told her without wasting any more time.

'I don't hide anything from Jai and Mom knows what happened, so there's no point of excluding them from this conversation,' Sunidhi countered sharply.

'As you wish,' Karmarkar gave in.

'I will get some tea for you,' Jai excused himself and hurried out to give the family their privacy.

Karmarkar took the other vacant spot on the bed, next to Sunidhi. 'Look, Sunidhi, I know I offended you and hurt your feelings. But I was wrong. I want to apologize to you for not trusting you and for breaking your faith in us.'

'The faith is broken and I have no interest in rebuilding it.'

Karmarkar was gutted. 'Don't be so harsh.'

'Please try and recall how you spoke to me that day. When you tossed allegation after allegation at me without even bothering to hear my side of the story.' Sunidhi was still miffed by their altercation.

'I am so sorry about that, Sunidhi. I know I can't do anything to undo it, but tell me how I can make it up to you,' Karmarkar implored, but Sunidhi was in no mood to relent.

'I need my time and my space to recover from it. I will only talk to you when I feel like it,' Sunidhi responded curtly.

Suhasini was exceedingly disquieted by her aggrieved behaviour, but she didn't interrupt their conversation.

'I'd like to suggest something,' Karmarkar persevered. 'The flat at Worli is lying vacant and...'

'Mom has already spoken to me about it and the answer is no,' said Sunidhi, cutting him short. 'I want to be on my own, that is, I want to earn my own livelihood and stand on my own two feet.'

Sunidhi's confidence in her self-worth moved Karmarkar a great deal.

'Okay, in that case I have an even better suggestion. You can shift to the Worli apartment and give me the rent every month.' He searched Sunidhi's face for a smidgen of approval, but she evinced no such reaction. 'I will waive off the deposit. And if you wish, you can also take Jai along with you.'

'I will think about it and let you know,' Sunidhi replied stiffly and showed her parents out.

As they we walking towards the door, Suhasini nudged her husband and handed a bag to him.

'Oh! I almost forgot,' said Karmarkar. He removed what was in the bag and placed it on a well-worn table. Sunidhi's chin quivered. It was a scruffy threadbare brontosaurus.

21

Sania was cruising along the Bandra–Worli Sea Link on her way to Nimesh Mehta's office. Ever since she had set foot in Mumbai, he had left no stone unturned in treating her like a queen. She had a chauffeur-driven car at her beck and call. He had also offered her a five-star service apartment, but she had refused it. She preferred to stay at her dad's flat which was vacant most of the days in the week.

Mehta's conference table was buried under paperwork. Sania sat primly in one of the chairs and tried her best not to judge the disarray as she sipped on her chamomile tea. She sat opposite Mehta who was noisily slurping a Frappuccino.

'That controversy you raked up has done wonders for you, Miss Sania. Your name is already out there,' he said, pausing his straw-sucking for a moment.

'Neither did I rake up a controversy, nor did I stage it. I only shared what I felt was the truth,' Sania corrected him in a matter-of-fact manner.

'Well, in any case, your truth was lapped up by the media. Within three days, we have been able to finalize nine huge contracts for you. Your life is going to change completely, Miss Sania. Just go with the flow and you will have no complaints or regrets.' Nimesh's words seemed mighty inspiring to his own ears, but they only made Sania squirm uncomfortably.

'I guess. Thank you...' It seemed like Sania wanted to say something but was holding back.

'Is something bothering you?'

'It's just that I hope I will have the final say in deciding whether or not I want to take up those assignments, because I don't want to say yes to anything and everything.'

'But of course, you are the one who will be signing the contracts,

Sania. We are going to be mere facilitators. All we will be making out of this is a small commission.'

'May I enquire how much that commission will be?' Sania asked him, making sure she understood the fine print very well.

'Give me a moment!' A slightly irked Nimesh picked up the intercom and summoned Rohit to his cabin. He was there in the blink of an eye.

'Rohit, please take her through all the contractual details. I am surprised you haven't briefed her as yet,' Mehta told him, his voice laced with disapproval.

'We have been glutted with work, sir, all pertaining to Sania only. The entire team has been busy sorting out her paperwork,' Rohit explained and requested Sania to follow him to his cabin. He made sure she was comfortable there before heading back to have a quick word with Mehta. He had been working with Nimesh for so long that he immediately knew something was off.

'Is something wrong, sir?' Rohit asked.

'That bitch seems like a problem-stirring one. Manage her well. I want all her personal details—her family background, job stints, the schools and colleges she attended, her boyfriends—every damn thing. You never know when you'll stumble across a titbit that can be used as leverage.' Nimesh's wily mind twisted with glee.

Meanwhile, Sunidhi had swallowed her pride and moved into her father's apartment in Worli. Her father was barely taking one-third of the actual rent from her, and she knew better than to pass up on such an offer. The apartment was in a posh complex overlooking the Sea Link and the interiors oozed chic sophistication. Sleek, minimalist modern furniture was complemented with ornate light installations and abstract art. Even though she was expected to shell out just ₹50,000 as rent every month, she was unsure if she would be able to pay up regularly. But she was determined to do whatever it took to not mooch off her father.

Half knowledge is dangerous and when combined with

stubbornness, it is a fatal combination. The best modelling agencies nationwide would have been thrilled to work with Sunidhi, but she refused to part with her commissions. So, she decided to groom Jai to be her manager. The idea had germinated from the fact that Jai had always wanted to establish a celebrity management company. So, he trained briefly before approaching various production houses, representing her, to solicit work for her.

Ignorance is never bliss when it comes to working in a competitive industry, and Sunidhi paid heavily for hers. She started making some really bad decisions and slipped the rungs without even realizing it. She declined to do brand endorsements for her dad's company, Plum, because of her incurable hubris. Within two months, four of the five assignments that she refused had gone to Sania and she began to grow in stature.

Sania was everywhere. If she wasn't shooting for a commercial, she was cutting ribbons and inaugurating high-end fashion stores. Some of the top brands were being endorsed by her. She had turned the tables on her detractors. Her family was irrevocably in her corner now. She had bought a huge flat-screen TV for them, apart from gifting top-notch phones to Ayub and Sakina. But Sajid continued to be stroppy and rigid in his mindset.

But there was one person who was really upset with Sania, besides Sunidhi who had permanently struck Sania off her list. Shikha had called up Sania umpteen number of times. But unfortunately, most of the times, Sania was unable to talk to Shikha because she was shooting or catching up on her sleep or travelling. Whatever brief conversations they had did not benefit Shikha at all.

Shikha felt like she was stuck in a rut and she couldn't move forward. Ever since the pageant had got over, she had been travelling to Mumbai at least twice every week. It was fearfully frustrating to be on the road for ten hours a day without any results. Not having her own place in Mumbai was a huge downer for her.

Shikha hoped that she could move in with Sania. That was the primary reason why she had wanted to meet her for a while now. But Sania was, in principle, not in favour of Shikha bunking with her because of her brazen behaviour. But Sania didn't know how to put Shikha off gently. Every time they had planned to meet, it had not materialized. Sania was genuinely busy, but Shikha was indisputably inconsistent. The few times that Shikha did manage to call Sania, she was too embarrassed to ask her if she could move into her apartment. After a while, she gave up all effort and even stopped calling Sania.

Shikha's mother often asked her to take up a job—that way she would have a steady income and she could help her mother out in running the house. But Shikha was adamant; she wanted a break in the glamour industry and nowhere else.

Shikha was invited to some local beauty shows where she was introduced as a finalist of the Beauty Queen pageant. It did not excite her after a point, so she stopped going for those as well. She wanted to be in the Big Game. Watching Shikha bungle every attempt she made, Prajakta's resolve to become a pageant winner became stronger and stronger. 'I will achieve all that Shikha di has not been able to,' she would tell herself every day.

Sania, on the other hand, was unstoppable. After vastly successful photoshoot campaigns and endorsements, she got a break in ad-films. Viewers nationwide—old, young and in-between—sighed as they watched her twist and turn with glee as melted Cadbury poured into her alluring mouth. What a beguiling mess she made! Within just a few days of release, the video went viral on social media.

Sania's folks were very thrilled to watch their daughter on TV. Even Sajid's wife and daughter opposed the blanket ban he had imposed on them—to not see or watch anything associated with Sania.

'Have you watched Sania's new commercial for Cadbury?' Anirudh asked Simran who had just finished one segment of her celebrity chat show shoot. Anirudh brought his iPad out on the sets and showed it to Simran and she was floored.

'Wow! This girl has arrived, and how!'

'Exactly! That's what I was trying to tell you. Let's invite her as a guest on our show.' Anirudh played the ad again on YouTube for the cinematographer.

'That is not a bad idea at all,' said Simran, getting her last-minute touch-up done.

'She is destined to be a star. Some Bollywood big shot is definitely going to take note of her.' Anirudh sounded a little too enthusiastic.

'Aren't you taking it too far? I told you I'm convinced that we should have her on the show. Anyway, you don't approach her for this. I will invite her. We have a lot of catching up to do also. All four of us actually!'

22

A Telugu film producer flipped through pictures of Sunidhi on his tablet. He was a swarthy, portly man who wore a chunky gold chain around his fleshy neck. His attire was just as garish as the décor in his office. A couple of unrecognizable trophies and awards were displayed proudly on his desk. He scratched his coarse, frizzy chest with approval every time he came across a particularly titillating photo. 'The film is more or less complete,' he told Jai. 'We will launch the promo of the film as soon as we finish this item song, in about a week.'

Of late, Sunidhi had not said no to any of the offers that came her way. When Jai, her buddy-cum-manager, told her that she had an offer from a Telugu filmmaker, her only question was 'How much?'

Sunidhi was exhilarated to hear that the producer was willing to pay her ₹10 lakh for an item number, which wouldn't take more than three days to shoot. She chased down a disco biscuit with a kale smoothie. That wasn't to celebrate as much as it was her daily routine.

'I have already said yes and they have paid ₹2 lakh in cash as an advance,' Jai told Sunidhi as he poured himself a large peg of Grey Goose.

'We can have a blast!' Sunidhi exclaimed. 'Where is the flipping cash?' She could barely contain her excitement.

'I have it, Su. But we need to finish off some of the earlier payments first.'

'What earlier payments, Jai?'

'Your dad's monthly rent for one. I hope you don't want to default on that.'

'Okay. And what else?'

'Usman's outstanding is ballooning. He has been behind my life for it.'

'How much is it?'

'Must be around two or a little more.'

'You better take a good quantity from him when you are making the payment to him. We should build a good credit line with him. He is a very useful fellow. We have to keep him happy.'

'You know what is bothering me, Su?'

'Your erectile dysfunction?' she taunted.

'The fact that you are hooked onto it bothers me. It's extremely hard to quit this shit once you're addicted to it.'

'What crap, Jai! I can leave it right now…right now…if I want to.'

A midnight-black vanity van stood with its curtains drawn, not that one could have seen much through the impossibly dark tints. Inside, the van was furbished with rosewood and plush white leather furniture. One of the tables was marked with crystal-white lines. Sunidhi, along with the hero, Gundappa, and the leading lady, Garima, made those lines disappear. Sunidhi shut her eyes and sat down as a strong kick hit her.

'Damn good stuff, man. Where did you get it from?' Gundappa asked Sunidhi, slowly loosing feeling in his face.

'From my supplier in Mumbai,' said Sunidhi proudly as she opened yet another pouch and drew it up on the table. It was over before they even realized it.

Jai was in no mood to be a part of their snort-fest, so he sat outside on one of the sets, amazed by its magnificence and splendour. When he stepped inside the van, he caught Sunidhi eagerly choking on Gundappa's tongue while his hands explored her firm bosom. When her eyes found Jai glaring at them, she casually stopped Gundappa and untangled her tongue and body from his.

'He is my boyfriend from Mumbai, Jai Savarkar,' she introduced him.

'Baayfriend? I thought he was your manager *la*,' Gundappa said, with raised eyebrows.

'He is all in one la,' Sunidhi said, making Gundappa and Garima burst into a fit of giggles.

'All-rounder, good, good. Hi, Jai. Sorry we had to practise love scene before the shooting la. You must be knowing that all top stars do that for good chemistry la. Camera is very sharp; it captures every detail la, so passion has to look real.' Gundappa's vulgarity was too displeasing for Jai.

Fortunately, the assistant director knocked on the open door of the vanity van. 'Your next shot is ready, ma'am!'

The assistant was surprised to find Gundappa in the vanity van. 'Gundappa sir, *nēnu mīru śōdhiñcaḍaṁ jariginadi*. I was searching for you,' he said.

'I was here only. Where were you looking for me? When such a beautiful girl comes from Baambay what else am I supposed to do la?' Gundappa laughed at his cheesy statement and left.

Sunidhi, who was following Gundappa, stopped at the door, turned around to caress Jai's prominent jaw and angular cheekbones. She brushed her lips against his, before nipping his lower lip hard and leaving.

On the set, the music started playing. It was a loud gaudy number, a typical item song. Sunidhi was in a skimpy outfit that left no room for imagination. The crop top she wore was so low that she was one big bounce away from a nip slip, and the skirt she wore was so short that her womanhood would be on display if she bent over. But she was too high to care. She would even perform a strip dance for the director if he asked her to, or even shoot a porn video. Jai was excessively worried for her. And his bruised lip.

Simran received a link on WhatsApp along with a laughing emoticon from Divya, the editor of her channel. The link redirected Simran to a video on YouTube. It was a Telugu item number called 'Mīprēmanāagni'. Simran was equally appalled and amused to watch Sunidhi's raunchy video. She immediately forwarded the link to a dozen of her friends.

'What's wrong with this girl?'
'Shocking fucking song.'
'She seems to have lost her mind along with her clothes.'
The responses kept getting meaner and meaner. After a couple of hours, Sania replied to the forward. 'Not in good taste.'
'I concur,' Simran responded. 'So, what's up with you, rock star?'
'Don't ask, man. Everything is too hectic.'
'But you're minting, right?' Simran sent a winking emoticon.
'I am not complaining,' Sania replied with a P-faced smiley.
'Want to catch up this weekend? All four of us?' Simran was talking shop but in a veiled manner.
'Can't say for sure. Have you spoken with Shikha and Sunidhi?'
'Not yet, but they are not as busy as you, rock star.' Simran figured that her barely obscured jibe would make Sania quit being pricey and meet them. But Simran's analysis was gravely misplaced, because Sania was just as humble and grounded as ever. The only difference now was that her time was no longer her time because of her hectic schedule.
'Saturday, second half?' Sania asked after about half an hour.
'Done deal. See you.' Simran replied promptly.

'You do that every single time. Why do you schedule an audition for me on the same day you notify me? How the hell do you expect me to plan it out? It takes five hours to reach Mumbai and even if you can't inform me two days before, at least have the decency and common sense to give me a day's notice,' Shikha spoke heatedly on the phone.
'We don't do it intentionally, Shikha,' the executive on the other end snapped back at her. 'You can go for the audition if you want to, or don't. But stop expecting us to baby you,' he said curtly.
'What? You are my agent. How can you talk to me like that?' Shikha raged into the phone, realizing too late that he had already hung up. She was about to redial his number when her phone started to ring and she answered it. 'Hey, Simran. How come you called?'

'Just like that. What's happening?'

'Nothing much, man. Just the usual. I have been running around for auditions and call-backs.'

'So we were planning to meet up, Sania and I, and hopefully Sunidhi,' Simran cut the small talk. 'We'd really like it if you could join us.'

'When are you guys planning to meet?'

'Most probably on Saturday in the evening, around 4:30.'

'Okay, I think I'll be free that time, so I will join you guys,' Shikha told her nonchalantly before disconnecting the call. The truth was that she was desperate to meet Sania. Prajakta, who was lurking around and eavesdropping on her conversation, knew that better than anyone else.

'Is she finally meeting you, Shikha di?' Prajakta asked Shikha, who merely heaved a sigh and nodded. 'The other day you told me that it was because of you that Sania won the pageant. How did you make her win?'

'I will tell you some other time,' Shikha skirted that question.

'Tell na, Shikha di, how did you make Sania win? And if you could make her win then why didn't you win yourself?' Prajakta persisted.

'You have your prelims in a month. Go and study instead of poking your nose in other people's business,' Shikha reprimanded her sternly.

'You also didn't study in the tenth grade and you dropped out in eleventh. So why are you asking me to study?' Prajakta was beginning to get under Shikha's skin.

'Get lost, Prajakta,' Shikha barked at her harshly and pushed her away.

Gurpreet, who could overhear their tiff in the kitchen, called out to Prajakta. 'Prajakta, she wants you to study because she did not. Just before her tenth board exams, Baba passed away. That affected her results adversely and she lost interest in studies completely.'

'So, can't I lose interest in studies? Baba's death affected me, just as much as it affected her,' Prajakta contended.

'Don't argue with me unnecessarily. Go and work on your Maths exercise book. You haven't even finished the homework you got from your coaching class. Don't think I'm unaware of how lazy you're becoming.'

'I don't want to study.'

'Ok! Then come here and help me knead the dough,' Gurpreet ordered her strategically. She knew Prajakta detested cooking, so she deliberately gave her a choice between a rock and a hard place.

Prajakta surrendered meekly and went back to her room.

23

A white Tata Safari made its journey through the Konkan region. An enchanting view of flourishing verdurous hills rolling past in all directions, interspersed with occasional glimpses of the majestic Arabian Sea made this stretch one of the most picturesque drives in the country. But only one person was awake to appreciate this scenic view and it was Usman. Sunidhi and Jai were completely zonked out in the back seat. They were on their way back home from Goa.

Usman had made his way to Goa in a desperate frenzy. He had been hunting Sunidhi and Jai for his payment, which had shot up to a staggering ₹5 lakh—an amount that was astronomical in his line of trade. He had delivered a substantial number of packets to them in Hyderabad as well through his counterpart there. He had made a hawala deal with his agent and now had to fulfil his part of the payment to a man who was steadily getting more impatient.

The original plan was to drive to Mumbai directly, but since they had dawdled endlessly, they had barely made it to Chiplun, a halfway point. The driver staunchly refused to drive any further since it was nearing midnight and he didn't want to risk chancing upon perils along the way. He stopped the car at the erstwhile Taj in Chiplun, now known as the Riverview Resort.

Jai jerked awake from his slumber when the car stopped suddenly. 'What happened? Where are we?' he mumbled, smothering the sleep in his eyes. He heard Sunidhi's phone buzzing and answered it in a daze. 'Hi, Simran. This is Sunidhi's friend, Jai. She is sleeping now. Yeah, tomorrow, right? She's aware. We will be in Mumbai tomorrow. I will remind her. Okay, bye.'

'We can resume tomorrow morning. We will spend the night here in Chiplun,' the driver told them resolutely. 'You can stay in this hotel; it's a very nice one.'

'But it must be expensive. How much is it for one room?' Jai asked Usman casually, who looked at him with a resolve that made Jai uncomfortable.

'You have to pay me my full amount by tomorrow latest. I will be in trouble otherwise, as will you.'

'You don't have to bring that up again, Usman. I will manage it, don't worry,' Jai assured him.

Jai got off in the driveway and went inside to make enquiries regarding the stay. A security person asked the driver to move the vehicle to the parking lot. The driver parked it in a corner and headed out.

Usman was alone in the car with the girl he had been fantasizing about. He turned around, grabbed Sunidhi's knee and shook it, but she remained comatose. Without wasting another minute, Usman quickly scanned his surroundings before sliding his hand under her skirt. He was pleasantly surprised to find that she was completely bare underneath. He stroked her and even in her state of unconsciousness, Sunidhi's body registered the stimulation and grew excited. Usman's bulge was so severe that it chafed against the zipper of his pants. He looked around again to check where the driver was, but he had disappeared.

Usman unzipped his pants. He pulled a lever next to his seat so it reclined till he was almost at the level of Sunidhi's inviting duct. He tried to slide into the back seat but stopped when he realized it would be too difficult to manoeuvre himself and too risky to enter her. In a quick change of plan, he inserted his finger into her while simultaneously stroking his turgidity. He was so excited that he spent himself in under a minute. Sunidhi stirred a little. Frightened, he straightened up the seat in haste, zipped himself up and began to clean his stained hands. A tap on the window almost gave him a heart attack. The driver peered inside and gave him a look of disapproval. Usman was not sure how much he had seen, so he just pretended as if nothing had happened. He tapped on the window again and told Usman that he had seen everything. 'What you were doing was not right, mister,' he told Usman.

Usman lowered the glass window and slipped him two ₹500 notes. The driver took one look at the notes and pocketed them wordlessly.

By the time Jai was back, everything was back to being normal. 'I have booked a room for us. We will see you in the morning,' Jai told them as he tried to wake Sunidhi up. He shook her with force, but she barely opened an eyelid.

'What about me?' Usman inquired, unaware of his fate.

'I will take care of him,' the driver told Jai.

Jai then lugged Sunidhi to their room.

'Just go a wee bit shorter on the hemline and reduce the frills on her collar and cuffs. We don't want her looking like a tragic lead from a Shakespearean play,' a stylist briefed her assistant, who took notes on her tablet. The director, Hector, who had flown in from the U.S., was seated in front of a video console, looking at Sania's close-up shots as she patiently waited for the stylists to relieve her.

'Sania, you look *bene bellissimo*, beautiful, my love. All I want you to do is pout a little more. Great! Can you be a little more sensuous? Try and bring some more passion in your eyes, dear. That's good, lovely.' Hector cajoled his model to give him a varied range of expressions.

Sania's mobile had been constantly ringing, but she was not in a position to answer it amidst work. She usually had a spot boy who ran sundry errands for her, but he was on leave. So the executive producer was helping Sania, doubling as her personal assistant. 'Can you please answer the phone? It must be my friend Simran. Please let her know that I will be there by 8–8:30.'

'Of course! Hello? Hi, Simran. This is Sania's assistant. She has asked me to notify you that she is running late and will be there by 8–8:30.'

'Oh! Thanks for the heads-up.' Simran was not amused at all, but she hid her bitterness well. She hung up and left her phone to charge on a table. She turned towards Shikha, who looked at her expectantly. '8–8:30. As expected, Madam is busy with some fittings and look test with the director.' Simran plonked herself on the executive chair in Anirudh's cabin at the Dastak channel office. Being a TV show host, she didn't work there full time. As a result, she didn't have her own workstation or cabin, so she used Anirudh's most of the time.

Shikha was playing Temple Run on her mobile, while Simran finished sending out some emails. 'Do you want me to call for something? A dosa or an idli?' Simran asked Shikha.

'No, no, nothing, I'm good.' Shikha was engrossed in her phone.

'I wanted to ask you... In fact, if you remember, I had called you immediately after the pageant, but you had refused to divulge anything at that time.'

'About the finale fiasco?'

'Yeah! What exactly happened? Was Sunidhi drugged or was it something else?'

'I don't know what to tell you.' Shikha was making up her mind about whether or not to reveal the truth to Simran when she was stumped to see Anirudh enter the cabin.

'Hey, what are you doing here?' Simran asked him.

'It is my cabin, so I will be here at some point. Hi! Shikha, right?' Anirudh offered Shikha a smile.

'You guys know each other?' Simran was surprised.

'Sort of, right?' Anirudh winked at Shikha.

Shikha just responded with a lukewarm smile.

'What do you mean "sort of"? Have you been checking out other pageant contestants behind my back?' Simran tried to hide her inquisitiveness with some humour.

'Of course not! I just met her that day when I bumped into you backstage, during your pageant,' Anirudh clarified, trying to put to rest Simran's prying mind.

'Anyway, Shikha, Anirudh is my boyfriend. Just giving you a fair warning,' Simran jested. 'We are going to the Marriott to meet Sania.'

'And Sunidhi?' asked Anirudh.

'She hasn't confirmed as yet. She is on her way to Mumbai from

Goa or Hyderabad. I guess we'll call her up once again on the way.'

With that the two ladies got up and bid their adieus; Shikha with apparent unease and Simran with a cursory peck on her lips.

'What makes you think I would want to meet you, fucking whores?' Sunidhi disconnected the call and flung her phone on the seat. Jai looked at her with an air of reprehensibility. Sunidhi glared back at him. 'Why the fuck should I be meeting them? Are they my friends? Bloody back-stabbing bitches.' They were finally in the suburbs of Mumbai.

'You and I both know that something went wrong between Nimesh Mehta and Khambatta. These girls might not have had anything to do with it,' Jai spoke through a mouthful of wafers.

'That reminds me, how much money do you have?'

Jai frantically gestured her to keep her voice down, afraid that Usman would overhear them and get bellicose about the payment.

But Sunidhi shrugged him off and said, 'I will handle him, you don't worry. Tell me how much you've got.'

'Around one.'

'Remove 50k from that, go to the Marriott and throw it on that slut Simran's face.'

'You bet money?'

'Yeah, I don't want to lose face on this front at least.'

'Did she ask you for it?'

'No, but that's precisely why I want to smack it on her face and end this story. You have to go right now.'

'Hello, what about my money, fellows? I am not going to wait for a minute once we reach Mumbai.' Usman, who had been eavesdropping, couldn't remain quiet any longer.

'It is already nine in the night, Usman. I can arrange for your money tomorrow in the morning or early afternoon,' Jai explained.

'We were supposed to start at seven in the morning today, but because of your dilly-dallying, we left at 2:30. No more excuses. I want my money. I don't care if you have to rob a bank or murder someone, I will not go back without my money.'

'Usman,' Sunidhi trilled. 'Why are you getting so restless? I am there for you; I will pay you. You don't have to worry about your payment at all, baby. Okay?'

'You don't interrupt, Su. I'm dealing with him, let me do it my way,' Jai scolded her. But Jai's condescension engendered Usman's mounting rage.

'What do you mean you will do it your way? There is no other way but paying me my cash, bastard. ₹5.5 lakh! Do you get it, motherfucker?' Usman roared as the scar on his face twitched monstrously.

'There's no need to raise your voice. And you better not use such language, you fucking scum.' Jai spoke strongly for once, but the next instant, Usman pounced on his throat. 'What the fuck will you do if I use such language? I want my money. Do you understand, you milksop?' Usman's menace conveyed that he was ready to snap Jai's neck. While Jai mumbled a quick prayer out of sheer desperation, Sunidhi remained unaffected and twirled a strand of her hair absentmindedly.

'Usman, what are you boiling for?' she cooed. 'I thought you were a big player. You shouldn't be getting worked up for such a paltry amount, baby.'

'Madam, you don't know—this pansy tries to insult me every time. Last night, he did not even offer to book me in the hotel. Do you know how bad I felt?'

'Getting you a hotel room was not my responsibility,' Jai lashed back.

'When he had specially come all this way for his payment, we should have taken care of him,' Sunidhi defended Usman and reprimanded Jai. 'Anyway, let bygones be bygones. Jai, you go to Marriott. Driver, where are we?'

'Sion, Madam.'

'So, how will we do it?' Sunidhi turned to Jai.

'However you want to.' Jai was in no mood to play Sunidhi's juvenile games, but he didn't want to create an uglier scene.

'From Bandra, you take an auto and go to Marriott and I will go home to Worli. Usman, you stay at Mahim, right? So shall I drop you there?'

'Yes, ma'am, but what about the money?'

'When I told you once that I will be paying you, I don't want you to bring it up again and again. And you don't need to call me Ma'am. Call me Sunidhi, okay?'

'Ok, ma'am, I mean Sunidhi ma'am.'

'That's more like it.' Sunidhi winked at Jai, who was utterly displeased with the way things were proceeding. He shot a scornful look at Usman and spoke to her softly. 'I don't like this guy one bit, Su. You better be careful.'

'Can you please relax? I know how to handle him,' Sunidhi asseverated in a hushed tone.

The driver pulled up before the Bandra highway junction. Jai cleared the payment with him and clearly instructed him to drop Sunidhi at Worli. As soon as he got off, Sunidhi asked Usman to come and join her at the back. He was loath to comply, but she wouldn't take no for an answer. Jai was fuming, but he didn't want to risk inciting Usman again, so he left.

'So, Usman, have you cooled down?' Sunidhi placed a slender manicured hand on his shoulder.

Usman was instantly aroused but nervous at the same time. 'It is a money matter and I have to pay people also. Whatever I delivered in Hyderabad and Goa was from the local suppliers out there. They will not wait for money like my Mumbai supplier.'

'So, what is the big deal, Usman? You will get your money.'

'But when? If it is not going to be today, I mean tonight, then I will have to give additional penalty tomorrow. They are dangerous bullies.'

'So, you are no less dangerous, Usman.' The way Sunidhi crooned his name made Usman's head hurt delightfully and made his crotch warm and tingly. He could not think rationally. He crossed his legs and sat obliquely to hide his turgescence.

Sunidhi's phone cut their conversation short. Simran's name

flashed on her phone, sending her into a tizzy. 'I know you are calling me for the bet money. It will reach you in fifteen minutes,' Sunidhi spat into the phone.

'Are you out of your mind? You were high on drugs that day when you went blank and lost the title and perhaps even today you are high. In which case, there is no point wasting my breath on you. Goodbye.' Simran, who was in a taxi with Shikha, did not mince her words before hanging up on Sunidhi. 'She has lost it completely,' she told Shikha who reacted impassively, which was very unlike her.

Sunidhi called Simran back multiple times, but she disconnected her call every single time. Furious, Sunidhi messaged Simran, 'You fucking two-bit whores. I will show you what I am capable of. Just wait and watch.'

'We know exactly what you are capable of. We have seen your cheap item song.'

Sunidhi was so furious that she nearly punched the window. She called up Jai immediately. 'Jai, don't give the money to that slut Simran, throw it at her face, with all your might. Promise me you will do that.'

'What happened, Su?' Jai asked with concern.

'That bitch is opening her filthy mouth to bark too much. Talk to you later.'

In her anger, she had forgotten about Usman's presence. 'What have you got?' she asked him in a stark change of tone.

Usman, who was still struggling to conceal his overeager friend, was startled by her question. 'N... Nothing. Why?'

'I mean have you got something different, something good? I want to try something that gives me a high, like I've never had before.'

24

After all the hiccups, speedbumps and diversions, Sania was finally able to meet Simran and Shikha at the Bombay Baking Company, a nouveau patisserie at the Marriott Hotel in Juhu. The atmosphere was abuzz with young energy. There was a flurry of activities all around as people exchanged ideas in not-so-private meetings and waiters glided through the onslaught of take-away customers to serve giddying delights on a dish. Amongst the bustle, one could spot quite a few Bollywood celebrities who congregated there for their weekly dose of gossip, and aspiring film-makers who liked to throw around weighty names.

'Is she finally coming or not?' Sania, who was relishing a divinely dressed tuna salad, asked Simran.

'She is a complete nutjob. I don't think we should even bother. We're having fun, aren't we?' Simran winked at Sania and then looked at Shikha. 'Hey, hope you are enjoying the sandwich?'

'Yes, very much,' Shikha struggled to speak with a big juicy bite of roast chicken sandwich stuffed in her mouth. Shikha agreed to order only when Sania offered to pay. Shikha was so cleaned out these days that she was unwilling to buy anything.

'Shikha, I need to apologize to you. We had decided to meet so many times before, but it never materialized. I can't even tell you how crazy hectic my schedule has been. I have hardly been in town. You might be thinking that I was avoiding you or something but believe me, I wasn't,' said Sania, with genuine contrition.

'I am sure you haven't been avoiding me, but my situation has become critical. I don't have a place in Mumbai. I keep shuttling between Pune and Mumbai and each trip costs me at least ₹1,500. Until I have some money in hand, it will be all the more difficult for me to rent a place here, even a PG. Even the goddamn estate agents take two months' rent as their commission.'

'I know, you had told me,' Sania sympathized. She leaned forward and held Shikha's hand in hers. 'For the time being at least, you can move in with me. But just one thing, my dad has been travelling a lot lately and he comes over once a week, so he stays there. Of course, he has his separate room as you know from the time you stayed with me before the pageant.'

'Yeah, I remember. That is not a problem at all. I will manage. I just need to bunk with you for some time. Once I get some good work, I will be out of your hair.'

'Not to worry, you can stay for as long as you want, but strictly no getting any boyfriends.'

'Done! When can I move in?'

'Today itself, if you like.'

'But I haven't got my stuff.'

'You can get your stuff tomorrow or on Monday. You can't possibly go back to Pune so late in the night.'

'Can I butt in if you guys are through with your deal?' Simran chuckled.

'It's called helping a friend, Simran,' Sania smiled.

'Speaking of which, I have a request as well. I would like to invite you to my show as my celebrity guest, Sania.'

'Me? On your celebrity chat show?' Sania was surprised and slightly disinclined. 'Please, let's not get into all that, Simran.'

'You know, Anirudh saw you in that Cadbury ad and he has been after my life to get you on the show ever since. He says you are a star in the making and I believe so too.'

'So, you too wanted to talk shop? And I thought we were meeting as friends,' Sania teased her.

Just then someone tapped on Simran's shoulder. 'Hi, recognize me?'

'Aren't you that guy who used to come to meet Sunidhi at the hotel regularly during the pageant?'

'Busted! I'm Jai.' He removed a thick wad of notes from his pocket and placed it on the table. 'Sunidhi has sent this for you.'

He was just about to turn and leave when Simran stopped him.

'I don't think we were serious about the money. It was just a joke.'

'Sunidhi asked me to give it to you. If you have any questions, why don't you speak with her directly?' Jai didn't wait for her to respond.

Simran looked at Shikha and Sania, bewildered.

'Was Sunidhi into drugs?' Sania inquired naively.

'Of course! She was heavily into it. This guy Jai is supposedly her boyfriend. He was the one who introduced her to drugs. He is more or less out of it, but it seems like she's hooked on big time.'

'So, during the final round, she went blank because of drugs?' Sania's curiosity was piqued. Shikha nudged Sania's foot with hers, trying to convey to her to keep mum. Her reaction wasn't missed by Simran's keen eyes.

'I myself am very confused about the reason behind Sunidhi going blank. In fact, I had called up Shikha as well to ask her if she knew anything about it. Do you remember, Shikha?' Simran looked at Shikha intently.

'Yeah, I remember, but why would I know anything about it?' Shikha squirmed under the intense scrutiny of Simran's gaze.

In another part of the city, Jai was worried sick about Sunidhi. He had been trying to call her frantically for the last half an hour, but her phone was switched off. She never did that. The one thing that was Sunidhi's lifeline was her phone. She charged it diligently every single day and took care of it more than she took care of herself. And she never switched off her phone. When Jai reached their apartment in Worli, his worst fears had come true. He immediately called up Usman. 'Where the hell is Sunidhi?' he demanded.

'Why are you asking me? Why would I know?' Usman replied harshly.

'She was supposed to be here at the Worli apartment after dropping me.'

'So? I'm busy.' Usman disconnected the call.

Jai called him back, but Usman disconnected the call. Jai tried again. And again, he rejected the call. On his third attempt, he found that Usman had switched off his phone. Jai immediately sensed that something was not right. The fact that Usman hadn't even asked him about the outstanding money was suspicious. He got an unshakable feeling in his gut that Sunidhi was in some grave danger. He hurriedly called up the driver of their taxi.

'Ganesh, this is Jai. Where did you drop Sunidhi off?'

'At Mahim, sir, along with that other guy, Usman.'

'At Mahim? Why at Mahim? Was there a fight between Sunidhi and Usman? Did he force her to get off with him?'

'No, no, they were in very good mood when they got off, sir. I overheard Madam telling Usman that she wanted to try something new. First, Madam went with Usman to his house, and then, they sent someone to collect her bags. I gave them and left.'

'What?' Jai gasped, unbearably distraught. 'Where exactly did you drop them?'

'Do you know Mahim Church, sir? Just one signal after that.'

'Can you come with me to Mahim and show me the place?' Jai pleaded.

'Sir, I don't know where they went after that. You please go and find out yourself. I have to be with my family, sir. I haven't met them for a week. Why don't you call Madam? I have to go now.' Ganesh knew better than to get involved in somebody else's mess. Jai cursed himself for leaving Sunidhi alone with that thug. He left for Mahim right away. *Please be fine, Su*, he prayed.

Sunidhi was on a speeding bike with Usman, her arms trailing behind her body and her hair flailing in the wind. She was delirious with rapture. She could hear her heart thudding in her ears and the blood coursing through her veins. She shrieked in a state of exaltation, startling the passers-by, but she didn't care. She only registered the surge of ecstasy swelling inside her and nothing else.

Usman stopped his bike in front of a dilapidated and deserted building in a by-lane of Cadell Road in Mahim—an ideal place for him to operate from.

Sunidhi wobbled, staggered, swayed and tripped as she made her way. Usman's crony, Munna, hurried towards her in a bid to assist her when he really was simply looking for an excuse to touch her. Usman eyed him with distrust and didn't allow him to get too close to Sunidhi. Usman held her by the waist with one arm and kept Munna at bay with the other.

'Go and get the room ready,' Usman ordered Munna.

'I have already done that, Ustad. Pankaj is also there in the room. We have kept her bags inside. There is no cash in them, only clothes and shoes. What sexy underwear she has! Ustad, you had told me you will let me also have fun. I want to have her badly.' Munna was as shameless as he was blunt.

Usman looked at Munna menacingly and smacked him hard on his head. 'You motherfucker, I will have her first. For the next three days, you don't even look at her. Do you understand that? Otherwise, I will go and fuck your mother.'

'Are we going to keep her for that long, Ustad?'

'I will decide. And until I have made up my mind, if you so much as touch her without my permission, I will rip out your intestines from your ass and strangle you with them.'

'Of course, Ustad! First, you have your fill, only then, I will.'

Usman guided Sunidhi to a dingy room on the second floor of the building. The discoloured walls and grimy flooring would have appalled Sunidhi under regular circumstances, but right now, she looked at them with glee. Usman made Sunidhi sit on a dusty sofa which was worn to shreds. He then mixed two little white pills in a Diet Coke and handed the concoction to Sunidhi. Munna had been observing his boss keenly and he knew right away that Sunidhi was roofied. She glugged the drink down and asked for more.

'I am feeling dehydrated,' Sunidhi told him groggily.

In just a little over ten minutes, Sunidhi felt an uncontrollable drowsiness descend upon her. The drugs in her system reacted with the rohypnol to incapacitate her more quickly. She had a distant glazed look in her eyes and was fixated on some containers lying in the room.

'What is in that box?' she maffled, unable to enunciate the words clearly. She tried to repeat herself, but it took her great effort to stretch her mouth open and she still slurred.

Usman ordered Munna and Pankaj to make themselves scarce and shut the door on them. Not wasting another second, Usman led Sunidhi to a mouldy bed. He held her up as she had lost all motor functions and she complied without any resistance. He spread her out on the bed and began to undress her.

Unbeknownst to him, Munna and Pankaj were fighting fiercely outside the dingy apartment to get a view of Sunidhi from a peephole. They came to an agreement; Pankaj would let Munna watch first in exchange for ₹500.

Munna got a hard-on when he saw Usman removing Sunidhi's shorts. He unfastened his pants in a flash and started petting himself. Even with Pankaj watching, he didn't have the slightest inhibitions.

Sunidhi felt like she was floating in a dream, detached from her body. She fought to keep her eyes open but couldn't. Slimy, adamantine tentacles pinned her down. She tried to resist, but her limbs wouldn't listen to her. All the thoughts in her mind obliterated when she felt a warm, sticky tentacle brush against her breast. Her nipples stiffened. The tentacle continued its onslaught, now on her other breast. Down, down it went, making her moan and squirm with twisted, foul pleasure. She was drowning in ecstasy when the tentacle suddenly retreated.

'No...pleas...don't stop,' she garbled, forcing her eyelids open with enormous effort. The vision shifted in front of her bleary eyes.

Sunidhi was in a jousting tournament. Across her, stood a knight in shining armour, but he was spinning. In her phantasmagoria, she tried to wave at him but couldn't. She was spread-eagled and strapped vertically onto a wooden rotating board. Round and round she spun. First, the knight was glinting magnificently on his destrier, then he was upside down.

The knight lowered his lance and started charging towards her on his steed. Not stopping, he speared her mouth with unwavering precision. She gagged and spluttered, but he was relentless. The knight rode back, giving her a moment's respite before storming towards her again. This time, he speared her sacred altar, shafting it ruthlessly, till she felt his lance in her stomach. Somewhere during the act, the knight lifted his visor—it was Usman. A barely audible voice inside her head screamed with protest. Sunidhi remained paralysed as conflicting emotions of agony and gratification collided within her and ravaged her cloudy mind.

Outside, Munna grunted his release. Pankaj took over the peephole to find a disappointing scene of Usman groaning his climax. He fell on Sunidhi limply and crushed her insentient body. After a couple of minutes, Usman stood up reluctantly and got dressed. He found his lackeys hovering impatiently outside the door and tossed a pack of condoms at them. 'Don't do it without wearing this.'

Pankaj was charged with excitement, having preserved his spunk when Munna had spent it all. He stepped into the room like a ravenous scavenger. Sunidhi's insensate being was least aware of a beast plundering her body, while yet another waited to pounce on her.

25

Jai had been searching for Sunidhi with perseverance. He was in the vicinity, but no one would guide him to Usman's den. He finally bought the loyalty of a peddler on the street, who took him to the building where Usman was residing. Before he could even get into the building, Usman strode down the stairs and stopped in front of him. The peddler who had brought Jai there escaped, fearing the wrath of Usman bhai.

'Where is Sunidhi?' Jai seethed. He was particularly oppugnant and wanted answers. 'I asked you where the fuck is Sunidhi?'

'Where's my money, you bastard?' Usman had earned a name for himself for two reasons; it was impossible to intimidate him and he was brutally immoral.

'What makes you think you'll get your money by kidnapping Sunidhi?'

'Kidnapping?' Usman laughed bitterly. 'Your slag came of her own free will—in more ways than one, might I add. She will only be allowed to leave once I get my money. Now fuck off!'

Usman was all set to hoist Jai out of there when Jai cuffed him. Usman's words had fuelled the rage burning inside him. Usman straightened himself like nothing had happened and spat on the ground. Jai's fist throbbed. He tried to clout Usman again, but he was too agile and powerful for Jai. Within just a minute, Jai was in Usman's grip and his face was getting pummelled. Usman loosened his hold and Jai fell into a heap. A crowd had gathered, but Usman was not worried. He hailed a cab and deposited a bloody-faced Jai in it.

The cab driver was a local fellow who knew Usman very well. 'Where should I take him, Usman bhai?'

'Dump him anywhere in Worli, Javed.' He threw a few hundred rupee notes in the passenger seat in front.

'He won't die, I hope,' the cabbie asked him nervously.

'He won't die so easily, his lifeline is with me,' Usman told him and slapped the bonnet of the car.

A little further up, Jai came back to his senses and ordered the driver to stop the cab. He got off with great difficulty. A nasty wound on his knee made him cringe every time he took a step which, in turn, made his face sting. He fished out his phone gingerly and dialled a number. 'Sir, this is Jai. Sunidhi is in serious trouble.'

Karmarkar couldn't remember the last time he had driven a car. He had one trusted chauffeur who took care of everything related to it. But that day was an exception. He was driving as fast as he could towards Mahim in a BMW 8 Series, the least ostentatious car he owned.

'So, this guy is a drug dealer and he is demanding the money that you guys owe him. Right?' Karmarkar asked impatiently.

'Yes, sir. He kidnapped Sunidhi and is using her as leverage to extort the money.' Jai's voice resounded though the speakers in Karmarkar's car.

'Are you sure that he has kidnapped her?'

Jai had been filling Karmarkar in on all the events that had led to this dreadful point, not omitting much. Karmarkar's heart sank as Jai proceeded. One thing was clear; his daughter was in grave danger of being drugged against her will. And if she died of overdose, Karmarkar wouldn't be able to forgive himself.

He reached Mahim in record time and met Jai near a church. He handed a bottle of water to Jai for his blood-spattered face, but he declined it. He didn't want to waste another second. He straightaway took Karmarkar to the building where Sunidhi was being held hostage.

'They are on the second floor. We will have to be very careful. Have you got the cash?' Jai wanted to make sure everything was in order before they made their move.

Karmarkar nodded in the affirmative.

As Karmarkar climbed the dank, tenebrous staircase, an ominous feeling coiled around his heart. He cursed himself for not giving more time to his daughter, and for shutting the door on her when she needed him the most. *I have failed her as a father and now she is paying for my obstinacy.* He only hoped it wasn't too late.

The flat had no doorbell outside, just a rusty old door latch. Jai knocked on the door frantically. Munna answered it. He immediately closed it halfway when he recognized Jai.

'What do you want?' Munna asked him curtly.

'I have come to make the payment to Usman.'

'Give it to me.' Munna stretched out his hand.

'We would like to meet Sunidhi first,' Karmarkar demanded.

'Who the hell do you think you are? A cop?' He glared at Karmarkar. 'And you bastard, you think you can act smart with me and get away?' Munna attempted to slam the door shut on Jai, but he stuck his foot in the door and began to shove it open with his shoulder.

'This is Sunidhi's father,' Jai uttered as Karmarkar lent his strength and they managed to overpower Munna together.

When the door flung open, both Jai and Karmarkar were aghast by what they saw. Karmarkar was about to collapse out of shock when Jai put his arm around him and steadied him. But in the process, Jai lost his grip on the door and Munna managed to lock it from inside.

Jai pounded on the door, but there was no response. He continued hammering on the door till a fellow opened the door with the door lock chained in place. 'If you create a scene out here, we will kill her,' Pankaj told him in a menacing voice. 'You better skip out of here.' He slammed the door shut once again.

Karmarkar, who was recovering at the back, sprang up and kicked the door with all his might. He swore to make those lowlifes pay, spurred by a singular image seared into his mind—Sunidhi was lying on her bare back on a rotting bed with an unmistakable stain of blood around her pelvis. Her unusually pale body was marked with angry blue and purple bruises. Her lifeless face stared at him with dull, vacant eyes, unblinking.

Karmarkar and Jai had holed themselves up in his car right across Usman's crack den. Karmarkar had not wanted to involve the local police in the fear that their incompetency would botch things up. So, he had pulled some strings at the highest level, with the authority that had the power to assign officers of the Special Task Force, STF.

Meanwhile, Usman was thinking of ways to bump Sunidhi off. Jai had threatened to implicate Usman for kidnapping Sunidhi and with his location exposed, he feared arrest. The only way to clean this mess up was to make sure that there was no evidence of Sunidhi to have ever come there. He was on his way back from an important deal. He tried to call up his stooges but those witless buffoons had turned off their phones. He replaced the old sim card in his phone with a new one registered under a false identity and walked briskly through the narrow by-lanes of Mahim to reach his place.

Across the street, Karmarkar's phone rang. It was the home minister. Karmarkar had given him a complete low-down on Sunidhi's situation. 'The special task force officer will be in touch with you. They should be there in the next few minutes. You are doing the right thing by manning that place. But we will have to act fast before those thugs get time to plan their escape,' the home minister briefed him.

The special task force was directly under the home ministry to deal with emergency situations. Despite the fact that it had some of the best-trained commandos in the country, Karmarkar was anxious.

Inside the flat, Usman's flunkeys were having a sex fest. Munna was on his third round with Sunidhi. 'One for each hole,' he had joked to Pankaj as he used her like a blow-up doll. Pankaj was watching him in the act, aroused and impatient. 'Make it fast, I want to have another go before Ustad comes back,' he spoke in a haze of hedonistic lust, holding on to his erection. Just then, Usman entered the apartment using his key. When he saw Munna plundering a vegetative Sunidhi, he blew his lid off.

'Are you fucking her without caps?' Usman bellowed at Munna, kicking him so hard that he fell off the bed. 'You bastard, I had given you a pack of condoms. When were you planning to use it? On your sister?'

'Two of them I had used, Ustad, but the third one tore and I did not have another one,' Munna defended himself.

'Your mother must have fucked a chimpanzee to produce such a hopeless git like you. You will get us into serious trouble if you keep banging her like there is no tomorrow.'

'But there will be no tomorrow, Ustad. The bitch's father had come here. He was offering the money, full amount, but Munna shut the door on him,' Pankaj informed him as he put his pants on.

'What the fuck are you saying?' Usman roared. Why didn't you dumbfucks call me? We will have to act fast. Did she wake up even once?'

'She was becoming conscious, but Munna gave her another shot of roofies.'

'You idiots, she will die of overdose. We will have to put her away; that's the only way we will survive this shit-storm.'

'I think they're planning on making a move,' Jai told Karmarkar fearfully. 'Two of them had just stepped out in the balcony to scan the area outside.'

Just then the Special Task Force officer called up Karmarkar. 'We are at the location. Can you please guide us to the building? Without stepping out of your car.'

'The off-white building north-east to my car, about sixty degrees from north. Please speak with my colleague, Jai; he will explain it to you much better.'

Within the next thirty seconds, twenty odd black commandos

surrounded the building, armed with automatic rifles. Four commandos sprinted to the building entrance. Their timing was just right. Usman was about to shift Sunidhi to some other place with the help of his lackeys. As soon as he opened the door, about half the Force stormed into the house and asked them to raise their hands.

Usman, who had managed to get Sunidhi in his grips, instantly removed a gun and pointed it at Sunidhi's head. 'If you try to act smart, I will shoot her dead.'

The commandos held themselves back.

'Fuck! So many of you rascals are here? Put your guns down. Put your fucking guns down,' Usman yelled.

The STF leader subtly instructed his commandos to keep their guns down.

'What do you want?' the STF leader asked Usman.

'Right now, I want to leave this place for an undisclosed location. And I want my mon...' Usman was interrupted abruptly. His head fell backwards as blood and chunks of his flesh, bones and brains splattered on the wall. The very same moment, he collapsed. Usman had been shot by a STF sniper.

Sunidhi, who was in Usman's grip, also went down. It wasn't clear if she had been shot. One of the commandos pulled her out and checked her pulse. It seemed okay, but it was lower than the normal rate. He checked her for bullet wounds; there were none.

In the meantime, Munna had tried to escape from the balcony. He was immediately sprayed with bullets and his limp body dangled on the parapet. After seeing Munna being killed like a rat, Pankaj was too terrified to run. He raised his hands and surrendered himself. Two commandos checked him thoroughly and took him into custody. Another part of the team scanned the apartment meticulously, not sparing any nook or cranny.

'We can inform the local police to take over now,' the STF leader announced on his walkie.

As soon as Karmarkar saw the commandos carrying Sunidhi on a stretcher, he dashed out to meet her. But the leader of the STF squad stopped him. 'Sir, we had called for an ambulance without a siren which is already here. The home minister told me about keeping it away from the prying eyes of the media. Your daughter has already been transferred inside the ambulance. You should go with her to the hospital right away.'

'A simple "thank you" seems inadequate. I am indebted to you, officer.' Karmarkar shook his hand graciously and headed towards the ambulance, with Jai trailing behind him. The guilt of his daughter's plight weighed down on Karmarkar and finally broke him when he saw Sunidhi's frail frame on the gurney. He held his unconscious daughter to his chest and wept like he had when he had held her for the first time in his arms.

26

A cold blast of air from the AC vents made Sania shiver. She rubbed her arms to appease the goosebumps on her skin in protest. Sania requested that the temperature in the studio be raised a little. Simran handed Sania her pashmina stole.

'I am used to it. They have to keep it really cool because of the equipment,' she explained to Sania, while skimming through some notes. They were about to roll for her *Celebrity Chit-chat Show*.

Sania nodded as she tightly wrapped the stole around herself. She was sitting next to Simran on the set of the show, but she was not seen on the monitors; as yet. The cameras were focused on the host first, who would then introduce the celebrity guest.

'Full lights. Camera,' the director instructed.

'Rolling,' responded the cameraman.

'Action!'

'Good evening, friends. Today in the *Celebrity Chit-chat Show*, we have a brand new entrant, who till about three months back was a coy, undiscovered star in Aurangabad. Since then, she has won acclaim for her work and adoration for her persona. Our guest tonight is the current Miss India, the reigning Beauty Queen, Miss Sania Ahmed. Welcome to the show, Sania,' Simran introduced her vibrantly.

The cameraman widened the shot to include both Simran and Sania. They both could be seen beaming at each other on the monitors in the control room where the online editor was frenetically cutting shots from four different cameras. His ears were glued to every syllable coming from the headphones, and accordingly, he chose visuals that he deemed fit in the edited version. Although it was not a live telecast, most of the shows followed this format of online editing, as it saved an awful lot of time.

'Thank you so much, Simran! I liked the introduction you gave me. I don't know what your definition of a star is, but I don't consider myself a celebrity from any angle.'

'You are too modest, Sania. The fact that you are on this show means you are definitely a celebrity,' Simran jested. 'So let's begin, Sania. Was it a dream come true when you won the Beauty Queen title?'

'I had never ever dreamt of winning a beauty pageant. It was a fluke, to tell you honestly. I sent in my application just for fun and got selected. After that, winning the title was an even luckier trip I would say.'

'I don't think it was just your luck that brought you this far. So what's next for you, Sania? Are you planning to get into Bollywood or do you have something else in mind?'

'The problem with me, Simran, is that I never plan. I cannot plan beyond a few hours or a day. For instance, right now I know I have a shoot with you today and then a couple of meetings after this shoot.'

'So you like to take things as they come. What was your family's reaction when you won the pageant?'

'My parents were ecstatic. But I've observed some funny changes in their behaviour ever since. Before I won the pageant, when I would sleep for long hours, my mom would keep nagging me about how I hibernated like a bear. But after I won the pageant, even if I have slept for a long time, she is always after me to sleep even more. It's really strange how once you become successful or famous, you are forgiven for everything. You can get away with murder. All that you do is appreciated unquestioningly. But when you are not successful, even the good things are looked down upon and people find faults in everything that you do.'

'So it must feel nice to be successful, to be the reigning Beauty Queen?'

'I don't let anything go to my head, at least I try not to. This Beauty Queen title I have is only there for a year. Next year, someone else will win the title and I will be history. So why should I get attached to something which is so temporary?'

'Wow! Profound stuff! It's going to be really interesting to continue this conversation with you, Sania. We'll be taking a small break here, don't go anywhere. We'll be right back with the *Celebrity Chit-chat Show*,' Simran looked straight into the camera and spoke.

Inside the control room, the editor and executive producer watched the monitors on the switching panel intently. The monitors showed the interview being shot from various angles. Being the producer of the show, Anirudh was supervising the entire shoot. He rushed out to the floor as soon as Simran announced a break.

Anirudh handed a few sheets of paper to Simran and was about to head back when Simran stopped him. 'Rudy, come here. Why are you in such a rush?' Anirudh looked at Sania and greeted her. 'And Sania, this is my honeyrudh.'

'Honeyrudh?' Sania chuckled. 'I've heard a lot about you.'

'I hope some of them were good things,' Anirudh quipped.

Sania nodded. 'But are you really good?' she taunted him playfully and the two girls sniggered conspiratorially.

Anirudh just huffed good-naturedly and turned towards Simran. 'Hey, I have listed down some more questions in these printouts. Quickly go through them and put them across to Sania in your own way.'

'You want me to grill my girl?' Simran spoke gruffly, but her expressions gave away her jovial intent.

Sania excused herself to take a call. 'It's Shikha, she moved in with me just this morning,' she informed Simran before answering the phone.

'Good for her. But please make it quick.'

Sania acknowledged Simran's request with a thumbs up and spoke into the phone, 'Hey Shikha, what happened?'

'I'm unable to start the geyser, yaar. Can you please tell me how to?'

'Yikes, I forgot to tell you that our geyser is a little moody. For now, just switch off the main button and turn it on after a couple of minutes. Sometimes it heats up and doesn't start. We'll have to call the electrician soon but this should work for now.'

'Cool, thanks. How's the interview going by the way? Are you done?'

'It has been going pretty well so far, but it'll go on for some more time, I reckon. Anyway, I need to get back to it, the break is almost over. See you later.' Simran signalled Sania to hurry up, so Sania hung up and hurried back to her seat.

Nestled in the comfort of Sania's plush apartment, Shikha now understood what a hectic day in Sania's life meant. Sania was neck-deep in work and genuinely had very little time to spare. She had not been avoiding Shikha all this while, like she had assumed.

Shikha had a room to herself in the apartment but currently, a lot of Sania's stuff was lying around in it. Partially filled suitcases, scores of unopened gifts and knick-knacks were strewn all over. Sania had promised her that she would get the room cleaned up in the next day or two.

With nothing better to do, Shikha decided to snoop around the house; she started with Sania's room. It was a meticulously kept fully carpeted room. An entire wall had been utilized to cater to Sania's aesthetic needs. A ceiling-to-floor shoe cupboard housed the biggest labels in the world—Jimmy Choo, Louboutin, Manolo Blahnik, Weitzman and Brian Atwood—all stacked in neat rows. Next to it was a full-length mirror which had adjoining shelves for high-end make-up products. And at the end, she had a cupboard, big enough to easily fit half a dozen people in it. Sania's wardrobe was a well-balanced mix of chic contemporary clothes along with classic, evergreen pieces. A quick look at the tags told Shikha that they were all top designer labels, national and international. An inadvertent pang of jealousy crept into Shikha's heart.

'So, Sania, how was your experience at the pageant? Did you have any untoward experiences?' asked Simran.

The camera was rolling again and they were recording the next segment of the show.

'Untoward experiences? No, not really. We had a lot of jittery moments, a lot of fights and differences with each other but nothing very drastic.'

'Did you come across any weird characters around you? Because once you start spending so much time with others, you start despising them.'

'I don't think that's true. Not to mention, during the pageant you hardly have enough time to complete your own tasks. So you barely get to know the other girls.'

'But still, familiarity breeds contempt. Didn't you have a falling-out with anyone?'

'Familiarity doesn't *always* breed contempt, at least not for me. For me, familiarity means warmth. It means shedding your inhibitions. I can't let my hair down around someone I don't know very well. Like today, if it hadn't been you conducting this interview, I would never have even agreed to come for it, let alone prattle on about myself non-stop.'

'Lucky me!' Simran joked as both of them shared a laugh. 'Ok. Sania, tell me something. Did you at least come across participants who flouted the rules? Who did things that were unbecoming or improper?'

'I'm sorry, but what do you mean by that?'

'Like were there girls calling their boyfriends over or having alcohol or doing drugs?'

'I am not the right person to answer these questions, Simran. I was never bothered with what others were doing. I was only concerned with the people who needed cheering up when the pressure of the contest got to them. If there were contestants who violated the rules, then it was the management's responsibility to deal with them. They are called supervisors for a reason. Moreover, what someone does in their own space should not concern anyone else. You can't plant a hidden camera and start picking on what they do. It's an encroachment of their privacy.'

'So if you would notice someone doing drugs, you wouldn't report it to the management?'

'That is a hypothetical situation. But, I don't think I would report. I am not a mud-slinging backbiter.'

And with that answer, Simran wrapped up the second segment and called for a break. Something was nagging Simran. She asked the executive producer to fetch Anirudh. 'I need to talk to you alone,' Simran told Anirudh as she dragged him by the elbow towards a secluded corner.

'What is the logic behind the questions you have given me? Why are we bullying her with questions on drugs and substance abuse?'

'What is wrong if we know her take on them, Simran? Moreover, I want to spice up the show. It's going too flat.'

'Rudy, it is only once in a while I get a guest like Sania, who I enjoy talking to. I know her; she is not the kind of person to take these questions nicely. She is the last person to interfere in others' matters. And she definitely would not like to get involved in any controversy.'

'So, all the more reason to use her to scrape the bottom!' Anirudh's tone sounded off alarm bells in Simran's mind.

'Scrape the bottom? What the hell are you implying, Anirudh?'

'Don't read between the lines, Sims. We'll talk later. Right now, focus on finishing this episode.'

Even though Simran was not fully convinced, she finished the shoot with Sania. Sania was instantly in a hurry to rush for her next meeting, but Simran wanted to have a word with her.

'Sania, I have a confession to make. It is something really important that I...'

Even before Simran could finish her sentence, Sania was on her phone. She offered Simran an apologetic look as she spoke on the phone. 'But, Rohit, you will have to manage the dates. You can't expect me to ask the producer to shift the shooting schedule. I am sorry, Rohit, but this is not done. Anyway, I'm getting another call, I have to take it. It is the director of the TVC we are shooting tomorrow.' Sania was overloaded with work. Simran was really happy for her. A new version of Sania stood across her, one that was a lot more confident and self-assured.

Simran desperately wanted to unburden herself by coming clean. She wanted to disclose everything to Sania—about how she was at the pageant for an ulterior motive, and how she was looking for scoops rather than trying to win the title. More than anything else, she wanted to apologize to her profusely. But Sania was already on her fourth call.

'Yeah! I am starting from here in the next five seconds,' Sania practically yelled into her phone and hit the 'call end' button. 'I am sorry, Simran. I can't tell you how badly pressed for time I am. I need to dash. The agency takes my case if I am late for any meeting.'

Simran walked Sania to the exit. Her driver came and collected her bags. 'There is so much I want to talk to you about, Simran. You remember the fiasco that happened at the Aurangabad airport? It was the handiwork of my precious cousin Rashid.'

'What?' Simran was shell-shocked. 'That guy who was relentlessly pestering you during the pageant? The one who wanted to get married to you?'

'Yup, the very same guy.' Sania got into the car, rolled down the window and clasped Simran's hand. 'We will catch up soon,' she told her earnestly. 'I'm lucky to have a friend like you—fierce and loyal.'

The knot of guilt in Simran's stomach twisted uneasily.

27

'She is out of immediate danger,' the doctor informed Karmarkar and his wife. Jai, who stood behind them, sagged with relief. 'But she needs to be kept in the Intensive Care Unit for another day. Although she has regained consciousness, her body functions are extremely depressed because of the drugs. We'd like to monitor her till everything's back on track.'

'When can we see her?' Mrs Karmarkar demanded.

'I would like to give her some more time to recuperate before she meets anyone. The experience she had was traumatic, not only physically but also mentally. She needs some time. But you can see her from a distance if you like.' No sooner had the doctor uttered those words than Mrs Karmarkar scrambled to get a glimpse of her daughter.

'Is she aware of what happened?' Karmarkar asked the doctor.

'She doesn't have a single memory from last night. Based on the tests we did on her, we were able to identify that she was drugged with Rohypnol, the date-rape drug,' the doctor explained. 'My team had feared that she was going to slip into coma at one point, as she was not responding at all. Judging by the amount of Rohypnol that was administered to her, she's lucky to be alive.'

'How long will she take to recover completely?'

'As such she might feel woozy, confused and uncoordinated for a week or two. She may also have some difficulty moving her limbs normally. But no one can know for sure how much time she'll require to heal from the psychological damage she endured. If you'll excuse me,' the doctor gave a sympathetic pat on Karmarkar's shoulder and left to check on the other patients.

Mrs Karmarkar could barely recognize the girl lying on the hospital bed. Dark circles and haggard lines marked her cadaverous face. Her emaciated arms were pricked with tubes in numerous places. She looked like a mere shadow of the exuberant girl she used to be. Seeing her daughter in this condition, something inside Mrs Karmarkar splintered.

'This is all your fault! Your stubbornness is the reason why our daughter is in this state. How could you let her rot outside, without realizing how lonely and immature she was? I will never forgive you for what you have done to her,' she lashed out at her husband.

'I gave her that house in Worli. I put a roof over her head so she could be safe.'

'So giving the house to her was the end of your responsibility?'

'She is twenty-four years old damn it.'

'So? For all of these years, you have mollycoddled her and that is why she has the maturity of a thirteen-year-old. When have you ever given her the attention and love that she needed? Whatever she did was out of anger, out of frustration that she couldn't win over her father's heart. She has always struggled to get your attention. She always took a backseat next to your companies and work. You drove her towards this insanity.' Karmarkar was deeply gutted by the vitriol his wife spewed. He was about to tell her how terribly wrong she was when the doctor called for him.

'Mr Karmarkar, I would like to talk to you in person.'

Karmarkar nodded at Jai and indicated to him to come along. As they were about to step inside the cabin, the doctor stopped him. 'Mr Karmarkar, if you don't mind, I would want you to come inside all alone. What I want to share with you is extremely personal.'

'Jai is family. He knows Sunidhi better than me or perhaps even my wife.'

'I would still request you to come in by yourself,' the doctor insisted. 'At best, you can call your wife in but only after you have understood what I'm about to share with you.' The seriousness in the doctor's tone rattled Karmarkar. He asked Jai to wait outside and himself stepped into the consulting room.

'I hope nothing is wrong,' Karmarkar said worriedly.

'I am afraid I have grave news.'

'What is it?' Karmarkar panicked.

'There is no easy way of saying this, Mr Karmarkar, but based on the reports we got on some of the tests we did, it was found that your daughter has been raped multiple times after being drugged,' the young lady-doctor informed him with anguish. 'At least three people have sexually assaulted her, brutally.'

The floor under Karmarkar's feet began to spin. 'What?' His mind was numb with shock and he stared at the doctor vacantly.

'Mr Karmarkar, Mr Karmarkar.' The doctor tried to snap him out of his daze, but he did not respond. So she grabbed him by the shoulders and physically shook him. He blinked disbelievingly.

'But, she was there for barely a couple of hours. Who conducted the tests?'

'I did.'

'And who else? Were there any other doctors or nurses with you?'

'There was another doctor and two nurses who aided me.'

'I want this test report destroyed,' Karmarkar told her emphatically.

'But, sir, we have to inform the police. That is a statutory requirement,' the doctor protested.

'I will talk to your hospital authorities. From your end, please see to it that no one talks about this. If there is so much as a whisper about this, I will take you to task. Do you get me?'

'What will you achieve by hiding the truth?'

'I will save my daughter the embarrassment and stigma perpetuated by society and the ignominy of being persecuted in the media. And please, just do not give me a sermon about facing the truth or some nonsense.'

'I will not.'

'Are you saying you will not co-operate with me?' Karmarkar glowered at her.

'No, I meant I will not talk about it to anyone.'

'Can I trust you on that?'

'Yes, sir. Nobody should have to endure this.'

'You have such an insane collection of clothes and accessories, Shikha. Where did you get all this stuff from?' Sania asked her, dressed in her unicorn pyjamas.

'This all is courtesy my fan club,' Shikha giggled. 'You know how experienced I am at getting my gifts from people. Sometimes, I even manipulate them to get what I want. Men are so dumb.'

'Wow! What a conniving fox you are.' Shikha took it as a compliment and beamed at her.

'How was your interview with Simran?'

'It was nice but a little strange.'

'Strange in what sense?' Shikha was setting up her clothes and accessories in her new room, while Sania inspected her reflection in the mirror for imperfections.

'She suddenly started talking about girls at the beauty pageant doing drugs. I don't understand where that came from.'

'But she was right! Quite a few of the girls at the pageant were doing drugs regularly.'

'What are you saying? Did you see anyone doing drugs?' Sania turned around to look at Shikha directly.

'So many of them! Our great Sunidhi Karmarkar was also one of the many.'

'Are you serious? How come I never noticed all this?'

'You are too innocent to understand these corrupt things.'

'Shikha, tell me something. Why did Sunidhi go blank in the final round? Was it because of the drug abuse everyone has been pinning on her?'

'Are you so dumb as to believe that, Sania? I mean you of all people should not be making such ignorant comments about the finale fiasco.'

'But just now you said she used to take drugs regularly?'

'Sania, what did I give you in the loo that night of the finale?'

'You gave me that chit.'

'And what did that chit have?'

'It had that line. Ya, I wanted to ask you. How did you get that line?'

'Exactly, the line that you spoke as your final-round answer.'
'Yeah. "Youth and beauty fade away, but character endures forever." I remember that line verbatim.'
'Of course, you do!'
'So? What connection does that line have with Sunidhi?'
'That was the answer that Sunidhi had written. She was the last contestant. When her turn came, you had already said her answer out loud, word for word that too. How could she have spoken at all? It would have been a huge embarrassment for her. So she chose to go blank.'
'Is that why I won the pageant?' Sania was immensely disturbed by what Shikha had just unravelled.
'Technically, you won because of that chit I gave you. You would not have won otherwise,' Shikha told her obnoxiously.
'So I won because I cheated.' Sania's heart sank.
'No, you won because I helped you.'
'I don't feel good about this one bit. I've never felt so guilty before.'
'Why should you feel guilty about it? I gave you the chit of my own free will.'
'Where did you get the chit from?' Sania probed her.
'I guess there's no harm in telling you about this now. But you have to promise you won't mention this to anyone, anywhere outside.'
'Pinky promise!'
'The chit was given to me by this guy called Anirudh Bhattacharya, Simran's boyfriend.'
'What? I just met him today,' Sania exclaimed. 'But why would he do that?'
'From whatever I can see, there is a huge conspiracy involved. Karmarkar wanted Sunidhi to win the pageant, but Khambatta, who was the sponsor for this year, wanted someone from a small town to win the pageant. Sunidhi was too hoity-toity for Khambatta's two-tier target audience.'
'This is too complicated. I still don't understand it.'

'You hear me out first. Simran's channel was trying for telecast rights...'

'Simran's channel means Dastak, right? The one I went to today?'

'Right! Since Dastak did not get the telecast rights which they badly wanted, they decided to back Khambatta, who is the biggest advertiser on their channel. So to support Khambatta's game plan...'

'That is how Anirudh came into the picture,' Sania butted in. 'Does Simran know about this?'

'By the looks of it, I don't think she knows anything. If she did, why would she call me to find out why Sunidhi went blank? Ideally her boyfriend should have told her about this.' Sania was processing this deluge of information as Shikha continued, 'Do you know Nimesh Mehta and Khambatta had a very serious fight later on? It got very ugly.'

'So Sunidhi became a victim of their crossfire?'

'Precisely!'

'And we benefitted out of it?'

'Not we but you. You are the biggest gainer in this game, even though you were completely unaware of it.'

'I don't feel comfortable with this at all, Shikha. This means that I won the title unethically, and I can't live with that. I think I will renounce the title.'

'Don't be silly, Sania. You promised me that you would not talk about this to anyone. That's the only reason I shared all this with you. If you blab about this to anyone, there will be a lot of problems for everyone, but mostly for you.'

28

After shooting the episode with Sania, Simran attended the subsequent editing session for a couple of hours. The episode needed one final session with the main editor later in the week, either on Monday or on Tuesday, and it would be ready to air the following Sunday. Usually, Simran would spend Sunday evenings unwinding with Anirudh, but he was tied up with work that day, so Simran loafed around the apartment without any purpose.

She was indulging in innocuous gossip with Divya, the in-house editor of Dastak, when their conversation took an unexpected turn.

'Are you sure he is there?' Simran asked Divya.

'I am not hallucinating, Simran. And unless he has an identical twin that I don't know of, he has been here since morning.'

'He didn't even tell me that. When I called him earlier, he said that he was busy with some important work outside.'

'He is definitely very busy but with Gul and Khambatta. They've all locked themselves up in Gul's cabin.'

'Gul is at his office on a Sunday? Something major seems to be brewing. Let's hope they're increasing the budget for our show. Let me call up Anirudh and find out.'

'His phone is not with him. It's in his cabin. I tried calling him a bunch of times.'

'Do you have any idea what they're up to?'

'They have been working with some freelance editor on the episode.'

'Which episode? The one we shot with Sania?' Simran was astonished.

'Yeah. Didn't Anirudh tell you?'

'No, he didn't.'

'He told me that he had discussed it with you and that you had agreed to it.'

'What? I have not exchanged a word with him about this episode. Can you please knock on the door and give him your phone?'

'I don't think I can do that, Simran. We have been in a frenzy through the day. I had to transfer so much data, the entire footage. I've been busting my ass like some goddamn apprentice just transferring A rolls and B Rolls. We're uplinking it right now.'

'Uplinking what?'

'The flipping episode, Simran. Haven't you seen the promos?'

'What promos? What the hell is happening?' Simran immediately switched on the TV and put on Dastak channel. 'What are the promos about?'

'About the beauty pageant.'

'Which beauty pageant? IBQ?' Simran hurried to her desk and ransacked it for the hard disks she had used during her sting-op. They were missing.

'Simran, I will have to call you back later.'

'Listen, listen, Divya, one sec...' Simran was overwrought, but Divya had already disconnected the call. Panicking, she called Gul. The line rang a few times before going to voice mail. 'Call me back, Gul. It's urgent.' Simran was pacing up and down her house, and a million thoughts blitzed her mind. A voice from the television caught her attention; it was her voice. She darted towards it.

A promo was playing on the screen in which Simran was interrogating Sania. 'Do you at least know the names of drugs that are popular currently?'

A very sharp close-up visual of someone snorting coke played on-screen with Sania's voice in the background. 'I have heard of cocaine and ecstasy. But I really don't know much about either.'

'I hope you are not being diplomatic about it, Sania,' prodded Simran.

'No, I honestly don't know,' Sania's guileless voice reiterated.

That scene was cut to a still from the interview. 'The most daring *Celebrity Chit-chat Show* episode,' a deep voice narrated. 'The reigning Beauty Queen, Sania Ahmed, discusses with Simran

Thapar the ugly side of beauty business. Tonight at 9, only on Dastak.'

Simran was horrified.

'Damn you, Anirudh, you shit-eating rat.' Livid, Simran stomped to her bedroom to get dressed. A nasty surprise waited for her on the other side of her closet. Anirudh had taken away all his belongings—his clothes, his laptop, his books, his toiletries. It was a premeditated act of betrayal. Simran sprinted out of her apartment.

She was on the way to her studio when she got a call from Sania. 'I was just about to call...'

'What the hell is happening, Simran?' Sania interrupted her. 'What are these promos on your channel?'

'I myself don't know. I am heading to my channel office to find out. I'm really worried that these people are up to something sinister.'

'Who am I supposed to turn to? I came to your channel for the interview only because I trusted you, Simran. If this plays out badly, it won't bode well for us.' Sania ended the conversation with those words.

'My guess was right. Simran had come with an agenda. And all that is coming out in the open now,' Shikha spurred Sania on. 'She used you to play her game.'

Simran was wounded by Sania's curtness. She knew that no matter what happened, she would be the one liable to answer her friends. She tried Anirudh's phone again, but it was busy. She tried calling him repeatedly but to no avail. It was apparent to Simran that he was deliberately avoiding her. She decided to call someone else instead.

'Divya, why aren't you answering my calls?'

'Simran, these people have gone absolutely nuts. You need to go to the office immediately and put an end to this insanity. I told them I had to be with my kid at home and left.' Divya almost had a hysterical edge to her voice. 'How did you not know anything about this, Simran? You should have been there.'

'I am on my way, Divya. But it will still take me half an hour to get there. Do you think the telecast can be stopped?' Simran asked her nervously.

'I doubt it, Simran. They must have finished uplinking it by now. You should try and talk to Anirudh. He is the only one who can sympathize with you. Because Gul has gone batshit crazy.'

'Anirudh is no longer with me. He was the one who schemed and perpetrated this whole thing. Just a few days ago, he was talking about getting a position in the London office. And that swine seems to have double-crossed me for that.'

'Then I'm afraid you won't be able to do anything, Simran,' Divya told her, defeated.

By the time Simran reached the office, not a single soul was there. The security guard outside told her that everyone had left about half an hour ago. He handed an envelope to her as she was about to leave. It had her name scrawled on one surface. She tore it open to find just a single-lined message. 'Dearest Simran, do watch this show's masterpiece tonight. It was all courtesy you. Love, Gul.'

'Can you tell me why I am here?' Sunidhi asked her father, perplexed.

Ever since she had come back to her senses, that was the question that singularly preoccupied her mind. She had even tried to coax the answer from attending nurses and doctors but to no avail. Her body felt like it was made of lead and her perpetual state of exhaustion made her very emotional and irritable. She despised being feeble, but what she loathed even more were the straps that imprisoned her to the bed.

'You have been immobilized because of your recurring convulsions. Do you remember where you had gone?'

'I had gone to a friend's house in Mahim.'

'That drug dealer was your friend?'

'Was he a drug dealer? I didn't know that.' Even though she was battered down by fatigue, Sunidhi still lied through her teeth.

'He had drugged you.'

'Who told you that?'

'You have been semi-conscious for a few days now.'

'What? What is the day today?'

'It's Sunday evening. You were on your way back from Goa last Friday.' Karmarkar did not have the stomach to tell her about the assault as yet. She needed time to process what had happened; as did he.

Mrs Karmarkar felt like she had been hit by a freight train when Karmarkar told her about the assault their daughter had faced. Jai was so angry with himself when Karmarkar shared the same information with him that he started hitting himself. Karmarkar had to physically hold him back from doing any more damage to himself.

The home minister had assured Karmarkar that no news about Sunidhi would be leaked anywhere. The STF had handed over the case to the local police. The police records had classified it as a narcotics dealer shootout case. There was no mention in the report of a girl being raped or rescued. The third accused, Pankaj, who had surrendered himself, was later killed in an encounter when he tried to escape police custody in the wee hours of Sunday morning. That was the version given by the police to all the leading newspapers.

No news channel or newspaper got a whiff of what had really happened. Or, they did but didn't have the audacity to go up against Karmarkar; such was his clout.

Since he owned a multitude of brands, Karmarkar always bought bulk media space that he purchased at throwaway rates. He used this media space as currency—full-page ads in newspapers congratulating some or the other minister, praising those in positions of authority through cleverly veiled, planted stories and scores of TV spots for various purposes, including favours to ministers who wanted to give a present to their own backers.

So while the home minister scratched Karmarkar's back this time, he expected Karmarkar to return the favour with interest.

Simran was at her wit's end searching for Anirudh. She had visited most of the places he frequented, but he was nowhere to be found. She even went to Gul's house, but he had disappeared too. She had run out of options and now it seemed like all that was left for her to do was stand back and watch her whole plan misfire against her.

Dastak had been playing the promos for the upcoming episode every half an hour since the afternoon, but Karmarkar was utterly preoccupied in nursing Sunidhi back to health at the hospital. Nimesh Mehta, who would have been spitting fire had he seen this, was blissfully unaware. He was on a sixteen-hour flight, on his way back from the U.S.

Fifteen minutes before the dreaded telecast, Simran was so overwrought that she was sure she would get a brain aneurysm. Every minute felt like it had been stretched into an hour. *Why didn't I destroy the footage when I had decided not to go ahead with the sting-op? Why did Anirudh stab me in the back? What will my friends do after they see whatever is there in the episode?* Terrifying questions flopped around inside her head. *They will lambast me and spit on my face publicly.*

The clock struck nine and Simran turned on the channel, shaking with trepidation. The first segment showed footage of the girls at the pageant which Simran had shot from her hidden camera. Then, to her utmost horror, in the second segment, she saw edited footage of Sunidhi snorting coke and then going blank in the finale. There were shots of Shikha lashing out at the pageant organizers. Personal moments of the girls smoking, drinking and revelling were flaunted to the world in the worst possible way. Even Sania was shown in bad light, thanks to the sting-op footage which had been randomly interspersed with her interview. A voice-over maligned young 'immoral' girls and blamed beauty pageants for exacerbating the erosion of values in society.

Simran's phone started ringing before the episode even got over. Her colleagues from the pageant, who hadn't contacted her in months, called her with an unstoppable fervour. But she didn't have the courage to hear what they had to say. A deluge of vicious, pejorative messages flooded her phone; messages that were filled with choicest abuses. Simran read them and shuddered. Her guilt clawed its way upwards and around her neck and strangulated her till she became dizzy.

The hateful, bigoted views in the episode were not Simran's but whoever saw her hosting the programme would automatically ascribe it to her. Moreover, the personal vilification of some girls, including her three closest friends, her roommates, was something she couldn't even hope to be pardoned for.

Her phone buzzed again. This time it was Sania calling. Although she was an atheist, Simran mumbled a quick prayer and answered the call.

'Is this why you became so chummy with all of us, Simran? You should have been an actor, not a host,' Sania told her acidly.

'Can you please just give me a chance to explain...'

'You traded our trust and friendship for this?'

'Sania, please hear me out. I had canned this entire sting operation, but Anirudh...'

'You are too petty,' Sania interjected again and disconnected the call.

Simran was shattered by Sania's abomination of her. With inconsolable tears, Simran tried desperately to call her back. Every time Sania rejected her call, Simran broke a little more inside. She began to type a repentant message but halfway through it, she realized the futility of it.

Quite a few of the girls who had trusted Simran with their secrets were affected by the sting-op telecast. But the fallout on Sunidhi Karmarkar was easily the most severe. As soon as Karmarkar had gotten wind of the episode, he had rushed Sunidhi home. An entire battalion of nurses and doctors had been called to take care of her. Little did Sunidhi know that she was in the eye of *yet* another storm. When she learnt about it, Sunidhi was stupefied. As much as she disliked Simran, she had never thought her capable of such flagrant treachery.

The sting-op telecast had caught Sunidhi on the wrong foot and Karmarkar had to act immediately to do damage control. He called his lawyers and briefed them about the incident.

'The fact that she was caught on camera being in possession of a sizeable quantity of cocaine, and using it as well, puts her in danger of being arrested, sir,' Karmarkar's lawyer informed him.

'So what is the way out?'

'We should file for an Anticipatory Bail immediately.'

'What are the chances that we'll get it?'

'We should get it without any hassle. The source of information is secondary. We can claim that the footage has been tampered with. Moreover, there is no complaint against us, so we can argue that it's media hype and an attempt to malign Miss Karmarkar.'

Being a Karmarkar, Sunidhi's act and the news of her possible arrest had caught the media's attention like wildfire. Almost every news channel was beaming Sunidhi's coke-snorting clip, originally transmitted by Dastak. The next day, all the major newspapers carried Sunidhi's story under different versions of this title—'Karmarkar's daughter snuffs. Caught red-handed'. Karmarkar's house was under siege by reporters and camera crew from every TV channel across the country.

'It has turned out to be much uglier than I anticipated,' Karmarkar told his lawyer on the phone. 'You please go ahead with the anticipatory formalities and keep me updated.'

Sunidhi peeked furtively outside the curtains in her room, a prisoner inside her own house. She shivered as she looked out, from part withdrawal, part fright and part anger. She saw her father's car being mobbed by the media people. In spite of having security personnel, Karmarkar was forced to get out of his car and jostle his way back home.

'Your daughter was caught on camera snorting coke. What was your reaction to it?' one of the media guys thrust the mike in Karmarkar's face.

'Mr Karmarkar, who will you be bribing to get her bail?' yet another one tried his luck.

Watching the sharks attack her father for her mistakes broke a dam inside Sunidhi.

Karmarkar's burly security guys formed a protective ring around him and led him to his house. The media hooligans were thumping the car, which was still outside in the crowd, with their fists, feet and equipment as the driver tried to manoeuvre it. Jai was trapped in the chaos as well, struggling to find his way through. Luckily for him, Karmarkar spotted him and asked a couple of his guards to escort him inside.

'Bloody vandalizing ruffians! In the name of media and news, they ransack you.' Karmarkar was speaking on the phone to the CM's secretary, Salunkhe.

'Mr Karmarkar, I called to assure you that your Anticipatory Bail hearing will be taken care of. It will be at the sessions court at 3:00 p.m. Mr Joshi is the judge. You don't have to worry about a thing. Everything is taken care of,' Salunkhe informed Karmarkar with a certainty that comforted him.

A visibly relieved Karmarkar walked to his bedroom. His wife, who had just finished her morning prayers, turned towards him to offer *prasad*. Sunidhi stumbled into their room, trembling hysterically. She collapsed on the floor as a grand mal seizure took over her body. Simultaneous blistering and frigid flashes made her sweat and shiver at the same time. Her muscles convulsed of their own accord. Two nurses rushed in to hold Sunidhi down. One of them injected a sedative in her system and the convulsions abated. Karmarkar watched helplessly as the nurses hoisted away his unconscious daughter.

29

'We should do more of these sting operations. Reality television with a twist. It works like critter videos on YouTube.' Gul was practically radiant with triumph as he spoke to Anirudh.

The two were having their morning dose of caffeine in Gul's office.

'Absolutely! I got some stupendous feedback for last night's episode,' said Anirudh proudly.

'And your girlfriend was so sincere that she should be given an award for the most sincere host, in the most insincere act.' They both dissolved in a fit of laughter. But their cackling was cut short when the cabin's door crashed open. Simran stepped in, fuming with rage. Anirudh gulped and turned as white as a ghost.

'Hey, Simran! What's up?' Gul made small talk with Simran with no remorse for his actions. 'We were just talking about your episode last night. We are getting incredible feedback. We might get one of our best ratings for that episode.'

'Good for you, Gul. But it's just too bloody bad for me.' If Simran could burn a hole into Anirudh's skull by glaring at him, she would've gladly done that. She looked at him sharply while frantically searching for his metaphorical balls since his real ones had retracted into his liver. 'With whose permission did you take my hard drives, Anirudh?'

'I th...thought you wouldn't m...mind it,' Anirudh stuttered.

'So I am sure you won't mind it if I cut your dick off.' Simran's words made Anirudh nervous. He knew fully well that an enraged Simran could do anything, even the unthinkable. But he simply winked at Gul and gesticulated that everything was peachy and he'd handle Simran. Before he could utter another word, Simran picked up a paperweight from the table and flung it at his crotch.

It struck home and Anirudh bent forward, howling. Seeing him in a vulnerable position, Simran wasted no time and caught hold of his dangling tie. Anirudh stumbled as Simran dragged him.

'L... Let me explain, S... Sim,' Anirudh tried to explain himself but the words literally choked in his throat.

Gul yelled at Simran to stop, but she had already dragged him out of his cabin by then.

'I...m...s...s...sorry,' Anirudh gasped, struggling to breathe normally.

'You fucking snake, you are sorry now? It's too late to be sorry. You thought you could fuck my life up and I'd sit back to applaud you?' Simran summoned all her physical strength to drag him out of the office and into the streets.

A crowd gathered in no time. The bystanders were more interested in shooting the act on their phones than stopping it.

Anirudh desperately struggled to get out of her stranglehold, but she held on to him with unflagging determination. Seeing his face turn blue, some of the onlookers cautioned Simran.

'Let go of him!'

'His face is turning purple!'

'He will die, you crazy woman!'

Divya and her colleagues from Dastak channel hurried to stop Simran. Divya got a tight grip of Simran's arm and yanked her. 'He will die, Simran. Just let it be. Let go of him.'

'Leave him, Simran. If he dies, you will get into more trouble than you can imagine,' another voice intervened.

Simran, who was possessed by a fit of deranged fury, jerked out of her frenzied stupor. She released Anirudh, whose chest heaved as he wheezed, gasping for breath. He was sprawled on all fours in the street and remained there, trying to gain his consciousness. Simran tossed a scornful look at him along with one final string of abuses before turning her back on him.

There was complete chaos on the roads, as passers-by had stopped to gape at her manic act. Cars and autos had come to a standstill, bewildered by a scene that seemed straight out of a

Bollywood potboiler. Some of them actually thought that a film shoot was going on. In all the pandemonium, Simran found herself being dragged away by someone. She was nervous for a second before she recognized the familiar face in the entire hullabaloo. Jai whisked her away from the site in a car.

'Where are you taking me?' Simran asked him.

'I had come to meet you. I have been trying to call you for some time now, but your phone seems to be switched off,' Jai explained as he nudged the driver to start the car. 'Mr Karmarkar wants to meet you. I hope you are aware that your sting-op has put the threat of an arrest on Sunidhi.'

'I saw it on the news some time back,' said Simran meekly. 'But what can I do now? It was something that was orchestrated without my consent.'

'Don't worry! Mr Karmarkar is a very reasonable man. He will not harm you.'

'I'm not in the right state of mind to meet him. I would like do to do this some other time.'

'Just meet him for five minutes. If you think that the meeting isn't worth your time even after that, you are free to go.'

'Please stop the car. I don't want to meet anyone right now,' Simran insisted.

'Okay! Can he just have a quick word with you on the phone?'

'Fine,' Simran conceded exasperatedly. Residual anger from her confrontation with Anirudh still throbbed in her bones.

Jai dialled Karmarkar's number. 'Sir, Simran Thapar is with me right now. She says that she would prefer to meet you some other time. Okay, sir.' Jai thrust his phone into Simran's grudging hands.

'Yes, Mr Karmarkar.'

'Look, Simran, I don't want to sound too harsh. But in my opinion, it will be prudent for you to meet me right away. Because if we decide to take legal action against you, I don't think even your channel will be able to do much to save you.'

Karmarkar's words hit Simran right where it hurt. She paused for a moment before replying. 'Fine, Mr Karmarkar. I will meet you. Not because I am scared of any legal action, but because I want a chance to explain my side of the story.'

'Fair enough. I look forward to it.'

As they made their way to Karmarkar's office, Simran, totally exhausted, caught a few winks in the car. When she woke up, she found that they were somewhere midtown, around Shivaji Park. She turned on her phone absentmindedly to check the time, not realizing that she had kept it off for obvious reasons. A flood of messages hit her at once. Most of them were leftover curses from her pageant colleagues, but there were a few messages which congratulated her. Amongst them was one from her mother. 'You finally grew balls. I couldn't be happier. Love you a lot, my tigress.' Simran was baffled by her mother's message.

By the time they reached Karmarkar's office, unbeknown to Simran, the video of her tugging Anirudh by his tie had gone viral. It had got more than 3,00,000 hits within minutes of being uploaded. The link was being forwarded on WhatsApp and Facebook by umpteen youngsters with tags like '#whatguysdeserve', '#superwoman', '#takenoshitfrommen', '#whoruntheworld'.

Nimesh was noticeably hassled after watching Simran's video of her dragging Anirudh, with Karmarkar in the latter's office. Their impression of Simran had drastically changed in the last half an hour after seeing what she was capable of. When Simran stepped into the room, Nimesh shot up on his feet, not realizing that Simran's intimidating aura had weaseled its way into his cowardly heart.

'Come, sit,' Karmarkar urged Simran.

Karmarkar held his meetings in a conference room attached to his office. The room was kept immaculately and it exuded a fraction of the power that Karmarkar wielded. As soon as she sat down, an attendant offered her refreshments. Simran needed some caffeine to wash off the residual lethargy that had set in after the long drive and of course, her lack of sleep. The four of them—Simran, Nimesh, Karmarkar and Jai—sat in grim silence, waiting for one of them to speak up.

'Tell me, gentlemen, what can I do for you?' Simran was naturally the one to take the lead.

'Haven't you done enough? Or is there more to be done?' Nimesh Mehta's acerbic voice retorted.

With a nod, Karmarkar gestured Jai to get something. Both Nimesh and Karmarkar looked intently at Simran as Jai handed over a letter to her.

'We have taken cognizance of your irresponsible behaviour which has caused irreparable damage to our brand equity and to the individual reputation of our contestants. We want an urgent and adequate response to our queries here below, failing which we will be compelled to initiate legal action against you,' the letter read.

As Simran perused the list of queries, she realized the legal gravity of her actions. She began to feel the heat. If she put her response down in writing, she would get tangled in a legal muck. She considered talking to a lawyer before responding to this document. She felt badly cornered. With her back against the wall, she decided to use her most trusted weapon from the arsenal; her gift of gab.

'I take full responsibility for my actions. Yes, I had come to the pageant looking for an exposé. I thought Nimesh Mehta was commoditizing beauty, which was utterly immoral. So, I grabbed the opportunity which he himself gave me,' Simran shared.

'What do you mean by commoditization? Commoditization of the female body happens everywhere in the media; more so in films. Why choose the pageant?' Karmarkar was not one to be taken by abstract, idealistic talk.

'Because I had information that young girls were exploited in the show. In a bid to get fame and money, underage girls walk straight into the hands of sleazy monsters. Plenty of lives have been ruined by it and I wanted to put an end to it. Also, isn't the pageant a launch pad for girls to enter films?' countered Simran, throwing a sharp look at Nimesh.

Nimesh Mehta's face had turned puce by now and a very conspicuous vein danced on his forehead. He stole a quick glance at Karmarkar who was looking back at him. The fiasco at the hotel with Shikha played in their minds.

'And you think you are Rani of Jhansi who will protect all the women?' the words burst forth from an infuriated Mehta. 'Your words have touched me and how! Please, sir, please rise up to give this young woman a standing ovation,' said Nimesh as he stood up and slow clapped for her. 'Oh Supreme Devi! I don't think I can take any more of your gyan for the day,' Mehta spat bitterly.

Karmarkar gave Nimesh Mehta a subtle look of disapproval that silenced him.

Their conversation was disrupted by the ringing of Karmarkar's phone; he apologized and excused himself to his office. It was his chief lawyer. 'Yes, Deshpande, tell me,' said Karmarkar in a tense voice.

'Sir, we have been granted Anticipatory Bail. There will be a few compliances but nothing untoward.'

'What compliances?'

'Just the usual; surety that she won't be fleeing the city. She'll have to go to the police station every other week, but we should be able to nullify that condition after one or two visits.'

'Okay! So the matter is in our control, right?'

'Very much, sir.'

Karmarkar thanked him and headed back for the conference room to find Simran and Nimesh shooting daggers at each other. 'Yes, Ms Thapar, you were saying something.'

'I was wrong. I realize that now,' resumed Simran.

'What did you realize, Your Highness? Do share with us ignorant ones,' Nimesh mocked.

'I have realized that beauty pageants have become a part of our system. TV channels get a show which has a spectrum of emotional highs and lows with an inbuilt glamour quotient. Companies get better-suited brand extensions and the girls get a platform that showcases them to the media and the film industry. All in all, it is a win-win situation for all the parties involved.'

'Oh really? And what do you propose we do about the dung

that was flung on our faces?' Nimesh jibed.

'I had never wanted this footage to be telecast. In fact, I had completely shelved the sting-op, because I was convinced that I did not have anything to validate my point. I realized that I was intruding on the personal space of my friends. But in the same breath, I would like to say that I was betrayed by someone very close to me who stole the hard drives from my house. He short-changed me and our relationship.'

'We saw what you did with him,' Karmarkar butted in, before Nimesh could pass another sneering comment. 'But, Simran, do you understand that you have damaged the fabric of our property? And you brought a lot of public censure for my daughter personally.'

'I am really ashamed of whatever the fallout has been on your daughter, in particular,' Simran told him with sincere contrition. 'One of the major reasons for me to back out of this sting-op was because I found out that my bosses had a personal vendetta against your daughter, which, unfortunately stemmed from an ulterior motive of teaching you both a lesson. I immediately abandoned my plan but unfortunately, I didn't destroy the footage which my boyfriend, my ex-boyfriend, misused.' Simran's voice was beginning to get thick with unshed tears. She did not want to stay there any more. She could not break down in front of these strangers.

'What about the loss of face to our brand? Who will compensate for that?' Mehta demanded.

That was enough to harden Simran and dry up her tears. 'You can take legal action against me. You might be able to recover a very small fraction of your losses,' she retaliated. 'As for me, I have already resigned from that channel that back-stabbed me.'

Nimesh Mehta and Karmarkar were both zapped by her unreserved plain-speak. Karmarkar, who wanted to play the good cop, looked at Mehta, who always wanted to play the bad cop.

'Give us a couple of minutes,' Karmarkar told Simran. The two of them proceeded to Karmarkar's cabin for further discussion.

'The girl is gritty and honest,' Karmarkar observed.

'What are we going to do?' Mehta asked.

'I am not in favour of any legal recourse. It will rebound on us.'

Mehta picked up a jar of dry fruits kept on Karmarkar's table and took out a fistful. 'Don't you think we are letting her off too lightly?' he asked, little bits of candied fig and pistachios peeking out of his mouth.

'We have her at a disadvantage. You can extract whatever information you want from her. I have too much on my plate to make a bigger deal of this. It is futile.'

The two went back to the conference room where Nimesh grilled Simran, again. 'Who perpetrated the plan?'

'It was Gul, along with Khambatta. They wanted revenge. I think you rubbed them the wrong way.' Simran had gotten a low-down from her channel colleagues, who knew every scene that was happening backstage.

'But they targeted me and my daughter,' interjected Karmarkar.

'There is a famous saying about collateral damage that comes to my mind. I will be your mess, you be mine. That was the deal we had signed.'

'What are your plans now?' Karmarkar seemed impressed by Simran's devil-may-care attitude. He tried to hide it by adding, 'I mean, how can one get in touch with you, just in case we need to?'

'I am going on a hiatus now. I'm off to New Zealand to be with my mom. Later, who knows? I might just start my own show on some other channel.'

30

'Don't tell me you have earned so much in the last six months that you have enough money to buy an apartment of your own,' Shiraz told his daughter, pleasantly surprised.

'How much more do you think I will need?' Sania asked.

Shiraz's trolley bag and handbags were stacked next to a wall. They were all wreathed in Emirates tags and bursting at the seams with excess weight. He had come back from a business trip in Dubai.

'How big do you want your apartment to be?' Shiraz sat up straight, flexing his shoulders.

Sania had scuttled off to the kitchen. She poured boiling hot milk from a kettle into two cups that were partially filled with water, a tea bag and two sugar cubes.

'As big as this house!' Sania had a huge grin on her face as she handed one cup to her chuckling father.

'You want to be one up on your dad, is it? But an apartment this size will cost you a lot more. Do you want to wait or do you want to invest your savings right now?'

'Right away, Abbu. Even if that means I'll have to look for something smaller in the suburbs. I want to call Ammi, Sakina and Ayub to come over and stay with me.'

'Isn't Ayub working there with your mamu?'

'Come on, Abbu, you know what a stubborn mule Mamujaan is. Once he has made up his mind, he won't change it for even Allah. I don't think he'll renew business relations with Ayub and Sajid bhaijaan.'

'That fight is still going on? Your mamu is one despicable crook. What was the connection between your winning a beauty pageant and his partnership with your brothers? It's the most ridiculous excuse I have heard in all my life. He was just looking for a reason to snap off business ties with your brothers. Do you know he swindled me and usurped my business? Then just to pacify your mother, he took your brothers in business, denying them their true share. Your mamu is a scoundrel who deserves to be taken to court.'

'Why don't you talk to Sajid bhaijaan? Call him over to Mumbai.'

'You know very well that his mindset is too blinkered for my liking. He judges my personal life. He hates me and I don't think we will ever get along.' Shiraz unpacked his suitcase and stacked a pile of clothes and packets aside.

'Abbu, don't you think you are too Americanized?'

'You are free to think whatever you want to.'

'Why haven't you ever called Ammi and Ayub here?'

'You have been here in this apartment for nearly six months now. Why haven't you called them over?' Shiraz paused, giving his daughter a chance to speak. But looking at her brow, he continued. 'Tell me, how many days was I here? Barely seven or eight days in six months?'

'Yes, so?'

'So, does it make any sense in calling them here when I am travelling? Now that you are here, you can call them whenever you want to.'

'I understand, Abbu. Even I am so scattered everywhere these days that I hardly get any free time. It has nearly been two months since Shikha moved here and I've barely spent a handful of days with her. Ammi will kill me if I invite her over and I am not even around to spend time with her.' Sania checked her watch and realized she was running late. 'Anyway, Abbu, I have to leave for Pune in a little while, so I better get going.'

Sania peeped inside Shikha's room on her way out. Finding her awake, she ran in and jumped on her bed like an excited five-year-old. 'See what I have for you,' she trilled, stretching her arm out with a packet in her hand. 'Dad got us all this stuff from Dubai.'

Shikha smiled so hard that she thought the top half of her head might topple over. She tore open the packet eagerly. She fawned over her haul—an assorted set of midi rings, a pair of chandelier earrings, two stylish tops and an elegant sequined dress. 'Say a big thank you to your dad for me,' Shikha told Sania as she enveloped her in a bear hug.

'You can say it to him yourself, he's right here.' Sania was just about to prance out when she remembered something. 'Hey Shikha, I forgot to tell you that I'm heading to Pune for an assignment. You can come with me and spend time with your family for the day. We'll be back by night.' Sania was awfully pleased with herself for thinking of such a clever plan.

'No ya, not today. I met them just the day before,' Shikha yawned, stretching like a cat on the bed. Sania ruffled her hair fondly and left.

A yoga instructor corrected Sunidhi's posture as she arranged her body into the Ardha Matsyendrasana. Sunidhi completed the asana and then switched to the lotus position for Pranayama. The yoga session was an everyday routine that she had been following for more than two months.

At the dining table, Karmarkar read yet another apology message from Gul Mohammad while he finished his breakfast. 'Mr Karmarkar, I beg for your forgiveness yet again. I never imagined that the sting-op would have such an adverse effect on so many people's lives, especially your daughter, Sunidhi's. Please give me one opportunity to make amends.' He deleted the message as he got up to leave for work. He called out to Sunidhi who came hurtling out of her room and grabbed a sandwich from the table. 'I am ready,' she sang, giving her father a radiant smile.

Sunidhi had metamorphosed in such a drastic manner that an outsider would never believe that she was the same girl. Recovering from her addiction was the hardest thing she had ever done. But once she had done that, she decided to fix herself from the inside. With great difficulty, she purged herself of hatred, anger and envy. Affable, optimistic and warm, Sunidhi didn't have a single bad trait of her former self. She accompanied Karmarkar to his office every single day and worked diligently. She had invested her sweat and blood in laying the groundwork to start her own TV production house.

Sania was huddled in the back seat of their car, a Persian shawl draped loosely around her dainty shoulders. She snoozed peacefully with her head resting on a pillow propped against the window. She had deliberately put her phone on silent. Abdul chacha took extra care to make the car ride as smooth as was possible on Indian roads. They were at the Vashi toll plaza. Abdul chacha gently slid the window down and paid the toll money from a small gap on top. But at the next signal, he had to brake suddenly to avoid ramming into a car that had suddenly cut into his lane, without any indicator.

Sania was jostled awake. 'All okay no, Chacha?'

'Yes, Beta, the fellow in front is a complete idiot. I can't imagine who would give a license to such a fellow.'

'It's okay, Chacha! As long as nobody got hurt.' Sania instinctively put her hand in the purse and fished out her phone. Nineteen missed calls, the screen read. *And I was asleep only for an hour*, she marvelled. Most of the calls were from Rohit, apart from two calls that were from her brother, Ayub.

She immediately called up Rohit. 'Yes, Rohit, tell me. You have been desperately trying to reach me.'

'Didn't you read the message?'

'No, what happened?'

'Where are you right now, Sania?'

'On my way to Pune obviously.'

'And where have you reached, if I may know?'

'Where are we, Chacha?'

'We have crossed Vashi,' Abdul chacha replied.

'You heard that, we should be there in a couple of hours. What time is the event?' Sania asked Rohit.

'There is a slight problem, Sania. The mini-pageant has been postponed due to some technical reasons.'

'So what do you want me to do?' Sania indicated to Abdul

chacha to pull the car over.

'I am afraid you don't have a choice but to go back.'

'And what happens of today? I hope you are going to count it as an appearance because...'

'But of course, Sania,' Rohit interrupted. 'We will count today as a working day. We will strike a day off from your mandatory appearances.'

Sania thanked him and disconnected the call. As they took a U-turn and headed back home, Sania called up Ayub.

'Sania aapa, thank God you finally called back. Something really disturbing has happened here.'

'What is it?' Sania asked, worried. 'Is Ammi okay?'

'Yes, yes, Ammi is completely okay.'

'Then what is it?' she asked with a perceptibly less tense tone.

'Rashid miyaan has created a huge scene in his house. He thrashed his sisters very badly.'

'But why?' Sania was aghast. She doted on Noor and Shagufta.

'Because they wanted to participate in a TV show. They gave your example.'

'So what if they gave my example?'

'Rashid miyaan called up Ammi and told her a lot of mean things.'

'Such as?' Sania wanted to know what that lowlife was up to now. 'Ayub, are you there?'

'Yes, Sania aapa. He told some very dirty things,' Ayub dodged her question artfully. 'Ammi is very upset. You must talk to her.'

'What dirty things did he say, Ayub? Ammi isn't going to give me the details, so you have to tell me so I can decide how to tackle this problem once and for all.'

'Aapa, he called you a slut and a whore,' Ayub cringed. 'He said that you slept with people to win the beauty pageant; without that it is impossible to get anywhere in this field. He vowed that if either of his sisters got into this field, he would kill them and even you. He said that he will get *jannat*, paradise, if he does that.'

'Anything else?'

'Nothing worthwhile. He was cursing a lot, Aapa.'

'I will talk to Ammi, you needn't worry.'

After disconnecting the call, Sania felt a shiver of nervousness skid along her spine. She knew that Rashid was a demented fellow, capable of doing extremely horrific things. *He will have to be handled really tactfully*, she thought to herself. She called up her mother to explain the reality of the situation and calm her down. To her surprise, her mother was in a light, jolly mood and brushed off Rashid's lunacy.

'He is sulking because you spurned his proposal. I remember he was a brat since he was a kid. Once Sajid was playing with Rashid's G.I. Joe and Rashid took so much offense to it that he ripped off all the sofas and curtains in the house. I had stripped him and whacked him on his bums at that time, but I don't think I'd like to do that now.'

Both mother and daughter laughed heartily.

Before she knew it, Sania was back in her apartment complex. 'Ammi, I just got back home, I will call you later. *Khuda hafiz*, Goodbye.'

Sania unlocked the main door with her set of keys and called out to her father softly, not wanting to disturb him if he was sleeping. His bedroom door was ajar and she prodded it open to check on him. Startled, Shikha hurried to the bathroom in a blur and wrapped herself in a towel. Sania's father, Shiraz, who was caught in a crude position, frantically tried to cover himself with a bedsheet. He couldn't meet her eyes. Sania's whole world came crashing down.

31

The mini-pageant in Pune had been called off because the organizers had failed to get the number of entries they had wanted. That day, after sending Sania back, Rohit had given an earful to Sachin Kumbhar, the local manager in Pune. 'What the hell were you doing, Sachin? You couldn't find ten good-looking girls in all of Pune?'

That was two weeks ago, but the scenario had not changed much since. Even now, they were struggling to get good entries.

'Rohit sir, we have to get girls who are taller than 5 ft 6 inches. They have to be sexy but skinny. They have to be in the age bracket of eighteen to twenty-six. And to top it, they should not have participated in any other beauty pageant. How can we meet all these criteria? Especially when three big pageants happened very recently,' Sachin complained.

'I don't care how you do it. Do whatever you have to. I want to see those girls by hook or by crook. Period,' Rohit told him.

'If I can bend some of the rules, I will be able to pull it off. Rohit sir, give me just two more days. I will think of a way to get entries.' From his tone, it seemed like he had already figured out a way.

'Look, Sachin, Nimesh sir himself is going to be there for this event. If you can't pull it off, I am screwed. I will then sack you and find a replacement.'

'Once I've given you my word, you can rest assured that it will happen.' Rohit dismissively acknowledged him by grunting and hung up.

Sachin immediately scrolled through the contacts in his phone and dialled a number. 'Payal, where are you? Meet me in twenty minutes below your building,' he barked into the phone as he zoomed on his bike.

Payal was waiting for him at the entrance of her building. 'What happened now? Why the hurry-scurry?' she asked him.

'Let's do what we had discussed the other day,' Sachin told her over the revving of his bike.

'Are you sure?'

'I am one thousand per cent sure, Payal. The water has risen way above my head. I have to do something before I get axed. Hurry up, let's go.'

'But they will be free only after four. They will have their lunch break now.'

'Then let's go fast and meet them during their recess. Let me have a look at them first.'

Payal got onto the bike with Sachin and they zipped past the bustling traffic on Shivajinagar road and headed towards Camp. They reached Payal's school just a little while after the lunch break had started. Some of the students were collecting their lunch boxes from their mothers and some from their house helps.

Sachin waited outside the school premises as Payal snuck in. She was a current student of the school who was on 'sick leave' so she could spend time with Sachin. Her parents had gone out of town for a couple of days and Payal wanted to make the most of her vacant house. Within less than five minutes, Payal emerged with nine willowy girls. Shikha's sister, Prajakta, was one of them. Sachin was stunned by their allure. Payal introduced Sachin to the girls. 'Hi, I am Sachin. I hope you are aware why I have come here?' Sachin had suddenly developed a phoney accent and a swagger in his stance. Payal suppressed a chuckle.

'Yes, Payal gave us a brief idea about it,' one of the girls spoke up.

'Great! So we will talk in detail when we meet later after you're done with school, alright?'

The girls found Sachin's mannerisms a little peculiar. They simply looked at each other and then exchanged looks with Payal. 'What is this about? And are we supposed to participate?' the girl who had spoken earlier inquired, slightly confused and slightly curious.

'I will brief you all about it soon enough, Swati. It is a great opportunity for all of you. You will definitely like it. Even I am going to be a part of it,' Payal reassured her friends.

'Can you tell us if we are selected or if we will have to go through some selection process?' Prajakta asked impatiently.

Payal looked at Sachin and he shook his head discreetly.

'Not now but later when we meet. I would like to see you in casual clothes,' Sachin told them and motioned at Payal to sit behind him on his bike.

'We will meet at my place in the evening,' Payal strained her voice to be heard over the infernal noise of the bike.

'You guys change into something smart and come over,' Sachin reminded them again.

'If possible, bring a change of clothes as well,' Payal added.

'What do we tell at home?' one of the innocent-looking girls asked.

'Tell them that you are going to my place, that's all. I will call you,' Payal told them.

With that, the two of them left the girls in a cloud of smoke and confusion.

Later in the evening, only six of the nine girls showed up at Payal's place.

'As you girls know, I have approached you for a beauty pageant,' Sachin briefed them. 'Have you heard of Miss Pune Beautiful?'

All the girls murmured a hushed 'yes', except Prajakta; she was the only one who was audibly enthusiastic about the event.

'Good,' Sachin continued. The winner will be going for Miss India Beautiful. Based on your appearance, you girls look like a smart lot, so I am confident that you will qualify. But I will have to test you all once.'

'What kind of a test is it going to be?' inquired one girl nervously.

'Normal routine test. I will make you walk, I will make you talk and I will make you rock!' Sachin's cheesy gusto made the girls dissolve in hysterical giggles. But Sachin continued nonchalantly, his ego intact, 'You girls are smoking hot, I hope you know that. If you get an early success in this field, you could be like Kate Moss.'

'I know Kate Moss,' Prajakta chimed. 'She is a kick-ass model and my idol.'

'Did you know she started modelling at the age of fourteen? That is why she has had such a long shelf life. Do you understand shelf life?'

'Of course!' another one chimed in, eager to impress. 'You have to use things before they reach their expiry date. Similarly, models need to make the most of their career before they start growing wrinkles, right?'

'Well said,' Sachin chuckled. 'Before you expire, you have to make the most of life, so it is really better you start young. Can I take your pictures, girls?'

One by one, the girls started posing for Sachin and then checked their photos to give their approval. Sachin sent the pictures to Rohit who replied immediately on WhatsApp. 'Wow, where did you find these tight-assed muffins? They are too good; I just want to take a bite.'

'Before you get carried away, there's a small problem, Bro,' Sachin replied, splashing cold water all over Rohit's fantasies.

'What is it?'

'These girls are just fourteen, fourteen and a half, max fifteen.'

'Oh fuck, are you serious? They hit puberty much younger now. Let me run this by the boss.'

'Ok! Let me know soon. I will manage the show once you give me the green light.' Sachin finished sending the message and turned towards the girls.

'Girls, can we do something crazy? I want to know what your level of wildness is.' Sachin incited and challenged them.

The girls giggled coyly until one of them volunteered to do a belly dance. She asked Payal to connect her phone to the stereo and play an Arabic composition. The girl created a riot. Her flexibility and sensuality made the others cheer for her and wolf-whistle. Sachin was really impressed and it showed on his face. The mood rubbed off on the other girls who tried to one up each other with some bizarre acts. Prajakta got so carried away that she unhooked her bra, flung it across the room, stripped to her heart-printed panties and danced wildly. Sachin shot all of it and sent the video to Rohit who drooled violently on seeing it. He immediately wanted an audience with Nimesh Mehta.

'Sir, can I come to your cabin for a couple of minutes? There is something important that you need to see,' Rohit told Nimesh on the intercom.

Nimesh watched the video clip one too many times, rewinding and slowing it far too often. Rohit instantly knew Nimesh loved it, but he still kept his fingers crossed.

'Let's do it,' Nimesh announced. 'These girls are complete knockouts. But be very careful.'

Rohit almost peed himself with joy. 'Not to worry, sir. We will take care of it,' Rohit assured his boss.

'I have got a heads-up from the big guy. And we are in business, babes,' Sachin proudly announced to the girls.

Sunidhi had been going to her dad's office for the last couple of months diligently. But her static position was beginning to make her impatient and restless. She enjoyed her stint, working for her father, but she wanted more. The fact that none of her proposals got an approval from any of the TV channels nagged her.

'Remember, Su, Rome was not built in a day. You need to exercise patience,' Karmarkar tried to mollify his edgy producer-daughter.

'But, Pops, we are the biggest ad spenders for these channels. How can they not give us importance?'

'We need them just as much as they need us. We cannot twist

their arm and make demands. They have a system, a process which neither they nor we can supersede. You will get some preference, but they will not bend over backwards to accommodate you.'

'So what do I do?'

'Just wait. Waiting is an art. Focus on making new proposals and get your team in place. Make value-added presentations. TV programming is not our core competence. Let it take as much time as it takes to build an impeccable track record.'

'But, I wanted something going for me immediately.' Sunidhi's restlessness began to worry Karmarkar, who feared the worst. He could not let her relapse. He would not lose her again.

As soon as Sunidhi left, Karmarkar called his secretary. 'I want you to call up Mr Gul Mohammad of Dastak channel. Tell him I want to meet him.'

32

It had been a regular working day for Sunidhi. She was going about her work when she saw Simran waiting at the reception. She immediately ducked and snuck back to her cabin. She picked up the intercom and dialled the front desk's number.

'Why is Simran Thapar here?'

'She has come to meet Mr Karmarkar,' the receptionist replied promptly.

'Does she have a prior appointment?'

'According to Karmarkar sir's secretary, they had fixed the meeting in advance.'

That's all Sunidhi wanted to know. She couldn't believe her father was doing this to her now, when she had just begun to trust him again. Sunidhi walked briskly to her father's cabin, knocked curtly on his door and stepped in without waiting for his response.

'Why have you called Simran Thapar to the office, Pops?'

'We will talk about it later. I am sure that can wait.'

'No, Pops. I want to know now. I want to know what compelled you to call that trickster.'

'I still have to talk to her. There is a proposal I have in my mind.'

'Father, she is one person that I never want to deal with in my life and I hope that you don't entertain her either.'

Karmarkar knew Sunidhi was extremely displeased with him because that was when she addressed him as 'Father'. But he ploughed on determinedly. 'On the contrary, I think that she is the person I want you to deal with a lot from now on.'

'You cannot change my mind on this one, Father. She has completely ruined me.'

'Has she? In all honesty, tell me, are you really ruined?'

'Well, she tried to ruin me and I don't see how that is any better.'

'You are mistaken, Sunidhi. She never wanted to do any harm

to you. She actually fought with her colleagues and her bosses for you. She is the only person who can help you take off. She has what it takes. You should think of forming a team with her.'

'Have you completely lost your mind, Father?'

'You should consider it your good fortune that you learnt your lesson, Sunidhi. I would say she is the one person because of whom you are back on track,' Karmarkar told her with moist eyes.

'You don't need to sell her so hard to me.'

'We will talk later.' Karmarkar dismissed her and called his secretary. 'Send Simran Thapar to my office.'

Karmarkar greeted Simran as she walked into his cabin and shook hands with her. 'How have you been, Simran? I'm surprised to see you back from your holiday already.'

'It was great to spend time with my mom, but Auckland can get awfully boring after a couple of weeks. I still managed to survive two months there,' Simran jested. 'How are you doing?'

'We are making new forays against smaller companies, so that extra workload has kept me buried.' Karmarkar led her to his desk and requested her to take a seat. He went around the imposing mahogany desk and made himself comfortable in a high-wingback chair. He picked up a tablet from his desk and tapped it on with his stylus. 'Let me quickly refresh the points I had made for this meeting,' he told Simran.

Karmarkar had a habit of making copious notes before a meeting. No matter who the person was, Karmarkar did his homework and lined up an agenda. He believed that one could never be too prepared for a meeting. 'I usually share the agenda with whoever I am meeting, but I wanted to put forth these points to you in person.'

'That's perfectly fine by me.' Simran was beginning to feel a little anxious by now. *A man who is chased by top bureaucrats, politicians, channel heads, film producers, the who's who of the media industry, is giving so much importance to me?* She marvelled. And it's unbelievable how organized and down to earth he is in his day-to-day affairs.

'Do you remember anything from our last meeting?' Karmarkar had a way of testing people's approach to life. He tried to gauge their outlook by assessing their response to a simple, straightforward question.

'Yes, I had mentioned that I wanted to start an independent show on a TV channel.'

Karmarkar gave Simran full marks for the simple reason that amongst all the nasty things that they discussed that day, she recalled the only positive one. 'I like your way of thinking,' he remarked to a clueless Simran.

'Thank you but, sir, I still do not know why I am here.'

'You are here for exactly the same thing you just mentioned.'

'To start a TV show?'

'Precisely. A TV show which will be your own. Isn't that what you want?'

Simran tried to conceal or at least tamp down her evident surprise. 'Very much so, but since when did you want to back a TV show?'

'There is a reason, but I wanted to know your mind before speaking mine.'

'Sir, I came back to India for just one reason; to start my own show on a leading channel. I had no clue how I was going to reach that goal. But as they say, if you ask for something with all your heart, someone does listen. And it looks like you were listening,' Simran spoke with zeal. Her eyes were shining with hope and purpose.

'Don't let your horses run wild,' Karmarkar cautioned her. 'There is one condition though; Sunidhi will be the producer on the show. And right now, she thinks of you more as her nemesis than her friend.'

'So, my first challenge would be to win Sunidhi over?'

'Spot on. Once you have her on board, you will have my full support.'

'And if I don't manage?' Simran tested Karmarkar this time around.

'My topmost priority is to get Sunidhi on track. Everything else will have to take a back seat,' he told her bluntly.

'So, you would like to use me to further your daughter's goals.'

'If your goal can be a part of her journey or vice-versa, isn't that a win-win?'

'Well, for me, it is a win-win either way. I would like to clear the air with Sunidhi. I will give it my best shot. Can I meet her now? I saw her in the office when I was waiting, but she ran in the opposite direction before I could even say hi. Or sorry.'

Karmarkar gave her a sympathetic smile and dialled a number on his intercom. 'Can you come to my cabin?'

'To meet Simran?' asked Sunidhi disbelievingly.

'Yes.'

'I thought I made it amply clear before that I have no interest in doing so.'

'Can you just drop in for a minute?'

'I'm only doing this so you don't feel insulted in front of her. I will come down, but I am not interested in what that life-wrecker has to say.'

'Just swing by.'

Simran sensed the discomfort in Karmarkar's tone. 'She doesn't want to meet me, does she?' she asked dejectedly.

Karmarkar shook his head. 'I want her to get rid of all the bitterness she has been harbouring. I hope you are mature enough to handle this.'

Before Simran could respond, Sunidhi barged in. 'Tell me, Father.'

Karmarkar looked at Sunidhi and gestured subtly towards Simran.

'What about her? Hasn't she done enough damage to last a lifetime?' Sunidhi spoke about Simran like she wasn't present in the room. 'The fact that she has the insolence to show her face here after what she has done is enough to show what a shameless hag she is.'

'I called her over because I wanted her to start a show with you. And you have no right to insult my guests,' Karmarkar reprimanded her sternly.

'So why would you even call me to meet your guest?'

'I thought that it would be best if you girls forgave and for...'

'I am not interested in any conversation with her,' Sunidhi cut in. 'Let alone working with such a heinous human. Can I leave? I have people waiting in my cabin.' Sunidhi's voice trembled with anger.

Karmarkar realized he didn't have even an iota of control over the situation. He looked at Simran who sat stoically across him, blinking hard at her hands in her lap, as if she had expected this all along. He waved his hand and asked Sunidhi to carry on. She stomped off in a huff. A painful silence followed. Simran looked at Karmarkar, who had a forced smile on his face.

'I guess that's that,' he said, his disappointment palpable.

Simran had not overtly shown any expectations from the meeting, but deep down, she had really hoped it would work out.

'I'm extremely sorry, Simran,' Karmarkar told her. 'I know you have it in you, but until Sunidhi sees that herself, I don't think things will work out.'

'I have wronged her and I can't blame her for being brutally honest. I would like to leave now, sir.' Simran stepped out awkwardly with slumped shoulders and a strained gait.

Gul had been waiting in the conference room for Karmarkar who was taking his own sweet time to meet him. Karmarkar was not a vindictive person explicitly, but those who knew him closely knew better than to fall for his cordial countenance. He was ruthlessly single-minded when it came to getting what he wanted. He was an expert at manipulating people just enough to make them beg him for business or just his time. Being in an influential position, he could afford to flex his muscles, as he did from time to time.

As soon as he set foot inside the conference room, Gul stood up and offered his best obsequious smile. 'Mr Karmarkar, thank you so much for agreeing to meet me, sir.'

'Please sit,' Karmarkar told him, his innate civility hiding the steely edge in his voice.

'Only after you, sir.'

'Don't be a greasy tin, Gul. Where was this grand propriety of yours when you decided to fuck me over?' Karmarkar accompanied his scathing words with a withering look.

Gul's smile slipped right off his face and under his shoes.

'Sir, your anger is totally justified. If I was in your place, I would have been angry too, perhaps much angrier,' Gul bumbled on, but with a lot less confidence than before.

'You targeted my daughter,' Karmarkar went on implacably. 'I will never forgive or forget that. I am meeting you for only one reason, as you very well know.'

Normally Karmarkar's staff served his guests beverages, but he had deliberately instructed them not to do so this time. He personally used the coffee maker in the conference room to make a cappuccino for Gul and himself.

'Mr Karmarkar, if you could have understood the predicament I was in, you would realize that it is not easy to take some calls. Each option that presents itself has scores of repercussions, but despite that, you have to pick one.' Gul could not even dare to sip his cappuccino.

'Do you mean to say this call that you took of doing a sting-op was put forth to you as a condition?'

'Absolutely, sir! It was a question of losing out on my primary client who makes up 65–70 per cent of my total revenue.'

'Targeting my daughter was a part of that deal, was it?'

'Unfortunately that is the truth, sir.'

'In your messages, you kept naming Khambatta as the mastermind behind the entire sting-op. It's ludicrous to even consider that my own protégé would double-cross me.'

'Sir, did he come and meet you even once after this incident happened?' Gul took Karmarkar's silence as a sign of encouragement and resumed. 'Khambatta has been fostering a very strong grudge against you and your daughter over the last few years. According to him, you and your daughter had mocked his plans of making an entry in low-income products in front of some investor who had committed a huge amount to him. The investor who had met you to cross-check Khambatta's antecedents was swayed by your prejudiced opinion. Khambatta had just branched out that time and this setback caused a lot of damage to him. For nearly a year, he could not raise the money for his business venture.'

'That's impossible! I helped him set up his goddamn venture.'

'But that was much later, sir. Not only that, apparently someone from your office messed up with his suppliers who were quite close to you. He was refused any credit for quite a few months initially.'

'Why didn't he talk to me?'

'I don't think he ever will. He felt extremely betrayed.'

'I thought he acted out because Nimesh Mehta had rubbed him the wrong way.'

'Sir, Nimesh Mehta was the icing on the cake, if I may take the liberty to say so. He blatantly insulted me and Khambatta. That made our resolve even stronger.'

'Your resolve to teach me and my daughter a lesson, right?'

Gul remained mum. He had laid almost all his cards on the table and he wanted to mend his ties with Karmarkar. If Karmarkar decided to brandish his hatchet around instead of burying it, Gul would be neck-deep in trouble. He was in a very delicate position. He had flown to Singapore last week to appease the owners of Dastak channel, the Chandarias. He had literally begged for six more months' time to start generating positive cash flows. Karmarkar was his biggest hope to get out of this marsh.

33

Be it any city across the globe, Nimesh Mehta always carried two things with him—a shiny black World Elite MasterCard in his wallet and an irresistibly foxy lady by his side. For his Pune visit, he had decided to take his Marketing and PR associate, Pakhi, along with him. Most of Nimesh's lady-friends had been discovered and picked from the applicants of his beauty pageant.

When Pakhi was around, Nimesh's pomposity shot up ten times, much like the decibel level of his voice. He behaved like he could conquer the world and lay it at her feet. But Pakhi was not just a pretty face. Being the smart cookie she was, Pakhi handled Nimesh deftly, having fun on the run while making big fat commissions out of the deals she cut for him. She was not an employee, so she dealt with him one-on-one. Nimesh preferred to outsource a lot of his work instead of keeping too many people on a payroll.

Nimesh had back-to-back meetings since morning with brands that were prospective co-sponsors. He had made a few good deals and was fully primed to unwind. Back in his suite at The O Hotel, Nimesh and Pakhi were like animated dioramas of naked limbs. Nimesh was in the throes of pleasure when he got a call from Karmarkar. Nimesh indicated to Pakhi that she daren't stop as Karmarkar updated him about the meeting he just had with Gul.

'An Advertiser-funded Programme? How did you even agree to do that on Gul's downmarket channel, sir?'

'First things first, don't call anyone or anything downmarket ever again. We don't know about the circumstances that force someone into doing whatever they are doing,' Karmarkar rebuked him.

'I am sorry, Boss.' Nimesh felt himself going limp. Terribly embarrassed, he tried to cover himself with a pillow, but Pakhi was in the mood to play. She giggled uncontrollably, but Nimesh muted her using offensive hand gestures.

Having no clue about what was happening at the other end, Karmarkar carried on in a serious tone, 'Hear me out, Nimesh. The need is as much mine as it is his. I want to keep Sunidhi busy with something right away. Even she will get to know if TV show production is her calling or not.'

'Fair enough, Boss. Tell me what you require of me.' Nimesh wanted to cut short the conversation.

'Gul has insisted that Simran should be the host of the show, and I concur. She is a firebrand.'

'I would beg to differ, but if that's what you want then I will trust your judgement.' Nimesh didn't have a single good thing to say about Simran, but right now, he was unable to contain his excitement, thanks to Pakhi.

'I want you to line produce this show. See to it that everything starts off smoothly.'

'Done deal, Boss. I'll call you tomorrow with an action plan.' Nimesh cut the call midway, switched off his phone and tossed it aside. His action plan was crystal clear right now and it involved a certain PR agent.

'The toughest task on hand will be to get Simran and Sunidhi talking. They need to bury the past and put their heads together and work.' Karmarkar spoke into the phone.

A beep made Karmarkar realize that the call had dropped. He redialled Nimesh's number, but his phone was switched off. He sat glumly in the crepuscular light of his cabin, contemplating all the things that had happened in the last six months. He was normally never at the office so late in the day, but he had been genuinely worried about Sunidhi. The rehab programme entailed that she must be kept busy with something constructive.

Back at The O Hotel, Nimesh had just finished with Pakhi. Once he was satisfied, he didn't show the slightest tenderness or regard to his partners. 'You better get going now. I have a thousand things to do than watch you sitting on your ass, moping around. Be there at the venue on time and get all the new co-sponsors along with you.'

Pakhi's face flushed with mortification. She got dressed wordlessly, gathered her belongings and left the room. She was mighty peeved, despite being used to Nimesh's abominable attitude, realizing that she wasn't used to it after all.

'I will be attending the mini-pageant tomorrow,' Nimesh told Rohit over the phone. 'The representatives of the newly associated brands will be accompanied by Pakhi. Take extra good care of them. See to it that there are no mistakes, and meet me at the coffee shop in the morning at 11:30.'

Rohit felt the pressure. He didn't want to leave a single stone unturned in making the event successful. He saw it as a big opportunity to impress Nimesh. 'Boss, can we skip the meeting? I will keep you updated on phone. There are a lot of things that I need to organize.'

'Fine. And, Rohit, don't fuck up.'

'I am so glad that your hunger for success exceeds your appetite for egoistic gratification,' Karmarkar heaved a dramatic sigh of relief as he pulled his daughter's leg.

'I hope you are not lying about Simran. Has the channel actually asked for her?' Only Sunidhi could dare to ask Karmarkar such questions; there had to be some advantages of being his daughter, after all.

'Do you think I am some wheeler-dealer who would use such petty gimmicks to coerce you into meeting Simran? Neither is Simran such a great personality, nor am I willing to stoop so low. So if you two are meeting, you are meeting for your own good. I just conveyed the offer that Gul Mohammad made to me.'

One of the house helps brought an end to their conversation and announced Simran's arrival. Sunidhi felt her stomach twist into a knot as she made her way to the living room to confront Simran. *To meet, not confront*, she corrected herself.

Dressed in a classic combination of well-fitted denims and a white shirt, Simran looked simple yet chic. Incidentally, Sunidhi was also wearing the same combination. If it wasn't for the sombre mood, Simran would have shouted 'same pinch.' The two noticed the similarity in their outfits. Simran gave her a half smile as she ran a hand through her hair and fiddled with her bracelet.

Simran followed a simple code in life—if you want to be accepted by another person, you should be able to accept your own state of mind in all honesty. But before she could voice it aloud, Sunidhi spoke. 'I am really nervous.' Sunidhi's honesty disarmed Simran completely.

'So am I,' Simran admitted. Her confession eased Sunidhi a little.

'I have been terribly upset with you, with whatever you did under the disguise of a fellow contestant.'

'I'm sorry! I was always interested in investigative journalism, so I took up this assignment as an opportunity to pursue my dreams. To say that it ended in a fiasco would be an understatement of the century. But it happened because of...'

'I know, your ex-boyfriend.'

'Yeah, so you are aware of it.'

'You dragged him on to the streets. It surely could not have been for fun,' Sunidhi chuckled as she spoke.

Simran acknowledged her comment with a smile. A few seconds of silence passed, as neither of them knew what to say next.

'Your dad told me that you are producing an Advertiser-funded Programme, an AFP, and that I should meet you,' Simran remarked.

'Yes, it is for your old channel, Dastak.'

'I was not aware that it is for Dastak. I'm sorry, but I don't think I want to do a show with them again.'

'Anirudh is no longer working there. He quit the very day that incident happened,' Sunidhi informed her, answering an unspoken question in Simran's mind.

'In that case, count me in,' Simran smiled at her, feeling a lot more relaxed.

'I want to show you some of the shows that my team and I shortlisted for referencing. Do you have time?'

'Absolutely! We can use the entire day if you like. That is, if you don't have anything else to do.'

'No, this show is my top priority.'

And just like that, they became two girls with a shared passion.

34

The participants for the Pune mini-pageant had all lined up backstage. They were being introduced to the judges for the event. Sania, who was one of the judges, took a round in the wings, interacting with the contestants and asking them some basic questions about their academic background, their aspirations and their hobbies.

Finding one of the contestants very familiar, she stopped. 'Haven't we met before?' Sania asked the girl who giggled away.

'Of course! We have met, Sania didi. I am Prajakta, Shikha didi's younger sister. Remember?' Prajakta couldn't stop giggling.

As soon as she mentioned Shikha, images of her father and Shikha in compromising positions began to flash in Sania's mind. Sania shook herself out of that nightmare. She did not want that incident to affect her any more, at least she wanted to think like it didn't. 'Yes, of course! I remember. How is your little sister? Shilpi, right?'

'Yeah, she is doing well.'

'And how is your mom?' Sania realized that she had a very virtuous image of the family at the time she had visited their house. But that illusion had been shattered now.

'Mom is alright, Sania didi. But she does not know that I have come for this pageant. So please don't mention this to her,' Prajakta spoke in a low voice.

'Why will I tell your mom? But aren't you in the tenth standard, Prajakta? Don't you have your boards in a few months?' Sania indirectly wanted Prajakta to realize that what she was doing wasn't right. But she didn't know that subtlety was a lost cause on Prajakta.

'I do, Didi, but I have been studying properly,' Prajakta defended herself. She sounded like she was trying to convince herself of that lie more than Sania.

'I was just curious as to why your age is written as nineteen over here?' Sania asked her, pointing at the open file in her hand.

Prajakta looked around to see if the coast was clear. 'Didi, all the setting has been done. You know Sachin? He has done the setting,' Prajakta told her in a muffled tone.

'No, I don't know Sachin. Who is he?'

'That guy over there,' Prajakta discreetly pointed at a slippery spindly fellow who was listening with rapt attention to every word coming out of Rohit's mouth. And it's not just me. There are five other girls from my school as well.' Prajakta took solace in that fact.

'So this Sachin has done "setting" for all five of you?' Sania asked her in hushed tones.

Prajakta affirmed it with a nod.

'But shouldn't you and your friends be concentrating on your exams, Prajakta?' Sania asked, thoroughly displeased.

'I have taken care of all that, Didi. Actually I wanted to talk to you about something personal. Can I?'

'Yeah, tell me.' Sania wondered which googly this girl was going to bowl.

Prajakta led Sania to a spot where there were no people. 'Didi, you are the judge, right?'

'Yes, so?' Sania asked with a frown, having an inkling of where this was headed.

'Can you do some setting for me, Didi? Please. You can make me win if you want to.'

'Have you completely lost it, Prajakta? How can you even think I would do something like that? Just two minutes ago, I was trying to restrain you from doing something unethical. Why do you want to use such shortcuts? You are taking routes which have a dead end. What's the hurry?' Sania kept her voice low, but it vibrated with intensity.

Prajakta, who did not expect such a severe rap on the knuckles, was stunned. She was silent for a couple of seconds, choosing the right words to say. 'Do you even know our financial condition, Sania didi? Do you know why Shikha di borrowed tops from you?

Or why she tells her boyfriends to buy gifts for her? My mother can't even buy me a proper dress. Every time I ask her to, she says she does not have the budget.'

'Where are you getting at with that?'

'Didi, if I win this pageant, I will get a lot of money. Sachin has promised me ₹10,000 even if I don't win, only for participating. He was telling me it is called appearance money.'

'I know what appearance money is, but at this age, you should not get sucked into this world. You have to concentrate *only* on your studies, nothing else. And moreover, this contest is for girls above eighteen.'

'The age issue has been taken care of no, Didi,' Prajakta pleaded, sensing trouble.

'I will talk to you later, Prajakta.' Sania had caught Rohit glancing in their direction several times now and she headed straight towards him. 'I need to talk to you. It is urgent,' Sania startled Rohit.

'Tell me, is there any problem?' Rohit tried to gauge her frame of mind.

Sania saw the people around and felt uncomfortable broaching the topic in such a public eye. 'Can we talk in a more discreet place?'

Rohit walked towards one of the green rooms and checked if there were any occupants. As soon as he opened the door, he saw one of the underage contestants squashed between the wall and Sachin. Startled by the opening of the door, Sachin immediately pulled out his hands from under her clothes and jumped away. The girl began to quake on seeing Rohit.

'She was feeling nervous, so I...' Sachin couldn't think of a single reasonable excuse for the situation, so he dashed out of the room, shamefaced, and the girl followed.

Sania reckoned this was one of Prajakta's school friends and shuddered.

'Rohit, shut the door. What exactly is happening out here?' Sania's voice shook with bottled-up fury.

'Everything is rocking. Why? What happened?' Seeing Sania so upset, Rohit got defensive. 'Ma'am, is something bothering you?

Is there anything inappropriate that has happened? We have taken extra care to...'

'Let's cut the bullshit, Rohit,' Sania interrupted.

Rohit's eyes widened to the size of tennis balls on hearing Sania cuss like that.

'I want to inform you upfront that I cannot judge this mini-pageant.'

'But why, ma'am? Has someone offended you?' Rohit asked her, while inwardly using all possible offensive phrases for her.

'As a matter of fact, yes, *you have*.'

'I have offended you?' Rohit was taken aback. 'What have I done? May I know the things that were not in line with your expectations?'

'Who are these girls?' Sania held the list in front of Rohit's beady eyes.

'They are normal beauty contestants. Why? What happened?'

'Are they genuinely "normal" contestants?'

'Yes, of course, we screened the contestants thoroughly before shortlisting them.'

'Are all these girls above eighteen years of age?'

'Yes, yes, they very much are.' Small beads of perspiration formed on Rohit's forehead.

'All of them?'

'They are, to the best of my knowledge.'

'I happen to know one of them who is just fourteen years old, but your list says that she is nineteen.'

'How can that be?'

'Prajakta Azgaonkar. She is the younger sister of last year's contestant, Shikha Azgaonkar.'

'Is it? Shikha Azgaonkar? The name rings a bell, but I can't place who she was. Why am I not updated on this? Rest assured, Saniaji. I will get her disqualified if I find out that her age has been misreported.'

'Misreported? Please do not pass the buck. Your local man has forged the papers of not only Prajakta, but five other girls as well.

And all this has been done with your blessing and your higher-ups,' Sania confronted him.

Rohit had never seen Sania angry, let alone belligerent, and it rattled him. 'I will look into it, please give me a moment.' He walked out briskly, and made a call from his phone.

'Hello, Nimesh sir. There is a problem.'

'What is it?' Nimesh snarled.

'It can become a serious problem...'

'I will call you back,' Nimesh hissed and hung up on a pleading Rohit.

Prajakta and her friends collectively gave Sania a stink eye after they got a whiff of her conversation with Rohit. Prajakta was worried that she might be dropped from the list. Seeing Prajakta crestfallen, Sania's heart gave a squeeze and stuttered. She cautiously approached Prajakta but stopped when Prajakta tossed a hateful look her way and stormed off.

Nimesh was with Pakhi at a Japanese restaurant, savouring a meal of sashimi and miso soup. Having just closed a major deal with a brand, Mehta was in a celebratory mood, but Rohit's phone call had deflated his spirits.

'I will see you at the show,' Nimesh instructed Pakhi and got up to leave.

'Yup, and I will get the brand guys along,' Pakhi confirmed and stayed behind to enjoy the rest of her meal.

Although he would have liked to do a lot more with her, Nimesh merely exchanged air kisses with Pakhi for now.

'Let that bitch go back. Don't take any shit from her. Since the day she won the godforsaken title, she has been a pain in my neck,' Nimesh snapped on the phone as he bustled back to his suite.

'But, sir, the local media has been hounding us. They want to do a story on the mini-pageant. If they even get a hint of this, it could spell big trouble for...'

'Give the phone to her,' Mehta cut him off mid-sentence, tired of the pointless banter.

Rohit rushed towards Sania and handed the phone to her. 'Nimesh sir wants to speak with you.'

'What about? I thought I had made myself clear,' Sania told him bluntly.

'Can you please speak with Boss and put forth whatever you want to?' Rohit insisted and Sania was forced to talk to Nimesh Mehta.

'What are you so upset about, princess? Aren't you being taken care of?' Nimesh asked her unctuously, while cursing her under his breath.

Sania didn't appreciate his patronizing tone one bit. 'I am not willing to be a part of such an unethical event which exploits teenage girls.'

'You are doing so well in life; why do you want to create problems for yourself unnecessarily?'

'You are free to ask someone else to judge this show. I will simply look the other way.'

'Oh! That's so nice of you. But why don't you look the other way till we finish off our event?'

'No, thank you. I don't want to be associated with this.'

'Give the phone to Rohit,' Nimesh told her coldly, clenching his fists.

'Rohit, tell that cow to go shit somewhere else. I will get one of the co-sponsors to judge the event. They will be more than happy to see so many hotties,' Nimesh sneered and laughed manically.

'But, sir,' Rohit walked away from Sania before resuming. 'The girls are from a high-profile convent school. If anything goes out of hand, there will be a huge ruckus; we can get...'

'So, do you want to pamper her ego? You want to beg her to stay?' Nimesh attacked him.

'Let me see what I can do, sir.' Rohit's mind was in overdrive mode. He deliberated on his option for a moment before looking for Sania. She was seated in the auditorium, waiting to hear from him. 'There is still an hour to go before the show starts,' he informed her. 'Sania ma'am, we will disqualify all the underage girls. You need not worry.'

'Why would I be worried? It's you who should be worried. By the way, what do you plan to tell those girls when you crush their dreams? You should never have misled them with false hope in the first place.'

'That is my headache. I'll figure it out. As it is, these girls start building castles in the air the first chance they get.'

'You would know better.' Sania felt a twinge of guilt snaking inside her as Prajakta's downhearted face floated before her eyes.

But Sania knew she could have never condoned such a dishonourable act. She told herself resolutely that in the given situation, this was the right thing to do.

35

Pakhi and the co-sponsors were guided to their seats by an usher. They settled down in the front-most row of seats, specifically reserved for them. Nimesh sauntered in and joined them after a few minutes. That was the cue for the host to commence the show.

'Good evening, friends. I am your host, Darryl. I take great pride in welcoming the Miss India Beauty regional pageant to our beloved city of Pune. This regional pageant will be the gateway to stardom for The Chosen One.'

His embellished words didn't stir the audience as much as it affected Prajakta. In her mind, she could see a vivid picture of herself being felicitated for becoming 'the chosen one'. She had truly believed she was special all along. 'See, I have goosebumps,' she raised her arm so her friend could inspect it.

All of Prajakta's classmates giggled with nervous energy.

After the host finished spewing his spiel, the contestants started walking down the ramp. Sania was making notes on a sheet of paper provided to her. She glanced at the names of Prajakta and five other girls which had been struck off. Unaware of the reality, she felt sorry that they had to be thrown out unceremoniously.

'Our next contestant is Ms Prajakta Azgaonkar, a young nineteen-year-old lass, who wants to conquer the world with her oomph and sass,' the host announced.

Sania's head snapped up. Dumbfounded by what she saw, Sania looked at Rohit who was preoccupied in updating Nimesh. Sania simply rose to her feet and strode out determinedly.

Rohit turned pale. Sensing something was off, Nimesh looked in the direction that Rohit was looking in and immediately realized that the epicentre of the trouble was Sania. 'Concentrate. I don't want you to show your anxiety,' Nimesh told Rohit firmly.

Rohit tried to regain his composure, but when he turned his gaze towards the main entrance of the auditorium, he was flabbergasted. A bunch of reporters from the local media had thronged around Sania.

'Why are you walking out of the show halfway, Saniaji?'

'Did you have a fight with the organizers?'

'Are they not paying you your dues?'

Sania was taken aback by their bizarre questions and raucous mannerisms. Although he couldn't hear the conversation between Sania and the reporters, Rohit smelled trouble.

'She is talking to the media,' Rohit whispered frenetically to Nimesh whose brow broke out into a cold sweat.

'Sack those fucking school girls immediately,' Nimesh murmured harshly. 'Make an announcement that we have discovered some anomalies in the data provided to us.'

Rohit scrambled backstage and flailed his arms violently from the wings to grab the host's attention. Darryl, who was making an announcement at that moment, stopped midway and excused himself rather awkwardly.

'We have a major change in the list of participants,' Rohit informed Darryl.

'It has come to our knowledge that some of the girls who have participated today have misreported their data. As a result, they stand to be disqualified,' Darryl updated the audience. 'Their names are as follows...'

As Darryl read out the names onstage, Rohit tried his best to quell matters offstage. 'I am sorry, girls. Due to some unexpected developments, we have to drop you from the show,' he told Prajakta and her friends.

'What? No, you can't do that. This is happening because of that whore Sania, isn't it?' Prajakta was implacably enraged. 'That bitch! Who the hell does she think she is? I will not let her get away with this,' Prajakta roared and rushed out to confront Sania.

Sania was jostling her way through the horde around her, trying to get to her car when Prajakta dug her nails deep into Sania's head and yanked at her hair, dragging her backwards. She screamed as an excruciating jolt of pain seared through her scalp. She lost her balance in the tussle and caught hold of Prajakta to prevent a fall. Caught off guard by the sudden weight, Prajakta lost her footing as well and both of them crashed into the crowd around them.

The media reporters stood by, shooting the catfight, instead of stopping it.

'Somebody get a mud wrestling ring,' a voice from the crowd catcalled.

A pair of arms from the crowd tried to hold Prajakta back, but she was hysterical with rage and only saw red. She unshackled herself from that person's grip and pounced on Sania, yet again. The very same person forced his way between them and protected Sania obstinately. Much to her relief, Sania saw that it was none other than Abdul chacha, her trusted driver and now, part-time bodyguard.

Rohit and Sachin managed to make their way to the front of the crowd and caught hold of Prajakta. It took their combined strength to pin her down, but Prajakta spat defiantly in Sania's direction anyway.

Abdul chacha led Sania to the car. She was so stunned by what had just taken place that she staggered behind him blindly, while he pushed aside the media guys who shamelessly hounded her for a comment.

With Sania ensconced safely in the car, Abdul chacha tried to steer them out of the mess, even as some of the reporters banged on her window for her reaction.

One of the reporters had managed to sneak inside the venue and he recorded Prajakta on camera. 'Everything was going smoothly, but that bitch Sania's ass started burning with jealousy. She's insecure that younger girls will get her crown and she will no longer get any attention. That's why she ruined our chances. I will not let her get away with this. She will pay.'

'Which school are you from, Prajakta?' the reporter asked her.

'I am from St. Mary's.'

'Which class are you studying in?'

'Tenth.'

'Did you fail in some of the classes earlier?'

'No! Why would you ask that?'

'Just like that! Then you must be around fifteen, right?'

Although Rohit intercepted their conversation at that very moment, Prajakta had revealed enough to do some serious damage. Rohit tried to catch hold of the journalist who had recorded Prajakta, but he had already sneaked out of the place by then. Rohit pushed the media guys back and whisked Prajakta away.

'Underage girls racket in Beauty Pageant exposed.' 'Reigning beauty queen in a catfight,' the Breaking News ticker read on the TV screen.

Shikha and her mom were horrified to see the ugly fight between Prajakta and Sania being broadcasted nationwide.

Shikha repeatedly called Prajakta on her cell phone, but there was no reply. The entire brawl was being aired on loop. Prajakta's crude comments about Sania were quite a shocker.

Shikha reflexly concluded that Sania must have provoked Prajakta as payback for catching Shikha in her father's bed. But it was such a sordid incident that she couldn't even share it with anyone. *Who will I reason it out with? What will I tell anyone?* Shikha's mind was in knots.

The doorbell rang. Both Shikha and her mom rushed out to open the door, but it was only Shilpi who had come back from school. Gurpreet took her into her arms and held her tightly. Feeling the pressure of her petite frame against her bosom reassured her marginally. They shut the door and anxiously waited for Prajakta to come home.

As the darkness outside grew, so did their fears. There was still no news of Prajakta. Shikha had been calling her persistently but to no avail. She had even deliberately left some incendiary messages in the hope that it would compel her sister to reply, but that plan had failed as well. Realizing that it was an event organized by Nimesh Mehta, Shikha called Rohit next; she was sure he would be fully aware of the latest developments. But he disconnected her call all the three times she tried his number. She sent a strong-worded message as well to him and waited for his reply; there was none. 'Mummyji, give me your phone,' she told her mom who was making Shilpi eat *sheera*, a variety of sweet.

'It's inside my purse. Wait, I will give it to you.' Gurpreet went inside her bedroom to fetch her phone.

'Why did you let Prajakta go in the first place. Why?' Shikha called out to her mother.

'I didn't even know that she was going to take part in this contest. She had told me two days ago that she was going to get some money for just going there, but I had put my foot down,' Gurpreet defended herself.

But a part of Shikha's mind didn't believe it. 'So she did mention to you that she was getting paid for this appearance.'

'She made a passing reference when she had got that boy along with her.'

'Which boy?'

'Some Sachin or someone,' mumbled Gurpreet uneasily.

Gauging her mother's reaction, Shikha's scepticism strengthened. *Did Mummyji let Prajakta take part in this for the money?* Shikha was appalled by that thought, so she shook it away. She used her mother's phone to call Rohit, who immediately answered the phone. 'Hello. Who is it?'

'Your mother, you sleazebag. Where is my sister?'

'Who is your sister?'

'Prajakta, you pimp...'

Rohit had hung up on her before she could finish giving him a piece of her mind. Shikha redialled his number, but he rejected her call again. She was livid.

Shikha was furiously typing out a nasty message to Rohit when her mum's phone pinged with a WhatsApp text. It was from some fellow called Shiro. Normally, Shikha would not have bothered with it, but the first few words of the message caught her attention. 'What are you doing, love?'

The fact that her mom had a lover in her life evoked mixed reactions from her, but for the time being, her curiosity triumphed and she opened the entire chat. 'I will be passing through Pune tomorrow morning. Want me to book the room at the Blue Diamond like last time or do you have some other place in mind?'

Shikha tapped on Shiro's profile to find out more about the fellow who was dating her mother. Not only was the face that appeared familiar to her, but she was also well-acquainted with the private parts that accompanied it. It was Shiraz, Sania's father.

Shikha stowed the phone aside with trembling hands. A sudden wave of nausea washed over her as she slid down the wall and flopped down onto the floor. Her mind was numb and she stared blankly at the walls. She heard her mom's sharp but loving voice, and Shilpi's cribbing. She quietly snuck into the washroom when she heard her mother's footsteps.

She stared at her reflection in the mirror like she was looking at a ghost.

Thwack! She slapped herself so hard that her face swivelled. *What the fuck is happening?* she yelled at the girl judging her, in a tremulous voice. *Do something, you fucking loser. Move your ass and stop feeling sorry for yourself.* The girl glared at her. *You have stooped too fucking low. You should be ashamed of who you are. Maybe you should just fucking kill yourself and spare everyone the bother.* Fat teardrops started rolling down the girl's face, hitting the basin before going down the drain. Her body began to shiver uncontrollably.

A knock on the door startled her. 'Shikha, Prajakta has called.' There was no response. 'Shikha!' her mother pounded the door.

'I heard you, Mummyji. I will come out and talk to her.' Shikha gathered herself with great difficulty. She flushed the loo and splashed some water on her face to wash off the traces of any residual tears.

Gurpreet retrieved her phone from the floor. Her phone's screen showed the chat history between her and Shiraz, and she instantly knew that Shikha had read it. She was not at all happy about it. She didn't want her tryst to be revealed to her daughter; not in this manner at least.

'Where is the phone?' Shikha, who had finally stepped out, asked her mother.

'She had called, but she disconnected the line after telling me that she was on her way. What's the matter? Why do you look so pale?' Gurpreet inquired.

Shikha looked at her with puffy, vacant eyes. 'Nothing. I'm fine.'

36

The lane which led to Shikha's apartment was an unilluminated and secluded one; sometimes frequented by drunks. That was one of the reasons why Gurpreet could never sleep at night until all her daughters were tucked safely in bed. That night, it seemed like the darkness had taken a form—a thriving, throbbing and pulsating form—that represented everything that was wrong in the world.

A pair of headlights pierced the swirling mass. A black Mercedes slunk into the street and expelled out Prajakta and Payal from the rear door. The car zoomed out of there noiselessly.

'Please, come with me upstairs,' Prajakta implored Payal.

'Even I am really late, Prajakta. My mom has been calling me non-stop. I will come with you till your doorstep.' Payal was extremely agitated, but she wanted Prajakta to reach home safely. Prajakta rang the doorbell and her mom answered it.

'What happened to your face?' Gurpreet was aghast.

Prajakta's face was swollen with red and purple bruises. Her lip had a rusty crust where it had split. Prajakta was terrified, inexplicably terrified. 'I am so sorry, Mummyji,' she mumbled with quivering lips.

Shikha marched up to the door to confront Prajakta. 'What the hell were you thinking? You shameless girl!' Shikha took out all her fear and anger on Prajakta; anger that stemmed from her bad choices, the result of it on her sisters and her mother's new relationship.

Prajakta glanced behind, looking for Payal who had made a hasty retreat as soon as things had started heating up. Before Prajakta could even straighten herself, Shikha had registered a tight slap on her face. 'Who are you looking for over there? You stupid bitch.'

'P... Payal,' Prajakta stuttered as she broke down.

'To hell with Payal! You have your board exams in the next two months and you had the cheek to participate in a beauty contest? That too by lying about your age so blatantly?' Shikha grabbed Prajakta's collar and hauled her inside the house, conveniently forgetting that she too had lied about her age during the IBQ pageant.

'You leave her alone,' their mother shouted at her as she tried to stop Shikha.

But Shikha was in no mood to comply. 'You don't interfere, Mummyji. Now, I will take care of her. You could not bring her on track, so I will. You perhaps thought she would get some money and it will be handy, right?' Shikha's acrimonious remark left a bitter taste in her mouth, but she didn't pay any heed to it.

'Don't you dare say anything like tha...'

'Why? Why shouldn't I? The truth stings, doesn't it, Mummyji?'

'Are you trying to imply that I would exploit my fourteen-year-old daughter to make money? At the cost of her studies?' Gurpreet choked, her voice laden with emotion.

'You would know that better; as long as you're truthful to yourself, if not us. This is clearly the result of how much attention you've paid to her upbringing. It is not a hidden fact and neither is what you have been doing behind our backs.'

Shikha's acerbic words felt like a smack on Gurpreet's face. She decided to keep mum. Shikha looked at her mother menacingly as she dragged Prajakta inside the bedroom. 'Open your books and start studying.'

'Let her be. She is very upset right now,' her mother reasoned with her, but Shikha was in an uncompromising mood. She pushed Prajakta into a chair near the study table, removed a stack of books from her school bag and dumped them on the table with a loud thud. 'I don't want you to do anything else from now on but concentrate on your studies,' Shikha told her authoritatively and banged the door shut, pulling a frightened little Shilpi aside.

Prajakta sat motionless in the chair. She lifted a hand to her cheeks to wipe away her tears when she felt the swelling on her face. She turned around and studied her reflection in the mirror.

Cuts, bruises and bumps marred her face. Her chin wobbled as more tears tumbled down. She was horrified to look at herself.

A few moments later, Gurpreet opened the door gently, taking care not to startle Prajakta. Prajakta had her arms folded on the desk and rested her head on them. She looked at her mother blankly.

'Prajakta, I made hot chocolate for you. I added extra chocolate in it just for you.' Gurpreet offered her daughter a mug along with a brittle smile.

Prajakta regarded her mother with dull unmoving eyes.

'Drink that and go to sleep. I will set an alarm for you. Okay? And tell me whatever happened tomorrow.' Gurpreet stroked her hair lovingly, but Prajakta barely perceived it.

Prajakta gulped down the drink in one go and made her way to bed. A thin trail of residue on the whiskers of her lips further evinced her naïveté.

'At least change into your night clothes,' her mother suggested.

But Prajakta just stared at her vacantly.

Gurpreet woke up at six in the morning and turned off the alarm, bleary-eyed. It being winter, the sun had still not risen and the room was submerged in shadows. Shikha and Prajakta usually slept together, but owing to last night's clash, Prajakta slept with her mother, and Shilpi with Shikha.

Gurpreet grabbled in the dark, trying to wake Prajakta up, but she wasn't there. She looked around the room, her vision still unfocused because of grogginess. Then she discerned the outline of a person standing on the bed. For a moment, she was terrified. 'Prajakta, is that you? Prajakta? What are you doing standing there like that?'

Not getting any response from her, she sat up, irked. She squinted at the silhouette and it definitely belonged to her daughter. 'Prajakta, what are you doing up there? Get down this instant,' she said sternly as she got out of bed to turn on the lights.

With one flick of a switch, Gurpreet's life turned upside down.

She emitted a blood-curdling shriek and collapsed on the floor. On hearing her mother, Shikha rushed in from the adjacent room, her heart thumping in her chest with panic. 'What happened, Mum...' Shikha stopped mid-sentence, white as a sheet, and then retched uncontrollably.

The bedsheet she used to sleep in was tied around her bruised neck. Her bloodless face had a greyish tinge, and her forearms and legs showed signs of struggle. Prajakta's lifeless body was suspended from the ceiling fan.

The cops had taken over and were making a *panchnama*, an inquest report. None of the neighbours had a single thing to say to the cops about the unfortunate occurrence. But the bigger sharks were waiting to pounce on the development. A huge contingent of various news channels was parked downstairs at the entrance of Shikha's building. The cops had completely cordoned off the area, prohibiting any media personnel to even step foot inside the building premises. The news correspondents were filing reports with their respective channels.

'The underage girl who hit the headlines yesterday for having a scrap with the reigning Beauty Queen has committed suicide.'

'Fourteen-year-old Prajakta Azgaonkar's suicide could be a flash in the pan for the gory practices prevailing in beauty pageants.'

'The loss of an innocent fourteen-year-old girl only corroborates the argument that there is too much performance pressure on kids by parents and the society at large in the show business.'

Most of the news channels had carried Prajakta's story and fuelled plenty of heated debates. Nimesh Mehta knew that if he didn't handle this incident smartly at this juncture, it would snowball into something unmanageable. He immediately called a meeting with his right-hand man at his office. Both of them had returned late the previous night from Pune after managing the huge fiasco at the mini-pageant. Nimesh was huddled with his core team at the moment, which included his legal advisor, Brijesh. Nimesh was trying to understand the fallout of this development.

'Sir, you can get into trouble for the "underage" tag that has gotten attached to the incident,' Brijesh explained.

'Yes, I am aware of that. Karmarkar had called regarding the same,' Nimesh muttered contemplatively.

'Would you like to send a Caveat Notice to Miss Sania?' Brijesh suggested, knowing his client's temperament inside out.

'I have a better plan,' Nimesh announced, his eyes dancing with a sinister gleam.

'With a very heavy heart, I have to inform you that we have decided to strip Sania Ahmed of her Miss India Beauty Queen title. Her conduct in relation to the unfortunate death of a young and innocent girl is deplorable. We feel she should have handled such a delicate matter with a lot more sensitivity.' Nimesh Mehta was flanked by Rohit and his legal advisor, Brijesh, as he addressed the media fraternity. He had called for a press conference to specifically discuss the recent incident.

Anything that was worthy of being breaking news was lapped up. And this incident was reported from the newsroom with particular gusto. Stripping a Beauty Queen of her title because of her connection with the suicide of a young teenager was juicy enough as it is. But the fact that the same teenager had been featured in a story on an underage girls' racket just a day earlier was enormous.

'So, are you putting the blame of this young girl's suicide on Sania Ahmed?' prodded one of the reporters, unabashed.

'That is for the law and the law keepers to decide. I found her behaviour unbecoming of a title holder, so I acted,' Mehta replied smoothly.

'Why didn't you stop the fight between Sania and the young girl who committed suicide?' catechized another correspondent.

'I would like to state here that we were very prompt in

preventing anything serious at the venue yesterday. Although Sania did manage to physically abuse the girl, we stopped her in the act then and there. But it is extremely regrettable and I genuinely lament the fact that we failed to gauge the injuries that were inflicted on that young girl's psyche,' Mehta choked.

Rohit offered a glass of water to him and a wad of tissues. Mehta made a big show of wiping his crocodile tears.

'So, by stripping her of the title, do you want to state that you have punished Miss Sania Ahmed for being irresponsible?'

'Our title holders are our brand ambassadors. They have a certain responsibility towards society. They cannot be so uncaring. We have a clause in our agreement that gives us the right to revoke the title that we have conferred on a girl for reckless behaviour during her tenure. We have decided to use that now because Sania Ahmed's conduct was rash and irresponsible. It resulted in loss of life of an innocent fourteen-year-old.' Mehta systematically painted a rather sadistic portrait of Sania.

Questions were thrown at Mehta who dodged them with ease and conniving skill. In the consecutive days, this issue went ablaze like firecrackers during Diwali. The incident was being discussed in the parliament and it had caused a frenzy in the media, which was agog with anticipation over the next move. The social media was filled with hate messages for Sania. Soon, the situation was aggravated, as tremendous pressure was put on the cops. They were forced to act immediately and put the case on high priority.

37

Sania who had barely recovered from the previous day's episode, could not wrap her head around what was unfolding before her eyes. First, the early morning news of Prajakta's suicide had shaken her up, and now, it was Mehta's press conference that was being aired on all the news channels. She was systematically being defamed by Mehta and the vilification of her reputation by the press was unmerited.

Her phone had been constantly buzzing with news reporters who wouldn't stop harrying her. Her mother was also trying to call her repeatedly. Sania knew what her mother wanted to say. From the moment the video of her altercation with Prajakta surfaced online and aired on TV, things had quickly gone from bad to worse for Sania. Just about everyone, including her mother, had been giving her free advice.

'But, Ammi, believe me, I have not done anything wrong.'

'Be very careful, Sania beta. Since that girl has killed herself, this could escalate badly. People will try to pin the blame on you. Be very very careful,' her mother cautioned her.

'But, Ammi, at least you try and understand the truth. I didn't even touch that girl Prajakta. In fact, she pounced on me.'

'But you should have stayed away from her.'

'Ammi, she was disqualified, so she was very angry with me. I did not even once try to insult her. I just raised a very valid point. Her age...'

'Have you been reading your *namaz*, your prayers?' Shamim interrupted Sania.

'Every single day, Ammi, every single day. I haven't missed my namaz even once,' Sania told her exasperatedly.

'Then don't worry! Nothing will go wrong. Allah will protect you.'

Just then, the doorbell rang. 'Ammi, I will talk to you later. Someone is at the door.'

'No, first you tell me who is at the door.'

'Whoever it is, I will deal with them and call you later.'

'I fail to understand why you shifted out of your father's house. You have only gotten into trouble ever since you left that place. Can't you go back there? I have spoken with him. He said...'

'I will talk to you later, Ammi.' Sania had run out of patience, so she hung up on her mother for the very first time.

The house she had moved into a few weeks ago was a rented one. It was much smaller compared to her dad's apartment. Unopened cartons were strewn around the flat. Sania had no time to unpack and settle down in her new apartment because of her heavy workload.

'Miss Sania Ahmed?' An intimidating male inspector, accompanied by a female sub-inspector, were at the door.

'Yes, how may I help you?'

'You will have to come with us to the police station,' the sub-inspector told her woodenly.

'But why? What have I done?' asked Sania with apparent disbelief.

'We need to make some enquiries,' the inspector told her more firmly now.

'But why, I ask?' Sania demanded, losing her calm. 'I want to know what is happening. You can't expect someone to come to the police station for no rhyme or reason.'

'We have to interrogate you about a suicide that happened in Pune. An officer from the Pune police force has come to investigate the matter specially,' the sub-inspector told her sternly.

'You will have to come with us,' glowered the inspector.

'What investigation? You can't just take me with you without any notice,' Sania protested.

'Then we will have to get an arrest warrant and drag you out like a criminal from your own house. Would you like me to do that?' he said menacingly.

'Madam, you better come with us right now to avoid a bigger scene,' the sub-inspector reasoned with Sania.

Sania felt blood draining from her face as the world around her spun in slow motion. She supported her feeble frame against the wall, lest she should fall. 'Can I... Do I...do I have some time? I mean, can I have a cup of coffee and then come?' she asked weakly, her shoulders hung meekly and her head bent forward in defeat.

'You will get tea and coffee at the police station,' the inspector told her indifferently. He seemed to be in a hurry to finish off this ordeal, but the sub-inspector gestured to him to go a little easy.

'I would like to make a few phone calls,' Sania declared, clasping her mobile phone in her hand.

'Call up the prime minister or the president or whoever you want to. But you will be coming to the police station with us.'

'Be ready in twenty minutes. We will wait here,' the sub-inspector told her.

Sania thanked her and shut the door for privacy. She staggered inside, forcing her unwilling legs to move. She quaked as she sank into a chair and tried to process what had happened. *How could things get so messy? Where did I go wrong? What should I do now?* She kept running in circles, berserk, in panic. She could only think of calling one person.

'Hey, what's up? Are you at a shoot?'

'I need to talk to you about something very dire, Gaurav.' Sania's voice cracked as she broke down.

Gaurav had been Sania's well-kept secret for over five years. Nobody knew about him, except her cousin, Noor. Not being a Muslim fellow, she was scared of backlash from her family. But she desperately needed him right now.

'What happened? Is it regarding yesterday's incident?'

'Yes,' Sania spluttered, crying inconsolably.

'Sano, please don't cry like that. Tell me what happened, so I can be of help to you. Sano, are you there?'

'Yeah,' she whimpered. 'I am here.'

'Then tell me what happened.'

Gaurav was the only person Sania could talk to about anything without the fear of being judged. Although he was based out of Bangalore, the two of them had constantly been in touch to the point where they had become each other's emotional support system. She poured her heart out.

'See, Sano, I know that you are completely innocent. But our system is very corrupt. The law keepers will want a fall guy, a chump, to get the pressure off their heads. And it looks like they will try and make you the scapegoat.'

'What should I do?' Sania squeaked.

'I need you to be composed. Speak the truth. Don't ruffle any more feathers. I will take the next flight to Mumbai and contact my seniors in the IPS right away. Let me see if I can pull some strings.'

Sania felt reassured but only infinitesimally. She was still terrified about facing the cops. Her mom had been calling her whilst she was speaking with Gaurav. She did not return her call but instead phoned Ayub, knowing fully well that her mother would get deeply distressed if she got to know about the police's involvement.

'Sania aapa, can I suggest something? Don't take it the wrong way,' Ayub addressed Sania. 'Sajid bhaijaan and Rashid miyaan would be the right guys to involve in this situation. They have dealt with the police a lot and know how to tackle them well.'

'No,' disagreed Sania vehemently. 'Don't even mention this to them. They are just waiting for an opportunity for me to slip up and make one wrong move. You know that better than anyone else, Ayub.'

'But, Aapa, they have a lot of expe...'

'I told you once and I won't repeat it,' Sania told him emphatically. 'I am transferring a decent amount of money into your account. If there is any problem, you talk to Gaurav. I am messaging you his number. He will be the one-point contact.'

'You don't trust your own brothers. And you want me to deal with a total outsider for such a serious situation? What is wrong, Sania aapa? Hello?' Ayub realized that she had hung up.

The television in their house in Aurangabad beamed visuals of Sania being escorted to the police station. Sajid was lambasting Shamim and Ayub as they tried very hard to ignore his tirade and pack their bags for Mumbai.

'Do you see what your darling daughter has done now? You people did not listen to me that time. She will drag our family name into such deep, stinking shit that you will have nowhere to go,' Sajid hissed.

Now Ayub realized why Sania was adamant about not involving Sajid. 'Our sister is in trouble and instead of thinking about ways to help her out, you are giving your brash opinion?' Ayub overtly stood up against his brother for the first time. 'In the last seven months, she has done much, much more for us than you have done all your life. So don't you dare utter another ill word against her.'

Unable to take his younger brother's defiance, Sajid swung his hand till it came in contact with his brother's face with a loud crack. Ayub returned his brother's actions. Sajid was disconcerted by the animosity that radiated off Ayub. The two ended engaging in a physical duel which was spiralling out of control. In their rage, they knocked over a glass table that dispersed shards all over the floor. The pieces pierced through Ayub's feet, but he stood firmly on his feet, giving Sajid his most threatening look.

In a fit of rage, Sajid picked up a bigger shard with a long, pointed tip and turned towards Ayub. There was blood in his eyes. Before he could act on his bestial instincts, their mother stood between them and looked at Sajid with unconcealed contempt. He dropped the shard but to vent his anger, he reached for the fifty-inch LCD TV. Uprooting its connections, he lifted it and yelled, 'This TV was sponsored by your dear sister, wasn't it? To hell with all her tainted money.' Sajid smashed the TV set to smithereens. Sakina and Shamim were aghast at Sajid's insanity. Shamim held her head between her hands and collapsed into a chair.

'You are just jealous of your younger sister because she is doing far better than you. It must surely hurt your infantile ego to know that a girl who is ten years younger than you is making ten times more money than you. Shame on you, worthless vermin,' Ayub spat, even as his mother and sister tried to stop him from escalating it any further.

Sajid was about to retaliate, when Rashid walked in along with his dad, their mamujaan, who was as rotund as his son was stick-like.

Everyone straightened up and silence descended in the room. Sajid's body language shifted drastically. He offered a hesitant half-*adaab*-like gesture to Mamu. 'What brings you here, Mamujaan?'

'I could not stop myself after seeing the kind of publicity your sister is getting. I thought I should also bask in her glory,' Mamujaan jeered and laughed like the hyena. Turning his gaze towards Shamim, his elder sister, he became sombre. 'This is what happens when you give a girl free rein and let her loose; mayhem follows everywhere. Look at what is happening to her out there and look here,' pointed Mamu towards the wreckage of the television.

Ayub tossed a venomous look at Sajid for causing that destruction. He didn't even acknowledge Mamujaan who was standing right in front of Ayub, staring at him intently in a bid to intimidate him. 'So, Mr Ayub Ahmed, Chote Miyaan, is the new rebel in the family? I heard you are supporting Sania through her bad choices. Do you think you can handle her problems? You can barely wipe your butt without help.'

There was complete silence. If one strained one's ears hard enough, one would be able to hear Ayub clench his teeth and Shamim frown. He wanted to question his mamu's intentions, but no one had the gall to talk back to him.

'Banish her. Disown her. Break off all your connections with her and let her rot. It will be a good example for young girls in our community. That is my *farmaan*, my order.'

'Who are you to give such diktats?' Ayub objected, provoked by Mamujaan's insolence. 'She is my sister and I will do everything in my capacity to save her.'

'How dare you speak to Mamujaan like that?' Sajid roared. He charged towards Ayub and swung a closed fist at his face.

Ayub ducked instinctively. Sajid lost his balance and almost fell flat on his face in the debris. 'Stop this nonsense in my house,' Shamim shrieked, unable to see two people who had come out of her womb fight like barbarians. 'If your son had gotten into trouble, would you have helped him or not?' she demanded from her brother, who stared at her with ill-disguised hatred. But she stood her ground and repeated herself firmly, 'Would you have helped your child if he was in trouble?'

'Depends,' Mamujaan skirted the question.

'Depends on what?' she persisted.

'Depends on whether he is right or wrong; if he is offending the community sentiments or not. And whether he is willing to change himself for the better or not.'

'You can lie to me, but at least don't lie to yourself. I know you would definitely help your child but only if it was your son; not your daughters. Both Noor and Shagufta have shared their innermost thoughts and feelings with me on several occasions. They feel like you are their *jallaad*, their executioner. If my daughter has taken a decision to be on her own and I endorse her independence, I know she is already a villain in your eyes. You will try your best to expel her from this world the first chance you get. But your prejudiced mindset and chauvinistic behaviour are not welcome in this house. I will help my children unconditionally, irrespective of their gender, whether it is my son or my daughter,' asserted Shamim, her words resounded in the room.

Mamujaan belonged to an abundant species of men who felt threatened when their dominance was challenged. He feared that this confrontation would erode his following, namely with Rashid and Sajid who were both witnessing this development. 'I will get a fatwa issued against your daughter. I will not spare her,' aggressed Mamujaan, in a bid to aver his manhood.

'Are you so stupid that you will cut your nose to spite your face?' asked Shamim incredulously. But her brother was busy answering a call.

'Yes, I am just coming to the shop. Wait there,' he said and disconnected the call.

'You use the latest iPhone to be with the times, but what about changing your outdated mentality? The latest technology suits your needs, so you parade it around like an emblem of your modernity. But where it really matters—like giving freedom to your daughters or treating them equally—you behave like a caveman. Your kind exists in all communities, riding the horse of orthodoxy to trample on women and instil fear in their minds. You will commit atrocious acts just to make sure patriarchy prevails, not only today but forever,' asseverated Shamim.

Shamim might as well have been talking in Greek to Mamujaan. 'What are you trying to say?' he mumbled blankly.

'I am not trying to say anything, Yusuf bhaijaan. I have already said enough.'

Sania was being interrogated by a senior inspector and two of his assistants, including the female sub-inspector who had gone to Sania's house. Another *havaldar* was noting down all that was being said. The interrogation was being video-recorded simultaneously. Sania didn't have much to say, except for the fact that she had met Prajakta for all of ten minutes.

'How did the physical fight happen?' the inspector asked.

'I did not say anything to Prajakta directly which could have provoked her. I spoke to the manager, Mr Rohit. I don't know what transpired between them, but when I was leaving, she came out and attacked me.'

'Two people have filed a complaint, accusing you of being the cause of this suicide.'

'Complaint? Who has filed a complaint?' Sania was alarmed.

'Miss Shikha Azgaonkar and Mr Nimesh Mehta. The post-mortem report is awaited, but there were bruises on the girl's face, which, according to us, are a result of the fight you had with her.'

The constable removed a sheet of paper from his file. It was a form in Marathi. 'You have to fill this. It is an arrest form. We will be producing you in court for a formal arrest tomorrow morning.'

Sania's blood froze in her veins.

Shiraz was accompanying Shamim and Ayub to the sessions court where Sania's bail hearing was underway. Simran was there as well, outraged by the charges laid on Sania. She made it a point to go and meet Sania before the hearing commenced. The police had encircled Sania to form a barricade around her.

'I am here for you,' Simran told her earnestly.

But Sania was in a daze, dissociated from the reality. She barely acknowledged Simran with her swollen, bloodshot eyes.

'The cops have cornered the case completely. Their palms have been greased by the prosecution,' Gaurav told Ayub.

'What are the chances of bail?'

'Very bleak. It'll be very difficult for us to get immediate relief. I have met my seniors, but they refuse to interfere at this stage, especially since it has become such a high-profile case now,' Gaurav explained infuriatedly to Ayub, who was almost in tears.

The prosecution had mounted a scathing attack on Sania, accusing her of being solely responsible for Prajakta Azgaonkar's death. They were pressing for her detention, so that she could not influence any of the witnesses and evidence. The bail application was denied. The order of the judge was like a sledgehammer that crushed whatever little hope Sania had to fight this battle in a dignified manner.

'Your mother is becoming senile. Just because your father has been sending money to her, she subscribes to his beliefs,' Rashid openly derided Shamim.

Sajid nodded in agreement and added, 'My father preaches and practices the ideology of infidels.'

'Absolutely! All his trips abroad have made him unsound. As

soon as he started turning into another Westernized puppet piece, my father began distancing himself from him. And then he had the nerve to accuse Abbu of taking away his business. Didn't Abbu take you and Ayub in the business?'

Sajid dithered on that one. He realized that not responding to this comment would put him in an awkward position. 'My dad was determined to take me abroad with him. He insisted so many times, but Maamujaan put his foot down every single time,' Sajid told him with a twinge of regret and longing.

'Hasn't that helped you? Otherwise, you too would have turned into one of those Westernized buffoons, disillusioned, and turning to drugs and alcohol. Abbu has always wanted to establish you in the business, so that you can run your house on your own. Rather than being grateful to him, your mother insulted him today. I will not take this lightly. Your mother should know who is right and who is wrong. Do you see any other girl from our community indulging in such unpardonable things? She will have to pay the price. I will make, no, *we* will make her pay the price.'

Sajid masked the tremor in his voice and the trepidation in his heart. 'What do you have in mind?'

38

Simran was fiercely typing away a rough flow of the sequence of events that led to Prajakta's suicide. She then made a list of people who had come in contact with Prajakta on that particular day. She reconstructed the entire day's events. Most of the timelines were blank, as she didn't know about Prajakta's whereabouts before and after the pageant.

'Hey, I want to sit with you and chart out a plan. Are you free?' she intercommed Sunidhi.

'Yeah! Coming right away.' Sunidhi was equally enthusiastic about solving this case.

'We need to know exactly what happened from the day Prajakta was shortlisted for the mini-pageant to the time she killed herself,' explained Simran.

Sunidhi nodded her agreement. 'What do you want me to do?'

'I want you to give me two assistants, so that I can leave for Pune with them.'

'Are you thinking what I am thinking?'

'To target this incident as our first episode?'

'I am so glad we are on the same page,' Sunidhi told her, giving her a high five.

'I will be reconstructing the events that happened on that particular day and before that as well.'

'That means you will be meeting Shikha as well?'

'Without a doubt! I fail to understand why Shikha would file a case against Sania, especially when Sania was so generous to her. What would she achieve by sending Sania to jail? Something just doesn't add up. I am convinced that Nimesh Mehta is involved in this.'

'Nimesh uncle? No way, Simran. He would never engage in such unpardonable offenses. If he did, he wouldn't be where he is today.'

'I know. I just hope I am wrong. But I will need your wholehearted support in finding the facts. Our show is about bringing the truth out in the open.'

'You have it...one hundred and ten per cent. But why do you think he is involved in it?'

'The way Nimesh Mehta called a press conference to strip Sania of her title and then put the entire blame on her was extremely odd. I felt that man was trying to hoodwink the investigation, as if he had pre-empted the gravity of the development. See, Sunidhi, I hope you understand that as an investigative journalist, I have to look at every possible angle of the story. It is not that I am cent per cent sure,' Simran backtracked, realizing that she couldn't afford to antagonize Sunidhi at this juncture.

'I get it, Simran. As the producer, I will give you a free hand. My job will be to deal with the channel, the production unit and whatever else my anchor wants. I want my show to be successful, that's all. I will not interfere with the content.' Sunidhi's words relieved Simran to a great extent.

Karmarkar set aside a book he was reading to talk to his daughter. 'This girl Simran has a really sharp and analytical mind. She is bang on as far as suspecting Nimesh's complicity is concerned.'

'Why didn't you say anything earlier in that case?' Sunidhi exclaimed, surprised by her father's admission.

'There are certain things you have to overlook. If I start judging the people around me, I will not be able to work with most of them. So I let them be, just as they let me be.'

'So, you too have such skeletons in your cupboard?'

'Give your father some credit,' Karmarkar chaffed. 'I don't need to resort to unscrupulous means to survive or thrive.'

'What will happen if Simran does find something against Nimesh uncle?'

'At the end of the day, Simran is merely a media person. She will not be able to indict anyone beyond making some noise about it. So a person in the eyes of the law remains innocent until proved guilty.'

'But why is Sania being held guilty if she has not been proved guilty?'

'Sania is at the receiving end of the law. As a result, she is guilty till she is proved innocent. The whole process of proving someone innocent or guilty is a long-drawn one.'

'If it wasn't for you, I would have been in jail or worse,' Sunidhi said aloud, her eyes glistening with gratitude and remorse.

Simran was having a meeting with Dipti and Shashank, the two assistants that Sunidhi had assigned to her. She was taking them through the material she had put together so far for the counter investigation.

'We have to meet Prajakta's friends. They will be able to shed more light on what really happened that day. But before that, we must find out how Prajakta registered herself for that pageant. She was clearly underage. Then, how did the people in charge of recruiting participants overlook the fact that she was four years short?'

'So, naturally, Sania being the judge, must have come in contact with Prajakta much later,' Dipti made a valid point.

'Correct. I wanted to talk to Sania myself. You two will be coming with me, but keep in mind that no one can know about our assignment. Or the fact that I am doing this show and this episode in particular.'

'But Mr Nimesh Mehta is the line producer for this show. His company is bound to know about it.'

'We will not reveal anything about this particular episode to them as of now. We will use it to our advantage at the right time. Shashank, I want you to draw up a list of all those who were involved in the mini-pageant from Nimesh Mehta's office. Dipti, I want you to work on the look of the episode. Give me a rough line-up. As we get more information, we will fine-tune the flow,' Simran delegated responsibilities to each of them. She then called up Shashank discreetly. 'Hey, you have a bike, right? Let's go for a ride.'

39

A rancid smell clung to the dank walls which housed the incarcerated. Sania was detained in an eight-by-ten-feet lock-up with seven other inmates. Most of them were sex workers or petty thieves or drug pedlars.

The rules and regulations in the police lock-up were not as stringent as the barracks, so Sania was allowed to have visitors. Shamim and Ayub had gone to meet her, carrying her favourite burger from the world's unhealthiest fast-food chain. The way she attacked the burger tore at her mother's heartstrings and a lone tear traced its way down her cheek.

'Gaurav has been trying to mobilize support from his seniors. There is a strong feeling of resentment in the media fraternity. There has been a flood of scornful messages on Facebook,' Ayub told her gravely.

'Keep praying. Allah will protect you, my child,' choked Shamim as tears rolled down her cheeks and Sania kept wiping them gently.

'Be strong, Ammi. I will find a way to get out of this mess. Please don't worry,' Sania gushed with unconvincing optimism.

'Your friend, Simran Thapar, had taken my number yesterday at the court. She called me quite a few times to inquire about you and guide me about how to tackle this situation. She is planning to go to Pune to find out about what happened there,' Ayub shared.

'Who is this guy Gaurav? Why is he so worried about you?' Shamim tried to keep her voice nonchalant, but her curiosity sneaked in.

'You remember Professor Dhanrajgir who used to live in our neighbourhood?' Sania asked her mother. Sania looked a little less pale after eating the meal.

'Is he the professor's son, Gaurav? He has grown so big.'

'He is an IPS officer now. Posted in Bengaluru.'

'But they had left nearly fifteen years ago.'

'We had been in touch all along. Earlier we used to exchange mails.'

'I know about it, Aapa, from Hotmail to Gmail and Orkut to Facebook and now WhatsApp,' Ayub teased, making Sania smile just a little.

'Is he your boyfriend?' Ammi frowned momentarily.

'No, Ammi. I like him and he likes me, but that does not mean we are in a relationship. But yes, I would like to be in a relationship with a man like him, at some point,' Sania told her, hopeful that this crisis would blow over and she would be able to start her life afresh.

Shamim realized that her daughter had metamorphosed into a level-headed mature person and beamed at her with pride. 'The things that you are going through will make you a lot stronger. Take this as a learning experience.'

'No, Ammi. Being wrongfully indicted is not a learning experience,' Ayub confuted. 'They think they can put anyone behind bars in the name of investigation and get away with it. I have spoken to Gaurav, and together, the two of us will expose the people involved in bringing shame to my sister.'

'Oh my little Bhagat Singh, you don't get worked up unduly. I am sure I am being subjected to this because of some wrongdoing I perpetrated. Maybe I caused a lot of anguish to that girl.'

'Aapa, don't you dare feel guilty. You weren't at fault. Don't worry about us. I will take care of things.'

'You have really grown up, Yu-yu,' Sania pulled his cheeks. 'You are behaving like you are my elder brother.' An unintended reference to Sajid deflated Sania's brief moment of happiness. She stared at nothing in particular on the table and blinked back her tears.

Sajid was drumming his fingers impatiently on the dashboard while he waited in Rashid's SUV. Rashid had driven him to the industrial area of Aurangabad without intimating the purpose of this trip. He stopped bobbing his knee when he saw Rashid walking back, cradling a two-litre bottle in his arms.

'Is this acid?' Sajid asked him nervously.

Rashid replied with a smug sinister smile that made Sajid's blood curdle. He saw a minatory cloud settle on Rashid's brow and cloak his prudence. In the last few days, he had quietly observed Rashid's rapid downslide into the quagmire of fanaticism. He could not fathom what had triggered this extreme behaviour.

Dumping the bottle in the boot of his SUV, Rashid spoke as he got into the driver's seat and slammed the door shut. 'You were asking me about the fatwa on Sania Mirza, right? I have the answer to that. There was no one devout enough to carry on that fatwa; otherwise, things would have been very different. Mark my words. When Abbu gets the fatwa this time, we will create history. Our deeds will be honoured.'

'Has Mamujaan discussed this with the *maulvi*, the high priest?' Sajid cut short his daydreaming.

'Of course! Abbu is the last person to make any false claims. I am preparing for that. Even if it doesn't happen, I am getting ready to give this story the end that it deserves.'

'But that flouts the law, Rashid.'

'When you are working for Him,' Rashid pointed upwards, 'there is no other law but His.'

Simran had been trailing Rohit for the last hour on the bike with Shashank. Finding an opportunity, she 'accidentally' bumped into him. 'Hey, Rohit, where the hell have you been?' she crooned and hugged him so tightly that Rohit was bewildered. 'Don't you recognize me?'

'Of course, I do! Simran Thapar, the one who dragged her boyfriend onto the streets,' Rohit sniggered, but Simran remained unaffected.

'I'm flattered to know that you have been keeping tabs on what's happening in my life. Let's grab coffee sometime? My treat,' Simran ambushed him, not giving him a nanosecond to think. 'I read about what happened to Sania. It's a damn shame.' She watched him like a hawk, about to devour its prey.

'Yeah, but she was reckless,' Rohit mumbled uncomfortably.

'By the way, did Sunidhi speak with you?'

'Sunidhi? You mean Karmarkar?'

'Obviously! How many Sunidhis do you know?'

'No, she hasn't. Why do you ask? Is there something I should know?'

'Sunidhi and I have started a TV production company. Just this morning, we were talking about you.'

'What about me? Do you guys want to hire me?' he asked unabashedly.

'We are hiring people, but we want someone with a lot of experience in television. How long have you been in this business?'

'I have been in the television industry for barely three years. I have worked in event management predominantly. I am sure the money in TV is very good.'

'You bet! Why don't you meet Sunidhi?'

'I think it will become messy. Our bosses are too close for comfort. Nimesh sir will not like it if I abandon him to work for Mr Karmarkar. Moreover, Mr Karmarkar would never poach Nimesh sir's staff.'

'Growth opportunities can present themselves from the most unexpected places. You have to be open-minded about it and figure out if you want to be stuck in the rut or aim for something higher.' Simran knew undoubtedly that she had him in the palm of her hand. 'I will line up a meeting with Sunidhi. We will be completely discreet about it,' Simran winked at him, putting his mind at ease. Just as she was about to leave, she leaned in close to him and whispered in his ear, 'Will one be good enough?'

'What one?' Rohit asked her, baffled by her question and distracted by the oriental scent that wafted from her.

'Crore.'

'One would be the minimum I would be looking for if I am taking a jump.'

Go drown in your own piss, you toad-spotted urchin, Simran cursed him in her mind as she gave him a parting smile.

Simran had been given a very small window of time to meet Sania. She wasted no time in getting to the crux of the matter. 'Look, Sania, I am telling you this in strict confidence. I am doing a show in which I will be revealing the truth about this girl's suicide. I want you to be absolutely honest with me, so that I can help you.'

'I was honest even the last time when you had recorded me on a hidden camera.'

'I know, Sania; can't you let bygones be bygones now?'

'I am in a quicksand, so I will latch onto even a straw at this point. I have no choice but to trust you.'

'Do you know why Shikha has taken such an intense hatred towards you? I mean, she has accused you for her sister's death and even filed a police complaint against you.'

'She was staying in my house.'

'I know that. Did something go wrong between the two of you?'

'In her complaint, she stated that I doubted she was having an affair with my dad.'

'What? Why would she make such an allegation?' Simran was flabbergasted.

'I caught her red-handed with my dad,' Sania told her in a trembling voice. 'I never brought it up, but she thinks I took my revenge by bullying her sister and pushing her over the edge.' Unable to hold it together any longer, Sania set all her supressed emotions free. Even though she didn't let it on with her family, she felt terribly helpless. And Simran saw it.

'I will do whatever it takes to get you out of this,' she promised Sania, her voice cracking with feeling. Simran realized that whatever had transpired was not as simple as it appeared to be.

'Did you have a scene with Shikha?' Simran asked Shiraz, point blank. Her questions made him so acutely uncomfortable that his first reaction was to tell her to get lost. But Simran held her ground. She always preferred to grab the bull by its horns and toss it down.

'I know something happened. I don't know how grave it was but whatever it was, I am afraid you will have to be honest if you are serious about saving your daughter,' Simran told him bluntly.

'How will this piece of information help save my daughter? You think I am some teenybopper who will buy your silly argument?'

'Whether you like it or not, you are mentioned in the complaint filed by Shikha against Sania. So, if you...'

'What?' Shiraz interrupted Simran.

'The complaint document is a fifteen-page-long thesis which is written in Marathi.'

'I will tell the truth and only the truth to you. You can make whatever you want of it. By the way, are you the lawyer who is going to be defending Sania?'

'Yes, I am the advocate's assistant,' Simran lied, desperate to reach to the bottom of this.

'I had just returned from Dubai that fateful day. I had got some gifts for Sania and Shikha. As soon as Sania left for Pune for work, Shikha came to my room and woke me up. I told her I was too sleepy and that I had a terrible body ache. So, she offered to give me a massage, claiming that she was really good at it. I was very reluctant, but she was insistent,' Shiraz told her defensively. 'As it is, she was dressed provocatively and easing the tension from my body, so I just did not stop her. Suddenly, she started doing some weird things and I was taken aback. I'll admit that I was a little aroused, but I was in complete control of myself. As luck would have it, Sania walked in on us at that very moment. She hasn't spoken to me ever since. I tried to contact her in every possible way, but she refuses to answer my calls or read my texts. To be honest, I have been seeing Shikha's mother, Gurpreet, for a while now. It seems Shikha got to know about us and is giving her mother a lot of flak for it as well.'

'If need be, are you willing to repeat this statement in front of people?'

'I will do anything, anything to save my daughter,' Shiraz broke down.

'Please do not worry, sir. Please stop crying,' she told him awkwardly.

'Sania is the apple of my eye. If she is going through this hell because of me, I would rather end my life.'

'Don't ever say that again,' Simran told him firmly. 'Any such step will harm her even more. Whenever you get the chance, confess all your sins to her. She will forgive you.'

40

'He's already here. I am talking to him about the job responsibilities he has been entrusted with at Nimesh Mehta's office. Once you reach the office, buzz me or just come over to the conference room,' Sunidhi spoke into her phone. 'It was Simran. She wanted to meet you as well. She will join us in a few minutes. Anyway, you were telling me about your responsibilities for the event that was organized at Pune,' Sunidhi prompted Rohit.

Rohit was the kind of person who auctioned his loyalty to the highest bidder. For now, it was Sunidhi, but if a better offer came along, he would switch sides in a heartbeat.

'Like I told you, I usually oversee the entire operations. Right from venue selection to the final draw of contestants to finalizing the hosts and handling the suppliers, sound, lights, decoration—every little thing that goes into organizing an event.'

'So, you are virtually in charge of the complete production.'

'Sunidhi ma'am, the production manager reports to me. I am in charge of the complete operations. I am the COO, as is mentioned on my business card that I handed to you. Apart from that, I manage Nimesh sir's daily routine. He has a secretary, but she also acts on my consent only.'

'That's quite a handful. How much are you drawing, if I may ask?'

'Whatever figure I tell you, can be easily cross-checked with Nimesh sir by Mr Karmarkar, so I will tell you the truth. I get almost ₹3.5 lakh per month, but I make a good amount on the side.'

'Under the table?' Sunidhi quizzed.

'Simran madam told me the package will be roughly ₹1 crore. Once I get that kind of money, I won't need to take cuts. I hope you understand.'

'But of course, Rohit.' Sunidhi didn't know how or where to take the conversation any further, so she just sat with a polite smile plastered on her face. Sunidhi was saved by a knock on the door.

'Hi, Rohit. So how's it going?' Simran pitched in, sensing that Sunidhi was struggling to keep the conversation going.

'Rohit was just telling me about his job profile. And he also spoke about the Pune event.'

'Don't even talk about the Pune event,' Simran scoffed. 'It is being hailed as the biggest botch up of the decade in event management companies. I think they goofed up big time,' Simran intentionally brushed it off.

'No, I would like to clarify that there was no goof-up at all,' Rohit disagreed.

'Then how was Sania arrested? There must have been slip-ups,' Simran goaded him.

'Actually, Sania asked for trouble. She was clinging to her stiff-necked pride of following principles, so Nimesh sir taught her a lesson. In a country like India, if you are so uptight about adhering to regulations, you will never be able to organize any event.'

'Tell me something, that girl Prajakta and Sania had a fight, but where did Prajakta go after that fight? I heard you took her somewhere in that black Merc which is Nimesh sir's, I think,' Simran cleverly engaged Rohit in the conversation.

'See, this is very confidential stuff. I don't know why this girl committed suicide, but Nimesh sir was very harsh with her. I told him so many times that she is too young and easily alarmed, don't frighten her so much. But he was very angry with her and when he is angry, he is like a raging bull on a rampage.'

'What exactly did Nimesh sir do?'

'Simran madam, I don't think...'

'Oh, never mind. We will not talk about something that you are not comfortable sharing. I was thinking of making him meet Mr Karmarkar,' Simran discreetly winked at Sunidhi.

'Definitely! So we can keep him in the loop. Let me call...'

'Don't you think we should go to his cabin?' Simran interrupted, but Sunidhi gave her a leave-it-to-me look and phoned her dad. 'Pops, can you please drop by the conference room?'

Simran excused herself and stepped out of the conference room. She briskly paced towards Karmarkar's cabin and saw him emerging. 'Sir, you just have to nod in agreement. Let Sunidhi and me do the talking, and please make it look natural,' Simran briefed him.

'What is happening? What jugglery are you guys up to?' Karmarkar wondered out loud before entering the conference room.

Simran followed behind and almost giggled when she saw Rohit shoot up like an arrow on seeing Karmarkar. 'Good evening, sir.'

'Good evening. Aren't you Nimesh's right-hand man, Rohit?'

Rohit nodded with fervour, his ego more inflated than before on finding out that Karmarkar knew him by name.

'We are planning to get Rohit on board for our TV production house,' Sunidhi explained.

'We might be taking him on,' Simran hurriedly added, giving Karmarkar a hint.

'That's great!' Karmarkar caught on. 'But won't Nimesh be upset?'

'I think you can handle that. You can explain to him that we want, no, we *need* Rohit very badly,' Sunidhi told him eagerly.

'But right now, please don't tell him anything,' Simran added.

'All the best and welcome aboard, Rohit,' played along Karmarkar.

'Once we have finalized the terms and conditions, sir,' Simran added carefully to give an authentic feel.

Karmarkar nodded and took his leave. Rohit looked like a child who had been given the key to Candyland. Little did he know that Simran would be waiting to make him pay for his gluttony.

After practically 'living' at the Dastak office for three years, Simran had mixed feelings about going back there again after a gap of almost four months. She was looking forward to meeting some of her old colleagues but not Gul. She had not forgiven him for his monumental part in the sting-op fiasco that had happened. But she knew that she could not hold a grudge against him for a lifetime.

'Let us meet Gul first,' suggested Sunidhi, who was walking along with Simran.

'No, I will head straight to the studio floor. I won't meet him in his cabin. He doesn't deserve that much importance or respect. If he wants, he can come and meet me on the floor,' said Simran stiffly.

Simran met Divya and Jatin who were the only ones left from the earlier ensemble. At complete ease with the cameras, Simran posed for stills as instructed by the director and cameraman. Next, they shot a promo for the show on a blue screen.

'When truth is kept hidden, the world crumbles with the burden of lies. This is *A Moment of Truth*,' Simran mouthed the words for the promo, but she didn't seem convinced by the hyperbolic language used in those lines. 'What are the other line options?' she asked one of the assistants, who handed her a sheet of paper.

'In times where views are sold as news and beliefs are packaged as facts, let's face *A Moment of Truth*,' she read out loud from the paper. 'Shortlist this one.' Simran got a prickling sensation at the nape of her neck, the kind she got when she was being watched. She looked up and found Gul standing barely three feet away from her. 'Hey, when did you come here? I didn't even see you come in,' Simran spoke in a characteristically phlegmatic manner.

'Am I too small and diminutive to be noticed now?' Gul jested but didn't garner any response in his favour.

'No, you are obscure.' Simran bit back an expletive and Gul forcibly laughed her comment off.

'How have you been? Long time, no see, no hear,' Gul side-hugged Simran who stood stiffly and gave him a tight-lipped smile.

'Ok, first things first. The show should be called something else. *A Moment of Truth* sounds too heavy and grim. What do you say, Sunidhi?' asked Gul.

'I agree,' Sunidhi seconded him.

'In fact, I have already discussed it with Sunidhi and we both have thought of renaming it *The Simran Thapar Show*,' Gul announced. His revelation was met with a half-hearted applause from the unit. 'So is it decided?' Gul looked at Simran expectantly.

But she had an inscrutable mask in place. Gul was immediately nervous and his mind was in a flurry; he did not know whether it had gone down well with Simran or not. Sunidhi shot her an inquisitive look, but Simran just shrugged indifferently.

'It's final then, we will be called *The Simran Thapar Show*,' Sunidhi declared with glee and the team cheered with excitement.

'Please shoot the promos accordingly,' Gul directed them; he had to have the final say.

'Hello, at least have the courtesy to ask for my opinion about it,' opposed Simran in a lighter vein. 'Won't it become a personality-driven show if we renamed it to that? What if I can't live up to those expectations?' Simran voiced her self-doubt.

'Simran, we feel that you connect very well with the audience. You are strong and vibrant; that will be the show's USP,' Sunidhi encouraged Simran.

'You are firebrand,' praised Gul.

'You are not going to start airing the promos till I give you the go-ahead. I hope that is very clear,' warned Simran and looked at Gul for an acknowledgement, who simply nodded and raised his hands in submission.

Shikha had not responded to Simran's calls or messages in over twenty-four hours. But Simran was now armed with some clinching information that she didn't have before. She had taken Gurpreet's contact details from Shiraz as a backup plan, just in case Shikha chose to ignore her.

'Dipti, you will accompany Simran in her car. I want you to be in constant touch with me, updating me about all the big and small developments. Shashank, you take your bike and reach Pune. Your mobility will come in handy.' Sunidhi was delegating duties to those two while Simran was busy making notes on her tablet.

There were several times when Sunidhi felt like she had been relegated to a facilitator. Every time an insidious thought like that creeped into her mind, she squashed it with undebatable rationale.

But isn't this the job profile of a producer? At least get one show on air first, then you can see what you want to do further.

Shashank and Dipti were watching footage of the mini-pageant with Simran in the backseat of her SUV. The vehicle was parked in a lane that led to Shikha's house. 'This one here is Sachin and this is Payal,' Dipti pointed out.

'Why did Rohit help you organize this footage?' asked Shashank, puzzled.

'Because I have given him an offer he can't refuse,' said Simran, trying to pull a Marlon Brando. She suddenly shushed everyone in the car. She had spotted Shikha.

Simran dialled Shikha's number and watched her. Shikha removed her phone from her handbag and disconnected the call when she saw who it was. She crossed the SUV and continued walking, looking for an auto-rickshaw. Simran asked the driver to follow her.

Shikha hailed an auto-rickshaw and was just about to get into it when Simran emerged out of her SUV and called out her name. Shikha turned around to see who it was and immediately rushed into the auto.

'Leave immediately,' Shikha ordered the rickshaw driver as she craned her neck behind to look for Simran, not knowing that she was jumping into the rickshaw from the other side.

'I need to talk to you, Shikha,' Simran told her with urgency.

'Have you been stalking me?' Shikha asked her, annoyed.

'It's a question of Sania's life. She will be ruined if we don't act.'

'Why do I care? I don't want to talk to you. Get lost!'

'Shikha, I know what has happened. I know everything that has happened, every damn thing.'

'You don't know jackshit, Simran. Just leave me the hell alone,' Shikha yelled.

'I know what happened between you and Sania's dad, and I know what is going on between your mom and Sania's dad as well,' Simran told her in a frighteningly calm and even voice. Shikha gulped and

Simran hooked her claws into her emotions and apprehensions. 'Shikha, I want you to understand we are dealing with a much bigger villain here. I have clinching evidence with me. He is someone who will keep devouring young and gullible girls like Prajakta and scapegoating innocents like Sania and you to his advantage. We need to stop him.'

'I am not interested in your big talk. You tried to expose his wicked ways before as well but what happened? You got exposed, not him,' Shikha resisted.

'Just tell me one thing, do you want justice for what happened to Prajakta?'

'Dead people get no justice.'

'On the contrary, the biggest irony in our country is that till the time you are alive, no one cares for you, but once you are dead, people revere you and cling onto your memory for as long as they can.'

Shikha kept quiet as Simran's words washed over her and stirred repressed emotions. All the anguish and agony she had bottled up inside her ruptured forth and crushed her. The sobs ripped through her uncontrollably, and felt like they were shredding her muscles and splintering her bones. She clutched onto her chest with her hand and felt her heart press into her lungs and explode into a million shards. 'I have done a gross injustice to Prajakta. I don't deserve to live. Poor girl, she didn't know what she was doing. She was so n...naïve and s...stupid,' Shikha hiccupped inconsolably. 'Prajakta was in a hurry to achieve success, j...just like me. I should have understood her weakness, but I did not. Even after she died, I did shallow and petty things. I... I...h...have sold my s...soul.'

Simran wrapped her arms around Shikha and held her close. 'Don't blame yourself for what happened, Shikha. 'Let's go somewhere quiet and discuss this. It still isn't too late for retribution. Do you want to go to a coffee shop?'

'No. Let's go to my house instead, if you don't mind.'

Shikha's house told the saga of a recent loss. A sense of despair hung in the air which was punctuated with sporadic bursts of sobs. It was just four days ago that Prajakta had given up on her will to live. Gurpreet went about her household chores listlessly. She would never be able to forgive herself for not understanding her daughter's state of mind that night—the person who she had nursed inside her, for whom her hips had cracked, with whom she was literally connected with a tangible bond for nine glorious months.

Meanwhile, Shikha's youngest sister, Shilpi, was removing clothes from the cupboard and trying them on. She put on a dress which was too big on her and spilled over her little arms and down to her shins. 'Mummy, at least now I can wear Prajakta didi's dress?'

Gurpreet gagged herself with her dupatta just to stop herself from screaming.

Shikha walked into her home at that very moment, opening the door with her set of keys. Shilpi repeated the question to Shikha.

'Yes, you can. Now go inside and leave us alone,' Shikha told her coldly.

But Shilpi's curiosity had piqued when she saw Simran, and she followed them into the room. 'Hello, Shikha didi's friend. I am Shilpi. My other sister has gone somewhere, so I will get all her clothes now,' she said delightedly.

'Shilpi, go inside,' Shikha commanded, thoroughly disturbed with what her little sister had just said.

Simran was equally appalled, but she indicated to Shikha to calm down. As Simran looked around the house, she realized Shikha's financial plight. Though it was no excuse for engaging in the kind of behaviour Shikha did, Simran finally understood why she did them.

As she looked around the room, she spotted pictures of Prajakta, along with her other belongings which gave her an insight into the aspirations the teenager had. Her eyes swept over the ceiling fan and they brimmed with tears. But she held them back.

'I am shitting bricks, man,' Sunidhi looked really nervous, sending alarm signals to Simran who knew that this girl was just out of a trauma. *I hope Sunidhi doesn't have a breakdown,* a thought crossed Simran's mind. With the channel announcing it as a live show there was bound to be a lot more pressure on the producer.

'Don't let the live telecast thing bother you. It is the headache of the technicians. We have your dad on the show now. It will be smooth,' Simran tried to pacify her.

'Exactly! That is why I am stressed, babes. With dad sitting on the dais, I will not be able to manage it smoothly at all.'

'I will be there to take care of any untoward things. Your production team is all geared up I hope.'

'Yep!'

41

'Bounce the light. Put one multi to the right of centre stage. Tilt the HMI.' The director of photography was giving instructions to his light assistants on the shooting floor. The set had been designed to give the live audience and technicians a clear view of the stage. There were eight cameras that would simultaneously capture all the action. The online editor had the impossibly difficult task of juggling eight visual feeds at once and deciding which best shot to keep.

Sunidhi was on her walkie-talkie. 'We will be rolling in a couple of minutes.' She looked proudly at the impressive set on the floor and felt a frisson of excitement shiver through her. This was going to be the first episode of the show, and her very first episode as a producer. The unprecedented hype that the show had built had attracted a huge crowd. Every single seat in the audience was occupied.

'I came for this only because you insisted,' Nimesh Mehta told Karmarkar in a blatantly disgruntled voice inside the green room. They were both being preened by the make-up man.

'I couldn't think of a better way to encourage the kids. Having somebody like you on their show would give them a boost.' Karmarkar did not evince any overt involvement in the happenings as he pandered to Nimesh's ego.

'I agree, but I'm not in the right mental state for this. The media has been hounding me mercilessly after that Pune incident.'

'But why do you have to get flustered? You don't have anything to worry about, do you? Let the media do their job and you do yours.' Karmarkar prodded Nimesh's psyche.

'You know how it is, Yogesh. They will judge a book by its cover.'

'But in your case, the cover itself has as much content as the book. They will never get to read the actual book.'

'Why are you pulling my leg, Yogesh? I am an ordinary man,'

Nimesh complained before they heard a knock on the door. 'Nimesh sir and Mr Karmarkar, you will be required to come on stage very shortly,' Dipti informed them.

Chivalrous as ever, Karmarkar got up and greeted her. 'We are ready, young lady,' Karmarkar dimpled, making Dipti blush furiously. 'Ma'am, I am getting the panellists on the floor,' she spoke into her walkie-talkie.

'Full lights,' the director called out and the studio floor became brighter. The audience sat up a straighter. There was loud clapping and cheering as Nimesh Mehta walked to his seat on the right side of the stage, followed by Karmarkar. One seat remained vacant, next to Karmarkar.

The left side of the stage illuminated and Simran walked in energetically to a deafening round of applause.

'They say beauty is skin deep and ugly is to the bone. Can one of you explain what this phrase means?' Simran charged at the show head-on, without wasting any time on formal introductions. 'You?' Simran asked a young man, but he shook his head.

Simran passed on the mike to a petite girl who had raised her hand. 'It means that it doesn't matter how physically attractive you are, if you have an ugly personality, it will emanate from you like a foul stench that you can't shake off, and no cosmetic procedures or perfumes will be able to hide that.'

'Well said,' Simran acknowledged the girl as the audience applauded her. 'In the first episode of this show, we will try and understand beauty in its entirety. We will be talking about the beauty business or if I may take the liberty to rephrase it, the ugly beauty business and whether it is surreptitiously eroding societal values. To debate this hot and sensitive issue, we have on our panel Mr Nimesh Mehta, arguably the most renowned name in beauty pageants across the country today. And giving him company is the man we all know as the media mogul of India, Mr Yogesh Karmarkar.'

The audience welcomed them on stage amidst a round of applause.

'Okay, Mr Nimesh Mehta, I would want to know from you what

beauty is. And what according to you are the criteria for someone to be called "beautiful"?'

'Hello, everyone. I feel beauty is a very subjective concept. As they say, beauty lies in the eyes of the beholder, so what I may define as "beautiful" might not be for someone else. One man's food can be another man's poison,' Mehta replied easily.

There was a slight murmur in the audience, but he remained unperturbed.

'So, you think there is a hunger for beauty in the public at large?'

'I am sure there is.'

'Are food and beauty co-related according to you?' Simran intentionally played with the words.

'No, I quoted that for want of an expression. Beauty actually is much more sublime, something which is inside everyone—inner beauty.'

'Is that why you have a swimwear round in your pageants where girls are made to parade in bikinis? So you can assess their inner beauty?'

The audience laughed a mouthful and Mehta gave an uncomfortable smile.

'Mr Mehta, what are the criteria for calling someone beautiful in your pageants?'

'To call someone beautiful, we do follow certain criteria, which include natural facial beauty, a well-maintained body, confidence and poise, and of course, the presence of mind and intelligence.'

'So, how do you find a girl's level of intelligence? Do you conduct some IQ tests?'

'Not really. If we do an IQ test, it might not give very good results.'

'So, you pick up girls who are not very bright and compare their intelligence or rather their lack of it, with girls who are even more dull-witted. Is that what you are implying?'

Why is Simran dumbing herself down so much? What the hell is she trying to do? Sunidhi wondered, watching the developments from the console room.

'I am sorry, but I would not like my girls to be called dull-witted. According to me, beauty is much higher than genius. The fact that it needs no introduction or explanation is proof enough. It can make the most powerful men weak in their knees, and make them kneel in awe. Beauty has that much strength and cannot be questioned. To me, a woman's beauty is the biggest wonder of the world.' Mehta seemed to have found his voice and the audience loved every word that came out of his mouth.

Simran gulped and exchanged a look with Karmarkar, remembering his words of caution. *Do your homework extensively.* Sunidhi was tempted to use the talkback and tell Simran to go on the offensive, but she refrained.

'But in your quest to give beauty a higher plinth than genius, isn't beauty getting reduced to a commodity?' Simran had found her bearings again.

'Says who?'

'Statistics, Mr Mehta. Statistics! There are an increasing number of beauty stores opening by the day, while bookstores are steadily shutting down. The sales of fairness creams are higher than ever before.'

'I am strongly against fairness creams. I feel they encourage a racist attitude in society. You will never find any of those brands, even as a co-sponsor, in any of my events.' More applause ensued for Mehta's comment.

Simran realized that she was playing into Mehta's hands, so she diverted her attention to the other panellist. 'Mr Karmarkar, do you think the beauty pageant industry is one of the reasons why women are seen as objects of desire?'

'I wouldn't think of it so reductively. These days, there are plenty of platforms for men as well where they are ogled at in equal measure,' Karmarkar replied.

'Fair enough. But it is a fact that 91 per cent of adult rape victims are females and women are nine times more likely to be victims of sexual harassment as opposed to men. Aren't women getting the short end of the stick?'

'I am afraid that is a problem with the way women are perceived in our society at large. In a nation steeped in patriarchy, I don't know how we can break away from this vicious mentality and make room for positive change, but I am willing to do my bit in bringing about change.' Karmarkar's egalitarian speech was lauded with emphatic cheers from the crowd.

'And Mr Mehta, do you think we need a change?' Simran turned her gaze back to Nimesh.

'Why not? Change is always welcome. But who will bring about the change? Everyone simply talks the talk, but no one really walks the talk. And realistically speaking, no such change can drastically alter the perception of society.'

'If someone told you to stop these pageants because it would definitely bring about a change, would you shut them down, Mr Mehta?'

'Why should I stop something that is running so successfully? Look, Simran, girls are so crazy about being crowned beautiful that they will do anything to get there. If I don't cash in on the craze, someone else will.'

'So, you admit that you are cashing in?'

'Not in the sense that you are trying to imply. I have made it into a successful business model, and now, I have the world at my feet. What else could an entrepreneur want?'

Simran switched gears and headed back to the audience. 'Friends, now I have a question for you. What kind of women would you like to see in the glamour industry?'

The enthusiastic audience started shouting out answers all at once.

'Young!'

'Hot!'

'Sexy!'

'Good-looking!'

There were some who had their hands raised.

Simran went up to a guy in his twenties and held the mike in front of him. 'I want to see women with very good figures,' he said, while tracing an hourglass shape in the air with his hands. He evoked a raucous laugh from the audience, but Simran was not amused.

'I would like to see all types of women—young, old, short, tall, portly, puny, straight-haired, curly haired, wrinkled, radiant—and not just the ones that are labelled "beautiful" by the media and fashion industry,' said a woman from the audience. She took her seat amidst bravos and cheers from all her female counterparts.

'But overall, definitely anyone would prefer young and good-looking women...' another man stood up and countered her.

'So, you all want to see young and beautiful women,' Simran interjected. 'But how young is the question?' Simran immediately had their attention.

'Twenty-one!'

'Whenever the girl gets a break!'

'Nineteen!'

'After the twelveth standard!'

'Twenty-two!'

'Once she has finished her studies!'

'Seventeen!'

Random answers emerged from the audience.

'Don't you want to see a girl as young as fourteen or fifteen, when her youth is just bursting forth? When she looks very fresh, vulnerable and nubile?' Simran's question caused a stir of murmurs and mutterings in the audience, but no one spoke up for a couple of minutes.

An adorable bespectacled girl got up and paused a beat before voicing her opinion. 'I think the audience has this morbid urge to see young girls who are just in their early teens, because they are naïve and easy to fleece. With the kind of lecherous men that are there around us, it is not easy growing up as a girl in India.'

'Hang in there, sweetheart.' Simran offered her a sympathetic smile before doing an about turn and marching towards the panel. 'Mr Karmarkar, what are your views on young girls being lured into the glamour industry?'

'The fault lies on both sides,' Karmarkar said contemplatively.

'Parents are also unable to refuse the tempting offers they get from rapacious producers or opportunistic agents who want to launch these young faces. Having said that, the system needs to be stringent about the age factor, because I believe minors are at a higher risk of being adversely affected by this experience, if things go wrong. Moreover, it would be equivalent to child labour.'

'You make a good point, Mr Karmarkar. Hold onto that thought. We will come back to it. I would quickly like to take this particular point to the audience,' said Simran, spinning around again. Audience, I want you to quickly tell me what is the age at which we get a driving license.'

'Eighteen!' they shouted in a chorus.

'And a voter's card?'

'Eighteen!' they responded in unison again.

'And what is the age at which you become lawfully eligible to get married?'

'Eighteen!' the group chanted.

'And you are not even allowed to consume alcohol before you are...'

'Eighteen!' they repeated.

'Actually, in India, you get a drinking permit as an individual only once you turn twenty-one,' Simran corrected them. 'In fact, in some of the states, it is twenty-five!'

The audience booed their disapproval of that fact.

'So what is the bottom line? You, the curvy-figure fellow,' Simran picked on the guy who had used the same hand gesture that he had used a while ago.

The audience was regaled.

'The bottom line is that we get to do everything only after we are eighteen, at least officially that is. Unofficially, it depends on us,' he retorted cheekily, making the audience laugh yet again.

Simran now pinned her gaze on Mehta who was feeling more and more like a sitting duck with every passing question. 'Yes, Mr. Mehta, I know you are eager to give your views, but I thought I should create the right atmosphere for you first,' Simran addressed him archly. 'Mr Mehta, please correct me if I am wrong, but doesn't your beauty pageant also have a minimum age limit for participation?'

Mehta nodded his response.

'Terrific. Let's get straight to it then. Mr Mehta, if you remember, you had mentioned earlier that the beauty business is a "game of fillers".'

'Game of fillers? I have never made such a statement.'

'Have you mentioned it otherwise? I mean among your own people?'

'No, I have never used that phrase. By the way, what does it mean?' Nimesh asked innocently, making Simran chuckle.

'You are funny, Mr Mehta. Don't worry! I will refresh your memory.' Simran signalled to the console room and the lights were dimmed down.

A big screen in the studio began to play a clip. It was an off-camera conversation between Mehta and Simran that had been captured.

'*This business is very tricky. Jo dikhta hai vo bikta nahi aur jo nahin dikhta vo bikta hai.* What you see doesn't sell, and what you don't see sells.'

'What do you mean by that?'

'A beauty pageant is a game of fillers.'

'How so?'

'You will get it at some point. You're quite sharp. In fact, you're the perfect combination of beauty and brains. Why don't you compete in my beauty pageant? You will win hands down.'

'How can you be so sure of that?'

'I will give you a position in the final five, straightaway. From there on, it will all just be a formality.'

'Are you making me a proposition, Mr Mehta?'

'How much more clearly can I spell it out for you?'

As the video clipping ended and the lights came on, Mehta's face had paled significantly.

'What do you have to say to that, Mr Mehta? I hope you will

not accuse us of doctoring those tapes,' Simran challenged him.

'You have shot this without my knowledge. You cannot broadcast this here without my permission,' Mehta snapped.

'It was an accident, sir. The camera was on and no one realized. I am sure you wouldn't have parted with these gems otherwise.'

It slowly dawned on Mehta that his decision to go to the mat would get his face slammed on the mat.

'So, friends,' Simran continued purposefully, 'at this juncture I would like to bring in someone who can shed some more light on this game of fillers, Miss Shikha Azgaonkar!'

Shikha walked on to the stage confidently and took a seat next to Karmarkar. Simran made the introductions between the panellists. Karmarkar acknowledged Shikha courteously, while Mehta shifted in his seat uncomfortably. Simran couldn't resist the chance to prod him further. 'Mr Mehta, do you need a hand fan? You seem to be sweating profusely.'

'No, I am absolutely fine,' Mehta glared at her.

'Shikha, could you fill us in about this "filler" business?' Simran emphasized.

'Where do I start, Simran? In beauty pageants, out of the twenty-five finalists every year, only four or five girls get somewhere and are able to sustain themselves through good, legitimate work. Giving another five or six of them the benefit of doubt, the remaining fifteen finalists are mere fillers, year after year. They are selected to merely fill the vacant slots in the first place,' Shikha revealed gravely.

Rankled by her words, Mehta looked like he wanted to cut in, but Shikha didn't let him.

'Resourceful, cunning and immoral guys, like Nimesh Mehta, have a well-oiled machinery in place,' Shikha glowered at Mehta and continued. 'They keep a track of these fillers, constantly monitoring them and maintaining a vigil. As soon as these girls start feeling low and frustrated with life, a discreet offer makes its way to them. Slowly but surely, they are brainwashed to walk the immoral path. It's a big, bad world of sin from there on—shopping in Dubai and London with sheikhs, escorting top businessmen and industrialists, entertaining foreign delegates and politicians. If you cross-check what the finalists in the last eight or ten years are doing right now, you will be shocked!'

'So, Mehta must be making a hefty packet for himself through these "filler" girls?'

'He makes much more money through the fillers than he makes in his legitimate businesses, that too in cash, tax free.'

'Who is this two-penny girl? On what basis is she spouting this crap?' Mehta raged back.

'This two-penny girl is the one you wanted to screw in your hotel room when you were caught with your pants down. Mr Karmarkar, weren't you there on that day as well? Don't you dare call me a two-penny girl, you glorified pimp.'

'Have you paid her to say these lies?' Mehta looked at Simran accusingly, while he was terrified to death on the inside. 'I refuse to take this shit!' Mehta sprung out of his seat and stormed off. Simran rushed to face one of the cameras and announced a break.

42

As he walked out, a flabbergasted Mehta looked at Karmarkar desperately and searched his face for an indication of whether or not he was a part of this carefully designed trickery. Although Karmarkar's expression was unreadable, he was remembering how after watching the visuals, Simran had procured that he was left dumbstruck.

'I can't believe this guy has gone so far. You tell me how I can help to get rid of him permanently.' A visibly upset Karmarkar had told Simran.

'I want him on the show. I want to expose him in front of the world for what he truly is.' Simran was fuming. All her pent-up feelings were coming to the fore in the show.

'We spoke with him, of course, without revealing what we have found. He refused to come in front of the camera. He said that at this juncture it does not make sense for him to be in the limelight and since it is a beauty pageant-related show, he wants to avoid it altogether,' Sunidhi had told her father while her eyes pleaded for his help.

'I have a feeling if you come on the show, even he will agree,' Simran had dared to invite Karmarkar himself. Sunidhi was surprised by her head-on approach, but she remained mum to see how he would react.

Karmarkar remembered how he had deliberated for a moment before he told them, 'I have done so much to create a monster like him. I will do whatever I can to put a leash on him, if not destroy him. But let me forewarn you, he is one wily fox. If you don't tie up all the loose ends tightly, he will turn the tables on you. Do your homework extensively.'

'Fuck! What do we do now?' Sunidhi asked Simran on the talkback as she rushed towards the shooting floor.

'We need to talk to your dad. Hurry!' Simran's ears hummed with hyperactivity.

'We are in a live telecast. Six minutes is the maximum amount of time we can defer the transmission for. We have lost more than two minutes already,' the director explained to Simran and Sunidhi frantically. No sooner had he finished his sentence than Simran ran towards Karmarkar's room, dragging Sunidhi along with her.

'Don't get worked up,' Karmarkar told them coolly, while sipping on a steaming cup of chamomile green tea. 'Nimesh is too gutless to go against my word and leave.'

'Can you please come with us and speak to him? He refuses to talk to us,' Sunidhi pleaded. 'Please, sir, we are extremely short on time,' Simran's sense of urgency made Karmarkar move.

'Okay, let's go to his room,' Karmarkar gave in.

'I want that whore to apologize to me in front of the audience, on camera. Only then will I agree to come back.' Mehta was in no mood to relent.

'Okay, I will go and talk to her. You guys please get ready till then.' Simran didn't want to waste a single second.

'I most certainly will not. He is a rotten piece of shit.' Shikha fumed.

'Please hear me out, Shikha. If we don't nail this bastard today, Prajakta will never get justice. He is too powerful. With his slimy connections, he can get away with anything. You have my word that we will edit that bit out before we stream it. I would never ask you to do this otherwise, not after all the things that moron has done. Please, Shikha, we are running out of time,' Simran tried to reason with her friend. Seeing the desperate but determined look on Simran's face, Shikha caved in.

The show was rolling again with all the panellists in their seats. In fact, an extra chair was placed next to Shikha, and Rohit occupied it.

Before we start our next segment, I have a special announcement to make. Simran nodded in Shikha's direction.

'I would like to take back some of the things I said to Mr Nimesh Mehta,' said Shikha with a saccharine smile. 'He is not a glorified pimp, but he is a pimp all the same.'

'What the hell is this, Simran?' Mehta hollered.

'Cut it!' Simran shouted. 'Shikha, please do not stretch this. I beg of you.'

'Fine. Are we rolling?'

'Roll cameras,' Simran shouted.

'Rolling!' one of the cameramen shouted back.

'Action!' Simran prompted Shikha.

'I apologize for using a derogatory term for Mr Nimesh Mehta,' Shikha said coldly, not looking one bit apologetic for what she said. But it did the needful and pacified Mehta.

'Thank you, Shikha. Now let's get on with our show. Welcome back, viewers! As some of you may have noticed, we have a new guest on the panel. Hello, Rohit,' Simran greeted him. 'Rohit Mehra has been working with Mr Nimesh Mehta for the past eleven years and virtually running his entire business. You could say he is the COO and CEO.'

There was a lukewarm applause from the audience.

'Hi, everyone. I'd like to start off by saying that what Shikha has said is not even 1 per cent true,' confessed Rohit, startling everyone.

Simran was quaking in her heels but did well to mask the devastation she felt inside, like all her plans had been torpedoed.

A smug smile was resurfacing on Mehta's face when Rohit spoke up once again. 'I am sorry, what I meant was that it is not even 1 per cent of the truth.'

Mehta's semi-smile froze midway and he glowered at Rohit with utter scorn. Rohit avoided Mehta's gaze.

'Mr Nimesh Mehta has a controlling stake in Chrysalis,' Rohit added.

'You mean the chain of cosmetic surgery clinics across India?'

'The fact is we actually wheedle and coax young girls who come to participate in the pageants. We convince them that if they get a nose job or a face lift or breast reshaping done, they will have a better chance in the pageant. Especially, if they get it done at Chrysalis. The girls are so obsessed with the way they look that they arrange for money by either blackmailing their parents or doing some unbelievable things.'

'So, if I had come to you, Rohit, what would you have advised me?'

'How can I say that, Simran madam? But I want to make a confession,' Rohit announced grimly. 'I have been a part of this gory business that Mr Mehta has established. I didn't know how this was impacting young gullible girls till I saw what you showed me.' Rohit didn't care about the repercussions he would have to face for his breach of silence, but he needed to atone for now.

Simran muttered a few instructions in her talkback. The lights were dulled again and the screen lit up with visuals.

'These are the girls who were cosmetically treated in Chrysalis. I want all of you to see the extent to which their cosmetic surgeries were botched up,' Simran narrated as a silent film played on the screen.

The film introduced enchanting young girls who were breathtakingly beautiful but had gone under the knife. They had come out with such unsightly distortions that they had attempted to end their lives. The audience was shocked into a silence.

When the lights came back on, a furious Mehta who was feeling cheated, fulminated completely. 'What are you trying to prove?' he demanded furiously with bulging eyes.

'I am just showcasing your achievements, Mr Mehta,' Simran batted her eyelids innocently.

'If there are some cases which have gone bad, there are hundreds which have been successful. Why don't you show the successful ones? How would my business prosper if my clientele wasn't satisfied?'

'Mr Mehta, at least twenty-five of them got your attention when they approached you with a lawyer, but the others weren't valuable enough to earn your time.'

'I don't think I am doing anything wrong. Whatever they have done, they have done of their own free will and accord. All these girls are over eighteen, legitimate adults. Each one of them had signed a contract which explicitly mentioned that Chrysalis would not be held responsible for any unforeseen mishaps. Can you prove anything in a court of law?'

'That's where we are headed, Mr Mehta, the court of law. You definitely know your last year's winner, Sania Ahmed. Don't you? In fact, she is going to be presented in the court of law later this week for her bail application, which has been turned down twice already. Why? We don't know. Why she was arrested in the first place is a mystery in itself. She has been held for abetting the suicide of a fourteen-year-old girl. We thought you could throw some light on that.'

'I don't want to comment on sub judice matters. Let the law take its own course,' Mehta told her coldly.

'The law will take its own course, but the media has to do what it has to do. Right, Mr Mehta? Shikha, I would like to know why you filed a case against Sania. Did you actually believe a benevolent girl like Sania could have killed your younger sister?'

'How can you ask anyone about a sub judice matter? You are not higher than the law,' Mehta blew his lid off.

Simran looked at Mehta with contempt and then at Shikha who had started crying.

'What happened, Shikha?' Simran asked, concerned.

'I will tell you, Simran. I want to tell the world that I have been an immoral, worthless bitch. I traded my sister's death, her soul. I want to make a confession in front of you, and the whole world that Nimesh Mehta gave me ₹10 lakh to file a case against Sania. At that time, I was convinced that Sania was responsible for my sister's death, but when you got Prajakta's friend, Payal, talking and you guys showed me the kind of animalistic treatment that my sister was subje...' Shikha could not finish the statement because of the sobs that wracked her body.

Rohit tried to hold her reassuringly, but she shrugged him off angrily. 'Don't touch me, you sleazy bastard.'

The mood in the studio became sombre. A doleful silence gripped the audience as they digested what was happening.

'Pull yourself together, Shikha,' Simran consoled her, soothingly stroking Shikha's back. 'I would now like to show you all the truth—the truth that will make you feel squeamish and make you realize that the law is not always right.'

'The person who shot this video did not want to come forward due to the fear of facing dire repercussions. The video had been recorded on the said person's phone and we are gracious for their willingness to share this with us,' Simran announced.

The video showed Nimesh Mehta pulling Prajakta's hair savagely and shouting into her ear. 'You cheeky whore, why did you have to talk to the media? Why the fuck did you blab that you are a tenth standard student from St. Mary's? Now I won't spare you. I will show you how to keep things in your mouth,' he swore diabolically. 'I will see to it that you never ever think of participating in a beauty pageant again.' Mehta thrashed Prajakta on her face with the back of his ring-studded hand.

Rohit, who was standing beside Prajakta, tried to stop him, but Mehta pushed him aside roughly and dragged Prajakta to the centre of the room by her hair. 'Undress. Come on. Remove your clothes and do a ramp walk for me,' Mehta gnashed his teeth at Prajakta, who stood there mutely, quaking and crying. 'I said, remove your fucking clothes. Didn't you hear me, slut?' Mehta slapped her with such force that she fell down on the floor face-first, and he kicked her savagely. 'I want you naked right now,' he bellowed. Unaware of its presence, Mehta turned towards the camera with a baleful look in his eyes. His features were twisted into a malevolent sneer. 'Watch what happens when you try to act too smart.'

The screen went blank.

'At this juncture, the person who was shooting this entire

incident on the mobile got scared and switched off the camera,' Simran explained. 'We do have the footage of young Prajakta being humiliated and disgraced in front of her friends and feeling mortified. Prajakta's sister, Shikha, and their mother, have requested us to refrain from showing the footage in public, but rest assured, we have enough to unmask this malicious double-headed brute.'

'HANG THE BASTARD!'

'FLOG HIM PUBLICLY!'

'HE SHOULD BE STONED TO DEATH!'

The audience, livid, rushed towards the stage.

Sunidhi was extremely worked up. She switched on the talkback hurriedly to speak with Simran. 'Wind up the episode, Simran. Do you hear me, Simran? Just sign off.'

'Stop right there, please!' Simran shouted and stood in front of Mehta to shield him. 'We have finally nailed this sorry excuse of a man. Let us be civil so that the show does not get a bad reputation. PLEASE!' She then looked straight into the camera and signed off. 'Thank you for watching *The Simran Thapar Show*, where the truth prevails.'

The online editor gave a huge okay sign to the director. 'This is a superhit episode. Mark my words,' the director shouted at the top of his voice, disrupting the mellow atmosphere in the console room.

Slowly, but steadily, a celebratory mood built up in the console room. Sunidhi, the one person who had been nervous all throughout, was feeling over the moon with what they had just achieved. With blurred, moist eyes, she observed the incident unfurling through the glass panel. Below, on the studio floor, Nimesh Mehta was being taken out of the studio by a posse of his security guys even as the audience hurled things and shouted abuses at him. Some members of the audience wanted to get their pictures clicked with Simran, but she excused herself and went to meet Karmarkar, who was still seated on the dais.

'You were phenomenal, Simran, absolutely phenomenal,' he beamed with pride and hugged her.

They both looked up at the glass panel of the console room

and spotted Sunidhi jumping up and down with excitement. She signalled to them to wait there, and sprinted to the floor. Karmarkar's eyes welled up seeing his daughter so delighted.

43

'If she gets bail tomorrow, she will emerge as a champion of women. That can be extremely detrimental for girls in our community,' Rashid explained to Sajid.

The latter was engrossed in cracking open the last leg piece of the mutton curry. Sajid had tipped his head back to guzzle the bone marrow when he spotted Rashid looking at him crossly.

'So what do you want to do?' Sajid asked, wiping the dribbled curry off his chin and avoiding his phone which was ringing continuously. It was his wife, Zeenat. A message flashed on his cellphone's screen: There is no way I will put our daughter in a madrasa. Sajid stared at his phone in deep thought, when Rashid's voice jolted him back to reality.

'An attempt to kill her will make her a hero, like that Malala, especially if she survives by any chance. I want to destroy her most valuable asset—her face. So that whenever she is called for charity shows and award functions out of sympathy, girls in our community will shudder to even think of following in her footsteps,' Rashid spoke with frightening determination and a maniacal glint in his eyes. He emptied the bottle of acid into two hip flasks.

'Are you sure this is what you want?' Sajid asked, dubious about the whole scheme.

'Of course! I have thought this through. Worst-case scenario, I will be caught or I will have to surrender myself to the police. You will simply need to get me a lawyer, and then, I will walk free, like all the other attackers in this country.'

'How will I get a lawyer if I am also behind bars with you?' Sajid countered.

Within a short time, each and every news channel had started airing excerpts from the episode with headlines like 'TV host rips Nimesh Mehta to shreds', 'Mehta could be arrested for abetting young Prajakta's suicide, among other crimes' and 'Nimesh Mehta— the ugly head behind the beauty business.'

Karmarkar was flipping through channels on his television. Gul had gone back home, but Simran had stayed behind to spend some more time with Sunidhi. A famous newscaster presented a news capsule on the screen. 'Trials by media have shaken up the judicial system earlier as well. The famous Priyadarshini Mattoo and the Jessica Lal murder cases are two instances that come to mind immediately. But this one seems to be getting even bigger. The innocence of Beauty Queen Sania Ahmed, who was stripped of her title in an underhanded move orchestrated by Nimesh Mehta, proved to be his nemesis. Public outcry against Mehta has reached such a crescendo that the police fear a law and order problem when the bail application of Miss Sania is presented at the hearing in the sessions court day after tomorrow.'

Visuals ranging from Mehta's press conference to Simran's episode where Mehta was excoriated were interspersed in the news capsule.

'Even if Gul had a personal agenda to annihilate Mehta, the coverage in the news channels will only help Sania's case,' Sunidhi opined.

'The home minister called me today,' Karmarkar revealed. 'He was quite harsh with his words. He said we might have exposed the inefficiency of the cops, but it will reflect on his ministry. He will have to face a lot of flak for this incident.'

'Big deal, Pops. Someone has to pay for the police's incompetence. We have unearthed a huge racket. We will be setting a new benchmark in investigative journalism,' said Sunidhi, upbeat, and, winked at Simran.

'Remember, you will be rubbing quite a few people the wrong way with a show like this,' Karmarkar warned her, always the protective father.

'I am absolutely prepared. I don't know about Sunidhi,' Simran shrugged as she took another swig of red wine from her glass.

'There's no two ways about this. We built this ship together and if it sinks, we will go down with it together,' Sunidhi told her in all seriousness.

'Let's raise a toast to your collective courage and tenacity in that case,' Karmarkar, holding his glass of Single Malt Scotch, summoned one of the house staff, and asked him to fix drinks for all

'But haven't the news channels picked up the story real fast?' Sunidhi wondered out loud.

'That is courtesy Gul's expert handiwork. He distributed the footage from the show to all the news channels. Exposing Nimesh Mehta was on the top of his bucket list. In fact, that was the only common ground I shared with Gul,' Simran smirked.

Sania's story was on the front page of all the major dailies. By default, she had become the nation's hottest topic. There were articles glorifying her sincere attempts to dissuade a young fourteen-year-old Prajakta from forging her age to participate in a beauty pageant, along with stories about how beauty pageants were corrupting young girls.

'Isn't commoditization of beauty harming society insidiously?' questioned one editorial.

'Are our law enforcers that dim-witted?' wondered a regional language newspaper.

Most of the articles went on to elaborate how, in an attempt to stave off pressure from their higher-ups, the cops arrested an innocent girl. Sania garnered a lot of public sympathy and the media gatekeepers filed this away as a simple open-and-shut case of being victimized by a corrupt system and scheming organizers.

The bail hearing had attracted a massive crowd. The youth had taken to the streets with great fervour. Everyone had come together to show solidarity for Sania. Zealous banners fluttered proudly and powerful slogans echoed in the wind. The city was brought

to a grinding halt. Mumbai, Delhi, Bengaluru and Ahmedabad had mobilized rallies in support of Sania as well.

When Sania was brought to the court, the crowd went ballistic with mass hysteria. 'Sania! Sania!' They chanted her name like a prayer and shouted slogans against the cops and Nimesh Mehta. As soon as they saw Simran, who had just reached there with Sunidhi, they mobbed her. 'Three Cheers for Simran Thapar! Hip hip hooray!' The crowd was delirious. Simran and Sunidhi were stunned to see the number of people who had gathered there to lend their support to Sania. Sania was neither a politician nor a movie star, but the fact that she suffered injustice with graciousness galvanized tremendous support in her favour.

Shamim, who hadn't eaten a proper meal in the last few days, recited one prayer in loop, that her daughter be exonerated.

'Simran is here, Ammi,' Ayub gently poked Shamim awake from her reverie. She was overwhelmed with a surge of emotions on seeing Simran, the most dominant of which was boundless gratitude. 'I watched your show. You have absolved my daughter. You really fought for her. It has done her so much good. All these people are here only because of your show. May Allah give you whatever you wish for,' Shamim hugged Simran fiercely.

There was a slight commotion as Sania was taken to the box in the courtroom. Simran stood in a corner, lost in her thoughts, with glistening eyes.

Simran, whatever harm you think you have caused to us, it was unintentional and more importantly, you have done so much to undo all that. You have resurrected me. And now even Sania. You have given both of us a second life, Simran. Sunidhi's voice replayed in Simran's mind.

The bail hearing, which should have been a mere formality, became a dramatic affair, especially when the judge gave a resounding warning to the cops and the government machinery. 'You are playing with people's lives here. Why didn't you investigate the matter at a preliminary level before making an arrest? How will you compensate for the trauma this girl has endured? I want a follow-up report from the police. Take this as a strict warning. If I do not get a satisfactory answer, I will suspend each and every officer on this case. Bail granted!' the judge roared.

The crowd went wild with exhilaration.

Sania, who had held herself together so far, suddenly collapsed. Gaurav, who was present there, and a couple of female constables tried to hold her up, but she doubled over. She had summoned every sliver of strength in her body to see this onerous task through. Now that it was all over, every cell in her body slumped with relief.

'Hey, are you okay?' Gaurav inquired, but she remained unresponsive. 'Look at me,' he urged her, cupping her face in his hand and coaxing her to open her eyes.

Tears trickled down through her closed eyelids and clung to her eyelashes. She opened her eyes with monumental effort and waited for her vision to refocus. Her face was a complete mess with tear-streaked cheeks, purple shadows and a runny nose.

'You are so beautiful,' Gaurav breathed, his eyes welling up.

As Sania stepped out of the courtroom, the crowd got totally unmanageable. Sania's name rippled through the air repeatedly, even louder than before. There was a tussle between the media people and the police who were trying to cordon off the area to prevent a stampede. But the crowd exerted such an immense force that the police barricade was broken off.

A few metres away, Rashid moved surreptitiously in the crowd, with dangerous designs dancing in his diabolical mind. After seeing how the crowd venerated his sister, Sajid suddenly found himself in a serious dilemma. 'We should not do something so horrific, Rashid, not after the people have forgiven her,' Sajid tried to reason with him.

'How does our plan have anything to do with people forgiving her? People are not going to be affected like we are. Girls from our community will start thinking they can do whatever they want to, without our permission. Are you okay with that?'

'Look, Rashid we should no...'

'You give me an answer, yes or no? Are you okay with that?'

'Wait for a couple of days and then do it. We can avoid being involved in the crime altogether if we make someone else do it.'

'What crime? This is not a crime. This is our duty. If we don't do this, some dumbfuck will do it and get jannat and the seventy-two virgins,' growled Rashid, exuding lunacy.

Sajid realized that he should have thwarted this extremist mentality in Rashid when he could. Now it was too late; he was unstoppable. Sajid dialled Mamujaan's number without Rashid's knowledge. With his head turned away and his hand firmly gripping Rashid, Sajid spoke on the phone. 'He is hell-bent on throwing acid on Sania's face. You please talk to him, Mamujaan, and tell him it is a sinful deed.'

For the first time in a very long time, Sajid felt an uncontainable swell of love for his sister. 'Speak with your father,' he handed the phone to Rashid with misty eyes.

Rashid threw a minacious look his way, as if he had been betrayed. He took the phone and tossed it on the asphalt, a couple of feet away. 'It is too late, Brother.'

Sajid instantly wanted to retrieve his phone, but he couldn't risk Rashid getting out of his sight. 'See, Rashid, I don't know much, but I do know that I don't want to destroy Sania's life. We don't have the right to...'

'Don't give me that bullshit, Sajid. Do you think she has the right to insult me? The right to be with a guy who is not even from our community? The right to mislead my sisters? Both of them want to act in TV serials now. Do you think she has the right to spread such evil ideas to girls in our community? You are getting cold feet just because she is your sister.'

'She is your cousin too,' Sajid pointed out.

'Get lost! I will do this on my own,' Rashid told him with bloodshot eyes.

'No, Rashid. Just think it through. You cannot do this to her. You will not be forgiven for this!' Sajid tried to clutch Rashid firmly, but he managed to slip through his fingers and disappeared in the crowd. Sajid was petrified for his sister. He hurried in the same direction as Rashid but could not trace him. So he hunted for his phone instead. By some miracle, he found his phone in spite of the mad rush. His display had cracked and there was an unmistakable outline of a shoeprint on top of it. Despite that, his phone was ringing, and it was Mamujaan.

'Why didn't you tell me earlier about his stupid plans?' Mamujaan was furious.

'I don't have the time to explain that right now. But what else did you expect after filling your son's mind with so much poison?' Sajid hung up.

In such a massive crowd, it was virtually impossible to locate Rashid. He called up Ayub. 'Listen, Ayub...'

'I will talk to you later,' Ayub disconnected even before Sajid could utter another word. Sajid called him again, but Ayub didn't answer. He himself was struggling to find his way through the milling crowd along with his mother.

'Sania! Sania!' he shouted to get his sister's attention, but she couldn't hear him in the pandemonium.

Sajid realized that he should head straight towards Sania. He elbowed the overwhelming crowd frantically in order to reach her.

'RASHID—ACID—SANIA'S FACE. STOP HIM ANYHOW,' he typed and sent a message to Ayub even as he elbowed his way forcefully through the horde.

Because of his massive build and tremendous height, Sajid could see farther than the rest in the crowd. He spotted Rashid's head only a few feet away from Sania. Sania beamed at Shamim and Ayub, who had almost reached her. Sajid realized he had run out of options. He took a deep breath and shouted at the top of his voice, 'AYUB, PROTECT SANIA FROM RASHID!'

Three people's heads immediately snapped in his direction—Ayub's, Shamim's and Rashid's.

EPILOGUE

Ayub sat on the edge of his seat, bobbing his knee nervously as he watched Shiraz pacing the hospital corridor. Lines of worry creased his father's forehead. The intransigent warden had put his foot down and refused to let Shiraz inside. More than two people were not permitted to enter the critical care unit, he had told Shiraz with a hint of annoyance.

Simran stood with her back against the wall, facing the door that separated the burn unit from the rest of the hospital. Sunidhi and Shikha were seated on connected metal chairs that lined the opposite wall on either side of the door. They had all come down to support their friend during an unfathomably dire time.

A painfully awkward look had been exchanged between Shikha and Shiraz when they had arrived at the hospital in the evening; one which had been instantly discerned by Simran's keen gaze. Even now, she noticed the discomfort lining Shikha's posture. Palpable anxiety throbbed through all of them. The door creaked open and the chief surgeon emerged.

'The burns are fourth degree ones that extend beyond the hypodermic area, causing necrosis of the underlying layers. It means that the muscles and tendons have been damaged severely. There was a portion where the bone was exposed as well,' the doctor informed Shiraz mechanically.

Sunidhi's face contorted in horror and Shikha desperately covered her mouth as the contents of her lunch threatened to make their way up.

'Multistage reconstruction will be required, which involves grafting, preferably from the thigh or stomach region. Fortunately, amputation won't be required, but it would take a miracle for all sensation to be regained. Rest assured, we will do our very best, Mr Ahmed,' said the doctor and excused herself.

Shiraz looked grimly at Ayub and seated himself next to him. Wanting to give the family some privacy, the girls left.

The hospital room was doused in a soft magnolia light, making the lacklustre grey walls seem even gloomier. A pungent smell invaded Shamim's nose. The distinct scent of sterility was punctuated by a coppery odour of burnt human flesh that hung heavy and thick in the air. She could almost taste it on her tongue. The oppressive silence was only broken by a recurring dripping sound from the IV. Shamim shuffled about in the room.

Within just a day, Shamim had acclimatized herself to the bleak surroundings and fallen in a routine that occupied her mind and kept her hands busy. Sania watched her mother rearrange the blanket, recheck all the medicines marking the bedside table and leave the room.

'Why did you risk your life to save me?' Sania asked Sajid. A plethora of emotions occluded her voice.

Because I encouraged Rashid's fanaticism all these years. Because of me he had the audacity to throw acid at you. Because I have given you nothing but misery all these years. Sajid wanted to tell her all that and more, but he kept his eyes firmly closed. Sania gripped his uninjured shoulder with care but despite her caution, a jolt of pain seared through Sajid's body. His eyes snapped open against his will and he suppressed a groan. The blurry silhouette of his sister loomed over him.

'Because I have been a complete jerk,' Sajid croaked, his parched throat making his voice crack.

Sania shook her head vehemently and laced her fingers through his unbandaged hand. 'What you did today undoes all of that,' she demurred, looking straight into his brimming eyes.

That tipped Sajid over the precipice and his chest heaved erratically as strangled sobs reverberated through his body.

'Your question kept nagging me,' he mumbled through watery eyes.

'Which question?' she asked.

'Why none of the Bollywood Khans have married a Muslim girl. I now know why they haven't. I want every Muslim girl to have the same opportunities as a Muslim boy.' He gave into the upheaval that raked his entire being and wept wretchedly, pouring out his guilt, his shame and his regret.

Sania felt the piercing jab of Sajid's outburst. She wrapped her arm gingerly around her brother's shoulder and squeezed it reassuringly. Upon hearing Sajid's cries, Shamim rushed inside. She made her way to the bed and stroked Sajid's head, trying her best to appease him. She sensed that bitter realization had finally dawned on her son.

The girls were on their way back to Mumbai. Simran and Sunidhi had decided to bring Shikha onboard as an executive producer for their show. To say that Shikha was ecstatic would be an understatement. But she contained herself surprisingly well. The mood in the back seat was relatively sombre. As she watched the vrooming cars pass by on the expressway, Sunidhi pondered over the last one year, inexplicably grateful for the changes it had brought, while Simran rested her head on the edge of the backrest and stared at the roof of the car unblinkingly. Thoughts of the next episode had started building up in her mind.

'Can you imagine a girl so divinely beautiful could have been desecrated by an orthodox lunatic? Her face would have been reduced to a mass of melting flesh and bones? And why? Just because her cousin, who must have dry-fucked her, was spurned by her? Or because he truly believed that her success would set a bad example for his sisters and the other girls of his community? Preposterous! I hope that bastard burns in hell for all of eternity!' Simran seethed.

Shikha partook by selecting the choicest expletives for Rashid.

'In some part of his heinous mind, that deranged maniac thinks he has the right to own someone.' Sunidhi spat with disgust.

'What do you think brought about the change in Sajid?' Shikha wondered out loud from the passenger seat. Her question was met with silence. 'Maybe it was his brotherly love for Sania finally,' mused Shikha credulously and looked back at the other two.

'It was the fear of the law,' countered Simran.

'Or, it could be that Rashid's extremism finally put him off,' Sunidhi chimed in. 'But whatever it was, he saved Sania just in time. He could have easily lost his own life in the tussle with Rashid,' she deduced and Simran nodded in agreement.

'It was like a scene straight out of a Bollywood film,' Shikha said with awe. 'Who were you reminded of—Sunny Deol or Salman Khan?' Simran asked Shikha.

'Tiger Shroff,' she said as the three of them looked at each other and dissolved into giggles.

Acknowledgements

While I believe I have a knack for telling stories, I had never imagined that I would write a novel someday. Now that I have reached here, I would like to take a moment to thank the people who played a major role in its culmination.

Simran Kaur Mundi, Miss India Universe 2008, was the first person I spoke to about this story. Being an insider, she gave me invaluable insights into the world of pageantry.

My ex-wife Sonam, for being there by my side when I needed her the most.

Anu Priya, who is a pilot by profession but gave me some surprisingly useful inputs about the motivations of the characters.

Atmaja, for reading the numerous drafts, the ruthless reactions and unfiltered but useful feedback.

Ritu Panchal, without whom this novel would not have seen the light of day. She breathed life into the manuscript, giving it a complete facelift and giving me the confidence to publish *Skin Deep*.

There are a couple of others who would not want to be named but have bared their souls to me and helped me tell this story.

Finally, I'm thankful to the team at Rupa—Elina Majumdar, Rudra Narayan and Manali Das—for giving the book its final form.